Surgical Audit

Related titles

Essential Surgical Practice, 2nd edition
Edited by A Cuschieri, G Giles and A R Moossa

Atlas of General Surgery, 2nd edition
Compiled by H Dudley, D Carter and R G C Russell

This above all: to thine own self be true,
And it must follow, as the night the day,
Thou canst not then be false to any man.

Hamlet, Act I, Scene iii, lines 56–58

Surgical Audit

Second Edition

Alan Pollock BSc, FRCS, FRCS(Ed)
Scarborough Hospital, Scarborough, UK

and

Mary Evans BA
Freelance Consultant Editor

Butterworth-Heinemann Ltd
Linacre House, Jordan Hill, Oxford OX2 8DP

 PART OF REED INTERNATIONAL BOOKS

OXFORD LONDON BOSTON
MUNICH NEW DELHI SINGAPORE SYDNEY
TOKYO TORONTO WELLINGTON

First published 1993

British Library Cataloguing in Publication Data
Pollock, Alan
  Surgical Audit
  I. Title II. Evans, Mary
  362.197068

ISBN 0 7506 0774 2

Composition by Scribe Design, Gillingham, Kent
Printed and bound in Great Britain by Redwood Press Ltd, Melksham, Wiltshire

Contents

Foreword I

There are those who regard the introduction of the concept of audit and quality control into clinical practice as recent and unwelcome infringements of professional freedom, but nothing could be further from the truth, for these ideas are as old as medicine itself.

Sir William Osler said, 'Medicine arose out of the primal sympathy of man with man and out of the desire to help those in sorrow, need and sickness' (1892. The Principles and Practice of Medicine, D. Appleton, New York).

It was, however, clearly recognised even in antiquity that empathy alone was not enough and that this compassionate ideal could not safely be left entirely to the discretion of individual practitioners, no matter how well intentioned. Thus it was inevitable that primeval codes of practice would emerge, and probably one of the most familiar of these was the Hammurabi Code of Babylon, circa 2000 BC. This attempted not only to regulate the practice of medicine but also quoted a scale of fees and the relevant penalties for malpractice. Similar principles of practice, such as those described in the Edwin Smith papyrus (circa 1500 BC) were also well established in Ancient Egypt and many of the ideas involved were subsequently promulgated by the great teachers of Greece and Rome. Hippocrates (460-370 BC), for example, emphasised the necessity for accurate case records and the importance of bedside observation, and demanded high moral and ethical standards; he also seriously questioned the efficacy of many treatments then in vogue.

The medieval crafts and guilds, while clearly containing some of the unsatisfactory propensities of the closed shop system, nevertheless played an important part in the preservation of standards. The Royal College of Surgeons of England has a copy of a parchment dated 1342 recording the appointment by the Lord Mayor of two Master Surgeons 'to oversee the practice of their art and report to him upon any colleagues who are defective'. A clear statement, albeit from an administrator, on the requirement for surgical audit.

The quest for quality control in our profession has therefore been a long one, but it is abundantly clear that the technological advances that have characterised the surgical renaissance of recent times have immeasurably added to the complexity of our moral and ethical problems.

This book is therefore most timely and it is particularly appropriate that it should emanate from the department of surgery at Scarborough. Mr

Pollock and his colleagues were early and enthusiastic advocates of the introduction of controlled trials into clinical practice and the standards they established were exemplary. Their studies have illustrated, on many occasions, the supreme importance of keeping an open mind and subjecting every result to a careful and critical analysis. The value of their contribution to this aspect of surgical practice has been widely admired and internationally recognised.

We live in an increasingly sceptical world and, moreover, one in which the demands for audit and quality control will inevitably increase. It is therefore essential that surgeons should appreciate this simple fact and with it the vital necessity of promoting our own appropriate assessment of standards of performance. If we neglect to do this it is already evident that others, who may not have the requisite judgement, expertise, or insight will be appointed to do it for us.

I hope that many surgeons will therefore find something of interest in this stimulating book. I wish it every success and congratulate its authors on the production of a very worthwhile and important treatise.

Sir Geoffrey Slaney, KBE, FRCS
Emeritus Professor of Surgery,
University of Birmingham

Foreword II

The appearance of a book on clinical audit is more than timely. As is so often true, there is nothing so fashionable as an idea whose time has come, and clearly this is the case. It is interesting that this belated but worldwide infatuation with the audit and assessment process is one that was broadly and systematically neglected as a clinical research tool for a very long period. However, at the moment, there is mounting concern about an opportunity to study the processes involved in clinical care and ultimately, of course, to examine outcome and determine how process and outcome truly interact.

An important factor, certainly in the USA, has been the influence of these considerations on the cost of medical care. There is a very realistic, and often dominant, concern that rising costs should be limited in every circumstance, hopefully with retention of desirable outcome. However, it is increasingly clear that cost control is an end within itself.

It is altogether appropriate that Mr Alan Pollock should undertake this kind of endeavour. The subject is undoubtedly closely related to his own long time interest in clinical outcomes and, most especially, his leadership in bringing the prospective randomised study of clinical permutations to the bedside, using the best of a well organised staff and the ultimate capacity of the National Health Service significantly to influence current clinical patterns. Those patterns include matters related to methods for selection of surgical incisions and of wound closure, and the administration of antibiotics to minimise perioperative infection. The same skills that the clinical epidemiologist and the nurse clinician have used to bring these data to the forefront in clinical trials are exactly those that need to be implemented in a broader audit of the entire clinical process.

One is not surprised to find the leadership of this volume coming from a surgical service since it has been traditional for surgical services around the world to have a meaningful and constructively critical assessment of surgical morbidity and mortality. Indeed, the ultimate application of audit is derived directly from the efforts of surgeons systematically to examine their untoward results with an emphasis upon correction and seeing that future avoidable events are indeed avoided.

Fundamentally, the outcome of many such endeavours will be influenced by the extent of patient disease, the promptness with which medical assistance is undertaken and numerous other factors. The capacity for misinterpretation of audit and assessment data is just as great as that for any other clinical data. For example, one can readily surmise that certain hospitals with low crude mortality rates for a given operation might indeed provide substantially less than the best possible care. This is especially likely if the element of self-selection of only the good risk patients into that hospital and the systematic transfer of patients with advanced primary disease and a high ratio of associated illness to another institution occurs; surely the outcome there will inevitably be worse, even if the overall medical care was better than in the referring hospital.

For all these reasons, this undertaking is more than timely, and the skills of Mr Pollock and Miss Evans have been well documented by their regular appearance in our most highly refereed and discriminating journals for many years.

Finally, it is also self-evident that an undertaking in the audit or assessment process is of merit only if mechanisms are established whereby such an audit leads to improved care for subsequent patients, both in the institution in question and in the broader domain of those who are fortunate enough to study and learn from the written and reported results of the audit. The ultimate improvement of patient care is the goal of such undertakings, and one must be certain that this end, and it alone, justifies whatever means are involved.

Hiram C. Polk Jr, MD
Professor and Chairman,
Department of Surgery,
University of Louisville,
Kentucky, USA

Preface to first edition

Lack of popularity is inescapable for any segment of the community that wishes to preserve or raise standards. H.A.F. Dudley (1981)

Why should doctors audit?

Everybody in the world is entitled to the same high quality of medical care. This must not be a pipe dream and the World Health Organisation aims at this target by the year 2000. Against this mainly epidemiological ambition is set the old fashioned concept of clinical freedom – each doctor treats his own patients as he thinks best, irrespective of changes in practice, developments in techniques, or the costs of treatment.

These two points of view must be assessed against the current background of 'managerial' medicine with, on the one hand its financial constraints and limitations on staff, equipment, and other facilities, and on the other hand, the technological developments that are making it possible to treat diseases that were previously untreatable, together with the fact that people are living longer and expecting more of the service. So why should doctors audit?

Theoretical reasons for audit

It is sensible to say that doctors should make the best use of their time – that they should be cost effective. It follows, therefore, that before they can improve they must know how they are actually spending their time and the resources of the hospital and the country. For example, a doctor who does two sessions a week at a hospital some distance away would be better advised to arrange to do those sessions on the same day, and not waste the time travelling to and from the peripheral hospital twice a week.

It is not only the doctor's time that can be saved. It is not cost effective to send patients regularly to a large centre many miles away for special investigations because the facilities do not exist at the local hospital. By buying the necessary equipment for the smaller hospital, the amount of money spent on ambulances, accompanying nurses, and so on would be saved within a comparatively short time.

Direct time saving of the sort we have just mentioned is not necessarily the best use of resources. The consultant may feel that he is making the best use of his own time by delegating the writing of discharge summaries to the junior staff, but is this the best way of teaching a young doctor? By the same token, is it in the best interests of the patient and the general practitioner if the consultant regularly delegates attendance at clinics to a doctor in training when the general practitioner needs the opinion of the consultant, and not that of a young man with comparatively little experience?

Practical reasons for audit

'Quality control', 'value for money', 'cost effectiveness' – such phrases as these are being bandied about more and more. But what do they mean? Are they trying to balance two concepts: that all patients should receive the same standard of care and that doctors should be entitled to clinical freedom?

'Never trust a surgeon who has never had a complication. He is either blind, or lying, or both'. All operations have complications; the aim must be to keep these complications to a minimum, and the most obvious way of doing that is to monitor all patients and, in cases where the rate is particularly high or particularly low, to investigate further, find out why, and make improvements.

It follows that surgeons must keep accurate records not only of patients who are operated on and who operated on them, but also of their clinical course, and the number of days they spent in hospital. This is already done in many places; what is not done and is equally important is to keep a record of the number and outcome of patients who did not have operations. This is important for several reasons.

Firstly, when patients die without being operated on, and only those patients who have operations are being recorded, a surgeon's mortality rate will be biased. Perhaps another surgeon would have operated on some of the patients and whether they survived or died they would affect his postoperative mortality figures. One of the hardest decisions a surgeon has to make is when not to operate. This argument can also be used in regard to morbidity. Criteria for operation have a strong influence on a surgeon's morbidity and mortality and perhaps go a little way towards explaining the wide differences published among units around the country. Surgeons who do not operate are the only ones who do not get complications.

Secondly, patients may be admitted because they are ill and require special investigations before being operated on. If there is a delay in these being done, patients may occupy beds merely because they are waiting for the investigations. They could equally well wait at home or in a convalescent ward, thus relieving pressure on the acute ward.

Knowing the length of time that patients stay in hospital under a surgeon's care while waiting for an operation can highlight overworked or inefficient diagnostic services, and can bring to light the misuse of laboratory or imaging facilities.

Thirdly, honest consecutive audit should be an integral part of both the teaching and the monitoring of the performance of junior staff. What stage of competence has a particular trainee achieved? What are his or her morbidity and mortality rates for particular operations?

Fourthly, clinical audit tells us who is actually doing the work. Is the consultant fulfilling his contractual obligations or is he leaving the work to his junior staff while he spends his time at the private hospital or on the golf course?

A computer 'bank' of information has recently been introduced in Britain so that patients needing a particular operation can call and find out where there is the least waiting time. There is as yet no centre that discloses information about mortality and morbidity. Whether disclosure of these rates would encourage or discourage honest audit is open to question.

Ethical and moral reasons for audit

Doctors owe it both to themselves and to their patients to audit their results accurately and honestly. An old Persian proverb says 'Fool someone else and you may be clever; fool yourself and you are stupid'. Without honesty audit is useless. This means that the progress of every patient that comes under a doctor's care must be recorded in detail, including all deaths and complications. Ideally the doctor should do this himself, perhaps at the time that he does the discharge summary and before selective forgetfulness has had time to creep in.

Obviously definitions must be laid down beforehand – for example, 'discharge of pus' for wound infection – and the definitions must be understood by all the members of the team. This understanding must also apply to causes of death; there are certain ones (for example, myocardial infarction, congestive cardiac failure, pulmonary embolism, and pneumonia) that, in the absence of necropsy, are nothing more than a convenient abrogation of responsibility by the doctor. Some people believe that every death within 30 days of operation is a direct result of the operation, whatever the immediate cause; in the absence of necropsy findings to the contrary this is perhaps the most honest view to take.

Economic reasons for audit

Performance indicators and diagnosis related groups are only two aspects of assessing value for money. For a long time doctors have ignored the fact that there are not unlimited funds for health care and that their work must be cost effective while at the same time giving patients the best possible service. 'New technology' is expensive and becoming more so, but there is still a tendency to demand the newest toy because it is available, and before it has been compared (favourably or unfavourably) with current methods of diagnosis or treatment.

In 1989 the Department of Health in Britain published a white paper entitled *Working for patients*. Among the Working Papers that followed this white paper was one entitled *Medical audit*, in which the government stated that every doctor must participate in regular systematic medical audit, defined as 'critical analysis of the quality of clinical care', to ensure the best quality of service within the resources available.

Quality control in the laboratory

Clinicians rely heavily on laboratory and imaging investigations, and they are entitled to know that the departments responsible are taking all reasonable steps to ensure that their reports are accurate. There are inaccuracies in every biochemical and haematological test, but these should be held to within two standard deviations of the 'true' result. In common with all other health care workers, laboratory and imaging staff can make mistakes, and these can compound the biases introduced by the test itself. At present, quality control is most easily attained in the departments of biochemistry and haematology, by the analysis of test samples submitted by central authorities. It is not, however, impossible to enquire into the accuracy of reports from the department of microbiology and that of morbid anatomy, histology, and cytology (including necropsy).

The most comprehensive programme of quality assurance at present is that of the American College of Pathologists, which sends check samples of varying levels of difficulty to all accredited departments every three months.

Audit of patient satisfaction

Managers want cost effectiveness, doctors want to cure patients and keep their morbidity and mortality down, but what do patients want? This question often gets pushed to the bottom of the list, if it gets asked at all, and it is really the most important. In general, patients want competence, courtesy, kindness, consideration, and information. They want continuity of care. They want the opportunity to decide for themselves, having discussed matters with their doctor, and be a partner in the decision about how to treat their disease.

They do not necessarily need or want an operation, but if they do decide to have an operation they will want to know what will happen, what complications are possible, how long they will be in hospital, and for how long they will be unable to work. They may be a little too awed by their surroundings and all the unusual and sometimes frightening things that are happening to them to ask spontaneously, so they must be given the opportunity to ask. If the operation is not designed to be curative they must be told how it will affect them and what disability they can expect. And finally, they want to be able to plan their admission with as little inconvenience as possible and be treated with courtesy and respect at all times.

Communication is the key. We are convinced that many law suits that are instituted against doctors and hospitals would never have been contemplated if open communication had been maintained throughout.

Legal reasons for audit

Consecutive audit of a doctor's practice can be of use if he is accused of malpractice. It could be seen from his records that his standard compares favourably with that of other doctors, and that his morbidity and mortality for a particular operation or other intervention are acceptable.

This will be particularly useful if the North American concept of relicensing is introduced into the United Kingdom. In Britain the Royal College of Obstetricians and Gynaecologists recommended in 1991 that specialists should be recertified every five years and should take regular revision courses.

Audit of publications

Doctors must also be concerned in auditing the way in which they communicate their results to each other. Peer review is perhaps not the best method, open as it is to all sorts of bias, but we have not yet discovered a better way. It is not perfect (as the cases of Darsee and Alsabti have shown) but it is the best we have.

In addition, once papers are published, doctors must apply common sense to evaluate the information and possibly apply one of the score systems, or even construct a simple one of their own, to judge the veracity of a paper.

Conclusion

Can audit achieve all these things? Certainly it can help, even if all it does is make a doctor consider his own practice and question at every stage the reasoning behind each decision. At most, if it is accepted and practised widely it may have far reaching effects on the distribution of staff, allocation of funds, and training programmes for junior staff.

Audit of structure and process are easy to define, and easier to carry out than audit of outcome. That is perhaps why they are practised more widely at present, and why more money is being spent on them. Doctors, however, must concern themselves with audit of outcome and patient satisfaction, which are far harder to define and monitor. It is those that should take precedence over other aspects of audit if treatment is not going to be regulated entirely by ability to pay. Audit covers all aspects of medical practice and all grades and specialties of doctors. What is needed is that it shall become as integral a part of every doctor's practice as outpatient clinics, ward rounds, and operating lists.

Alan Pollock
Mary Evans

Reference

Dudley, H.A.F. (1981) Academic surgery: future uncertain. *British Medical Journal*, **282**, 1771–1772

Preface to second edition

There has been steady progress in clinical audit in the past few years. New methods of measuring deviations from health, new techniques for recording and retrieval of data, and a widespread appreciation of the importance of patient satisfaction, have been noticeable during the past decade. The result is that much of the information and many of the opinions expressed in the first edition of *Surgical Audit* have had to be modified, revised, and updated. Some of our statements we have removed, but we have added more than we have subtracted. Two new chapters have been introduced: how to begin an audit (Chapter 4), and the use of scores and scales to evaluate outcome (Chapter 15).

We have been criticised for using the pronoun 'he' when we refer to doctors or patients, when clearly we mean 'he or she'. This is such a clumsy expression that we have not adopted it. When it was inappropriate to change to the non-sexist plural ('they') we have left the word 'he' (or 'him' or 'his'). It is time for that marvellous and ever-changing tool, the English language, to import a non-sexist singular pronoun. Our American friends, who are so prolific in neologisms, will surely find one and we shall soon be using the new construction and be able to avoid irritating some women.

History

Chapter 1

The history of audit

I beseech you, in the bowels of Christ, think it possible that you may be mistaken.
Oliver Cromwell (1650)

The verb 'to audit' dates from the sixteenth century when it meant 'to make an official systematic examination of accounts' (*Oxford English Dictionary*). It has retained this meaning and, if you leave out the words 'of accounts', it is exactly what we mean by clinical audit. Attempts to analyse the results of treatments have been made since antiquity though the analyses have often been biased by preconceptions or faulty logic. For example, among the writing of Galen (130–201) is the statement that is translated as: 'All who drink of this remedy recover in a short time, except those whom it does not help, who all die. Therefore, it is obvious that it fails only in incurable cases.' (Strauss, 1968.)

The evolution of national statistics

In the millenium before Christ, populations were counted from time to time by the Babylonians, the Egyptians, the Chinese, and later by the Greeks and Romans. It was a census ordered by Caesar Augustus that probably took Joseph and Mary to Bethlehem.

John Graunt, a London draper, has been called 'the father of medical statistics' (Anonymous, 1921). In 1662 he published *Natural and Political Observations upon the Bills of Mortality* in which he drew attention to the high infant mortality and showed that the overall mortality in towns and cities was higher than in country districts.

Until the eighteenth century, however, there was no systematic attempt to register births and deaths, and certainly no attempt to record the causes of death with any accuracy. The eighteenth century is known as the Age of Enlightenment, not always flatteringly. French philosophers of that century were often called 'enlightened' in a pejorative sense to indicate 'a shallow and pretentious intellectualism, unreasonable contempt for authority and tradition' (*Oxford English Dictionary*). It was certainly a time when long cherished notions were being overthrown and new ideas poured forth; among these was the recognition of the importance of national statistics. Births and deaths were registered nationally in Sweden from 1749. In 1776 an attempt was made in France to establish such a national register, but it was not until the nineteenth century that even moderately reliable statistics became available, first in France, in 1800, and later in other European countries.

In England the first national survey of lands and people was undertaken by William I soon after he was crowned in December 1066. This resulted in the publication in 1086 of the *Great Inquisition or Survey of the Lands of England, Their Extent, Value, Ownership and Liabilities*, known since the sixteenth century as the Domesday Book. According to the Elizabethan, William Lombarde, it was so named because, 'it spared no man, but judged all men indifferently, as the Lord in that great day will do.' John Stow, another Elizabethan, wrote that the word is a corruption of Domus-dei because the book was kept in a part of Winchester Cathedral called the House of the Lord – Domus-dei.

From the eleventh to the sixteenth centuries there were no more than sporadic enumerations of the population in England and such information as the expectation of life at birth and the death rate from infections can only be guessed at. Even the exact number of people dying of the Black Death during the medieval epidemics – the worst was in 1348 – is not known for certain. In 1538 (soon after he had broken the union with the Roman church and established the Church of England) Henry VIII enjoined his Lord Chancellor to instruct the clergy of every parish to keep registers of all the baptisms, weddings, and funerals at which they officiated. The records remained parochial, however, in spite of the recommendation of Lord Burghley, Lord Treasurer to Elizabeth I, that 'there should be yearly delivered a summary of the whole whereby it should appear how many christenings, weddings, and burials were every year within England and Wales and every county particularly by itself, and how many men-children and women-children were born in all of them, severally set down by themselves' (Nissel, 1987).

In 1597 an Act was passed requiring transcripts of parish registers to be sent annually to the diocesan registrar. This Act was more often ignored than obeyed and no proper national census was carried out until 1801 (Nissel, 1987). This census, and those of 1811, 1821, and 1831 were almost certainly inaccurate and little information was derived other than that the total population of England and Wales was about nine million. It was not until the 1841 census that the first reliable figures were available as a result of the establishment of the General Register Office in 1837 and the provisions of the *Population Act* of 1840.

The *Population Act* was based on the recommendations of the Statistical Society of London (Bonar and Macrosty, 1934). The Society's report to the government noted that: 'According to the system adopted on previous occasions, the officers employed in England were the overseers of the poor, who were for the most part avowedly incompetent to undertake a task requiring considerable intelligence, precision, and energy. The returns which they obtained from the inhabitants were not subject to any examination for the purpose of detecting error or fraud; nor was there any security for the correctness of the abstracts which were sent to the Home Office, or any ready or certain means of correcting error when it was detected. According to the system to be adopted this year [1841], the officers acting under the Registrar General, whose duties in the registration of births, deaths and marriages eminently qualify them for such a task, are to mark out districts of a convenient size, and to select a qualified enumerator for each. They are afterwards to examine and, if necessary, to amend the returns sent in by the enumerators, and the superintendent registrars will have to take care that no district shall have been omitted, or insufficiently examined by their subordinate officers.'

For the 1841 census 35 000 enumerators were appointed, each being responsible for between 25 and 200 houses, depending on the density of population. The name, age, sex, occupation, and place of birth of each person were recorded and, for the first time, the enumerators' sheets were sent to the General Register Office in London where they were laboriously counted and analysed.

This system remained in use for 70 years, individual cards replacing the lists in 1880. The Hollerith punch card sorting machine was first used in a national census in the USA in 1890 and was adopted in Britain in 1911. Another 50 years went by before computers were first used to process the data generated from British censuses.

Registration of births, marriages and deaths

The parish records of the seventeenth and eighteenth centuries make fascinating reading but they recorded details only of parishioners of the Church of England, and the registers that were kept with greater or lesser precision by other churches had no legal validity. There were, in addition, many people who did not go to any church.

The Reform Bill was finally passed in June 1832, the House of Lords having been threatened by William IV that if it were not passed he would create enough peers to swamp the Tory opposition. The result was the enfranchisement of an additional 250 000 men by the abolition of a large number of 'rotten boroughs' – boroughs with scant population that were nevertheless entitled to return members to the House of Commons.

One of the first actions of the reformed House of Commons was to appoint a Select Committee to enquire into the system of registration of births, marriages, and deaths. The recommendations of this Committee were finally embodied in the *Act for Registering Births, Deaths, and Marriages in England 1836*, and resulted in the establishment of the General Register Office in London in 1837. Thomas Lister's first task after his appointment as Registrar General in August 1836 was the appointment of registrars and superintendent registrars throughout England. Most of these were officers of Poor Law Unions and such was the efficiency of Lister's organisation that by June 1837 registration of births, marriages, and deaths was made compulsory and, 'every person who shall wilfully make ... any false statement ... shall be subject to ... fine and imprisonment with hard labour for a term not exceeding seven years, or to fine and transportation for the like term'.

During the first year of the new Act the General Register Office received certified copies of nearly a million entries, which were bound in 12 volumes and indexed alphabetically. There was, however, no provision at first for detailed analysis of the data generated. This deficiency was remedied in 1839 when Dr William Farr was appointed 'Compiler of Abstracts'; his title was later changed to 'Statistical Superintendent'.

The Statistical Society of London

A meeting of the British Association for the Advancement of Science in Cambridge in 1833 resolved to form a statistical society; this was accomplished in March 1834 and the Society received a royal charter in 1887. It was the brain child of Richard Jones, the Reverend T. R. Malthus (the author of *Essay on the Principles of Population*), Charles Babbage (the inventor of a calculating machine), and Adolphe Quetelet (director of the Royal Observatory in Brussels). Part of its 'Prospectus' read as follows: 'The Statistical Society will consider it to be the first and most essential rule of its conduct to exclude carefully all opinions from its transactions and publications – to confine its attention rigorously to facts – and, as far as it may be found possible, to facts which can be stated numerically and arranged in tables ... The collection ... of new statistical materials will form ... only one part of the Society's work. To condense, arrange, and publish those already existing but either unpublished or published only in an expensive or diffused form or in foreign languages would be a task of equal usefulness.'

The Committee on Vital Statistics of the Statistical Society was formed in 1838 and its objectives were: 'To collect the Statistics of Life, embracing enumerations of Births, Deaths, Marriages, and Population, with or without distinction of age, sex, climate and occupations. To point out the defects in existing observations ... and to recommend the objects of enquiry to which attention may most profitably be directed.'

In the Annual Report of the Society for 1836–37 the Council observed: 'As gold is collected in small particles united with dross, yet when refined and stamped becomes the most valuable medium of commerce, so statistical facts must be collected in small numbers and in crude forms, and it is not until they have been united in large masses and undergone the process of examination and arrangement that they will be admitted as sterling coin in the currency of science.'

The rule in the Prospectus that opinions must be excluded from the transactions and publications of the Society was unworkable and by 1851 it was recognised that the collection of facts was a sterile exercise unless they were used to draw conclusions. As Lord Overstone wrote in that year's Report '... facts may be accumulated under the name of a Statistical Society in a perfectly unintelligent and unprofitable manner, or they may be accumulated under some systematic arrangement and for some definite and beneficial purpose'. There is no doubt that the enquiries conducted by the Society had a powerful effect on public opinion and on legislation in the nineteenth century.

The Statistical Society did not at first concern itself with the statistical analysis of probabilities, and ignored the work of the Swiss and French mathematicians of the eighteenth century, particularly Daniel Bernoulli, Abraham Demoivre, and Pierre Simon, Marquis de Laplace. These men laid the foundations of the theory of probability and Laplace had published the 'method of least squares' to obtain a common value of a number of dispersed observations of an event. As early as 1855 the Earl of Harrowby wrote: 'By the employment of the doctrine of probabilities, one branch of statistics is brought into immediate contact with the higher mathematics' (Hill, 1984). It was not, however, appreciated that these methods could have a bearing on vital statistics until Francis Galton, FRS, published *Hereditary Genius* in 1869 (Hill, 1984). From his studies of deviations from an average the whole modern theory of mathematical statistics has proceeded. Francis Ysidro Edgeworth presented a paper to the Statistical Society in 1885 *On Methods of Statistics*, which brought the calculus of probability into practical use by showing that, 'in apparatus for eliminating chance the most important piece of mechanism is the law of error or probability curve'. Only in the closing years of the century did the names of Karl Pearson, G. Udney-Yule, and A. L. Bowley emerge as the champions of mathematical statistics.

Dr William Farr

Farr was born in 1807 and adopted at the age of two by Mr Joseph Pryce, the village squire, who paid for the boy's education. Farr was a prodigious reader and when he was 19 years old started studying medicine as an apprentice to Dr Webster in Shrewsbury. Mr Pryce died when Farr was 21 and left him a legacy, which he used to study medicine for 2 years in Paris. He gained the medical qualification of Licentiate of the Society of Apothecaries in 1832. In Paris he was influenced by the teachings of Pierre-Charles-Alexandre Louis, the exponent of the 'numerical method', and this probably determined the future direction of his life. After qualifying as a doctor he had a brief career as a physician in London, punctuated by numerous contributions on public health to *The Lancet*, of which the most important were two papers in 1838, *On Benevolent Funds and Life Assurance in Health and Sickness*. He devoted the rest of his life to the study of vital statistics. As Statistical Superintendent at the General Register Office he was responsible for over 40 volumes of *Reports on Births, Deaths, and Marriages* and produced what was at the time acclaimed as a 'great work', *The English Life Table*.

The story of the Broad Street pump and the major outbreak of cholera in London in 1854 is well known. The credit for ascribing that outbreak to contaminated water, long before bacteria were shown to cause the disease, belongs as much to William Farr as to John Snow. Farr had been elected a Fellow of the Statistical Society in 1839 and was President from 1871 to 1873. He read numerous papers to the Society and made many contributions to the library. He was also a Fellow of the Royal Society.

Farr continued as Statistical Superintendent until 1880 when, at the age of 73 (having unsuccessfully applied for the post of Registrar General), he gave up the job, became increasingly mentally incapacitated, and died in 1883. In his later active years he collaborated with Florence Nightingale in the statistical analysis of diseases and deaths in the army and was instrumental in achieving many improvements in public health, both in the army and among the poor in the cities. In his report on deaths he laid down 12 rules for the control of 'zymotic diseases' (Humphreys, 1885):

'1. This is the primary rule: place the population in the sanitary condition found by experience to be most favourable to health...
2. Fortify the body by a mild disease, if any such is known, against a severe disease. Vaccination, or even inoculation...
3. ... use specific applications in the earliest stage of invasion ... careful experiments are required...
4. ...To suppress plague, suppress the wretched sanitary condition of Egypt ... to put a stop to pandemic outbreaks of cholera, cleanse the waters of India, and improve the condition of the population; to extinguish enteric fever and typhus in our cities, extinguish the rookeries.
5. Syphilis is dealt with [by] forcible detention of infected women in hospitals ... why is the principle not extended to both sexes?
6. The destruction of the zymotic germs by chemical agents, by fire and by disinfectants should in all cases be enforced.
7. Water in rivers charged with sewage ... conveys the germs unchanged ... The pure water of the hills is the safest.
8. The diffusion of several zymotic diseases ... is probably effected by detached flakes floating in the air. This danger is lessened by some such treatment as Dr W. Budd has suggested [cleaning and isolation].
9. The assembly of large masses of men in pilgrimages, or in any way, produces often coalescence of zymotic elements ...
10. The vessels [ships] should be under strict sanitary regulation, to intercept the transit of epidemics.
11. ...quarantine ... should be kept within the narrowest limits.
12. ... similar methods of prevention should be pursued in dealing with livestock.'

The nomenclature of diseases

Doctors made little attempt to be specific in their diagnoses until the nineteenth century. The gradual emergence of a taxonomy of disease was a phenomenon of the nineteenth century, more than 50 years after the great botanical taxonomy, Linnaeus's *Systema Naturae Fundamenta Botanica*. The classification of diseases was stimulated by the acceptance of rationalism after the French Revolution. Descartes, the 'father of modern philosophy', proposed that all natural events, not only mathematics, should be submitted to reason. Body functions should be explained in terms of engineering and mathematics.

One of the problems that the General Register Office tried to overcome was the unhelpful content of death certificates. Despite pleas by the Registrar General to doctors to give authentic names to fatal diseases, the bills of mortality in 1840 contained such entries as aged, convulsions, dropsy, inflammation, water in the head, carcinoma, debility and (the most common single item) consumption. Thomas Lister did his best to ensure that causes of death were accurately recorded, but it was not until 1855 that progress was made towards an internationally acceptable classification of diseases. Farr wrote: 'The utility of a uniform nomenclature in the registration of the causes of death was so strongly felt at the first Statistical Congress that the members expressed their opinion in the subjoined resolution; and Dr Marc D'Espine and I were requested to prepare a report on the ground that we had for several years the practical direction of statistical inquiries on this subject in Geneva and England. The resolution is to this effect: *Il y a lieu de former une nomenclature uniforme des causes de décès applicable à tous les pays'*.

The classification that was eventually favoured recognised four main groups: 'epidemic, endemic, and contagious diseases; sporadic disease of variable seat – for example, cancer; sporadic diseases of special systems or organs; and deaths from external causes – poisoning, asphyxia, and injuries'.

In Britain the classification of diseases that was first published in 1785 was replaced by an anatomically based 'nosology' that was circulated to doctors in 1845. This in turn was replaced by the *Nomenclature of Diseases*, the compilation of which was started in 1859, the first edition being published in 1869. The fourth edition was published in 1906, price one shilling (5 new pence). The *International Classification of Diseases* was not adopted in Britain until 1911.

A further problem about the early records of the causes of death was that it was not until 1874 that doctors were required to issue death certificates. In spite of these shortcomings, important epidemiological studies were made by analysing death certificates. By 1840 the General Register Office had started issuing *Weekly Returns* of the causes of death in London; these were later extended to cover other big cities. They allowed the correlation of diseases with occupation and with place of residence.

Sir Edwin Chadwick

Until the middle of the nineteenth century, the creation of healthy living conditions in towns was not considered a responsibility of the central government, and the squalor of the towns and cities became worse and worse. Sir Edwin Chadwick, Secretary to the Poor Law Commissioners, argued that it would be cheaper in the end to eradicate poverty than to palliate it by increasing expenditure on poor relief (Flinn, 1965). He produced a *Report to Her Majesty's Principal Secretary of State for the Home Department from the Poor Law Commissioners on an Inquiry into the Sanitary Condition of the Labouring Population of Great Britain. Presented to both Houses of Parliament by command of Her Majesty, July 1842*. This report, which showed that poverty was closely linked with appalling sanitary conditions and ill health, included a 'tabular return made up from the registration for the causes of death in England and Wales, which is the most complete yet attained'. This table was the work of William Farr and was originally published as Appendix 1 to the *First Report of the Registrar General* (1839). In Bethnal Green in London in 1839 the average age at death in several classes was: 'Gentlemen and persons engaged in professions, and their families – 45 years; tradesmen and their families – 26 years; mechanics, servants, and their families – 16 years'. It was not until the *Public Health Act 1848* was passed that for the first time the government was charged with a measure of responsibility for safeguarding the health of the population.

The major cause of the poverty, overcrowding, and lack of sanitation in the 1820s was the unprecedented migration from the countryside into the towns. Between 1821 and 1831 the population of Manchester, for example, went up by 47% and that of Bradford by 78%. The Statistical Society investigated the occupancy of 27 houses in Church Lane in the St Giles district of London, and found that the mean density was 24 persons per house in 1841, and 40 in 1847. One of the chief concerns of the *Sanitary Report* was the incidence of 'fever', a term that probably included both typhus and typhoid, described by Robert Cowan in a communication to the Statistical Society as 'that unerring index of destitution'. Curiously enough the *Report* hardly mentioned cholera. The importance of pulmonary tuberculosis ('consumption') was clearly recognised; it accounted for more deaths than any other single cause.

In the early nineteenth century Edinburgh was the most important medical school in Britain, and one of the men most influential in widening medical horizons to include public health was William Pulteney Alison, Professor of Medicine from 1820 to 1856. Chadwick obtained most of his data about Scotland from Alison, and also sought opinions and data from sources all over the rest of Britain. The preparation of the *Report* took nearly 3 years and as soon as it was published Chadwick sent copies to many influential people, including Charles Dickens and the Archbishop of Dublin. *The Times* carried a leading article on the *Report* and other influential journals also commented on it.

Chadwick's main concern was the presentation of facts relating to poverty, filth, overcrowding and disease; he concluded that, 'the primary and most important measures and at the same time the most practical, and within the recognised providence of public administration, are drainage, the removal of all refuse from habitations, street, and roads, and the improvement of the supplies of water'. He made one specific suggestion, that instead of removing refuse and sewage by hand, it would be far cheaper to remove it in suspension in water in glazed circular bore drains. The sewers of the early nineteenth century were brick built square constructions that habitually became blocked and did not carry a sufficient volume of water to clear detritus.

A paper by Chadwick (Flinn, 1965) was published in 1844 in the Annual Report of the Statistical Society with the title *The Best Modes of Representing the Duration of Life, and the Pressure and Progress of the Causes of Mortality Amongst Different Classes and Different Districts and Countries.* The prevailing theory of the spread of infections at the time was the miasma theory, expressed by Chadwick's collaborator Southwood Smith in 1830: 'The immediate or the exciting cause of fever is a poison formed by the corruption or the decomposition of organic matter. Vegetable and animal matter, during the process of putrefaction, give off a principle, or give origin to a new compound which, when applied to the human body, produces the phenomena constituting fever.' This theory was contested by Alison in Edinburgh and the rift between these two men may have been partly responsible for the fact that the *Public Health Act 1848* did not apply to Scotland, and it was not until 1867 that the *Public Health (Scotland) Act* was passed.

Florence Nightingale

In 1863 Florence Nightingale observed: 'In attempting to arrive at the truth I have applied everywhere for information but in scarcely an instance have I been able to obtain hospital records fit for any purpose and comparison. If they could be obtained they would enable us to decide many other questions beside the one alluded to. They would show subscribers how their money was being spent, what amount of good was really being done with it or whether the money was not doing mischief rather than good!'

Florence Nightingale's revelations of the inadequacies of the British Army's administrative and medical services during the Crimean War led to a new wave of inquiry and reform in Britain. By the middle of the nineteenth century it was obvious to three great powers that the Ottoman empire was on the verge of collapse and each of these three – Britain, France, and Russia – was intent on securing its influence in Turkey. The Crimean war broke out between France and Britain on the one hand, and Russia on the other, because of a ridiculous squabble between Napoleon III and Czar Nicholas over the question of claims to the custody of the Holy Places in Palestine. Napoleon proclaimed himself the champion of the Catholic pretensions, and Nicholas of those of the Greek Orthodox church. War finally broke out in March 1854 almost accidentally, and certainly found the Anglo-French alliance inordinately unprepared.

The siege of Sevastopol was conducted in appalling climatic conditions and with practically no logistic support. It was to this scene that Florence Nightingale and a small team of nurses came to Scutari in 1855. It transpired that 3186 men died in hospital in January 1855, 83 from wounds, 2761 from infectious diseases, and 324 from other causes. *The Times* reported that 'Not only are there not sufficient surgeons ... not only are there no dressers and nurses ... there is not even linen to make bandages.' At its worst over 40% of the soldiers admitted to the Barrack Hospital in Scutari died there, but within six months of the arrival of Miss Nightingale's nurses, the mortality was down to 2%. These events had an enormous influence in improving the condition of hospitals in Britain in the second half of the nineteenth century.

Unqualified doctors in the nineteenth century

One of the problems about the gathering of statistics in the first half of the nineteenth century was the abysmal ignorance of many so-called doctors; this also accounted for the low esteem in which the profession was held in the community. In 1841 the Census listed 33 339 persons as practitioners in all branches of medicine, whereas eight years later the medical directories gave the names of only 11 808 qualified doctors (Vaughan, 1959): there were twice as many unqualified as qualified practitioners.

Even the doctors who were apparently qualified (or at least had been awarded a medical degree) often had little or no training. At the older universities it was possible to collect a medical degree merely by remaining in residence for the required time and attending two dissections. In

1840 medical qualifications could be awarded by any one of 19 separate authorities, including the Archbishop of Canterbury! The best medical training was probably by being apprenticed to the house surgeon of a hospital. Of the official medical schools, only Edinburgh and the private medical schools in London, such as Hunters, Brookes, and Dermotts offered good training.

Medical Reform Bills calling for uniform qualifications for medical practitioners were abandoned time after time, and it was not until 1858 that the first *Medical Act* became law. This Act proclaimed that, 'it is expedient that persons requiring medical aid should be enabled to distinguish qualified from unqualified medical practitioners'. This was to be achieved by the setting up of a General Council of Medical Education and Registration of the United Kingdom (the title later shortened to General Medical Council). The functions of the General Medical Council were first, to set and maintain minimum standards of medical education and, second, to publish an authorised pharmacopoeia. In no way did the Act prohibit the practice of medicine by unqualified persons, but it did prescribe a fine of £20 for anyone who professed to be a qualified practitioner but whose name was not in the Medical Register.

An *Amending Medical Act* was passed in 1886; wider representation of doctors on the General Medical Council was not required, and the Council was instructed to ensure that qualifying examinations in all three branches of practice (medicine, surgery, and midwifery) were held and reflected a satisfactory standard of proficiency. There is still no legal bar in Britain to the practice of medicine by unqualified people, provided that they do not pretend to be qualified, do not prescribe addictive drugs, do not profess to treat certain serious diseases, and do not sign death certificates.

As for patent medicines, a series of publications in the *British Medical Journal* on *Secret Remedies* was consistently ignored by the press, which derived a considerable income from advertisements for these nostrums. It was not until 1939 that the first inroads into this trade were made. That year saw the passing of the *Cancer Act*, which forbade anyone but a registered medical practitioner from treating, or offering to treat, cancer. In 1941 a similar restriction was placed on the advertisement of drugs for the treatment of many other serious diseases; the death knell of the lucrative business was finally tolled with the adoption of the *British Code of Standards in Relation to the Advertising of Medicines and Treatments* in 1949.

Conclusions

The nineteenth century was marked by profound changes in the collection of national statistics of births and deaths, and more accurate classifications of diseases. Without these advances no progress in the assurance of the quality of medical and surgical practice would have been possible.

References

Anonymous (1921) Medical statistics. *Lancet*, **i**, 985–988

Bonar, J. and Macrosty, H.W. (1934) *Annals of the Royal Statistcal Society 1834–1934.* The Royal Statistical Society, London

Cromwell, O. (1650) *Letter to the General Assembly of the Church of Scotland.* 3 August

Farr, W. (1838) On benevolent funds and life assurance in health and sickness. *Lancet,* **1**, 701–704; 817–823

Flinn, M.W. (ed.) (1965) *Report on the Sanitary Condition of the Labouring Population of Great Britain by Edwin Chadwick, 1842.* Edinburgh University Press, Edinburgh

Hill, I.D. (1984) Statistical Society of London–Royal Statistical Society. The first 100 years: 1834–1934. *Journal of the Royal Statistical Society,* **147**, 130–139

Humphreys, N.A. (ed.) (1885) *Vital Statistics: A Memorial Volume of Selections from the Reports and Writings of William Farr MD, DCL, CB, FRS.* Edward Stanford, London, pp. 250–330

Nissel, M. (1987) *People Count. A History of the General Register Office.* Her Majesty's Stationery Office, London

Strauss, M.B. (ed.) (1968) *Familiar Medical Quotations.* Little, Brown and Co., Boston, p. 492.

Vaughan, P. (1959) *Doctors' Commons. A Short History of the British Medical Association.* Heinemann, London

Chapter 2

The evolution of surgical audit

Trace science then, with modesty thy guide; First strip off all her equipage of pride.   Alexander Pope (1733)

The second half of the nineteenth century was an exciting time for surgeons. For the first time they could operate slowly and meticulously without inflicting pain. It was no wonder, then, that most of them were content to master new techniques of operating and were less concerned about the outcome of their efforts than about their ability to expand their expertise.

Joseph Lister, Regius Professor of Surgery at the Royal Infirmary in Glasgow from 1860 to 1869, is regarded as the father of modern surgery. He wrote about the beneficial action of phenol in compound fractures and severe lacerations. He published no detailed statistics but concluded his famous paper in the *British Medical Journal* (Lister, 1867) with the statement: 'But since the antiseptic treatment has been brought into full operation, and wounds and abscesses no longer poison the atmosphere with putrid exhalations, my wards, though in other respects under precisely the same circumstances as before, have completely changed their character; so that during the last nine months not a single instance of pyaemia, hospital gangrene or erysipelas has occurred in them.'

How was this achieved? By 'introducing the acid [phenol] of full strength into all accessible recesses of the wound by means of a piece of rag held in dressing forceps and dipped in the liquid' followed by 'employing a paste composed of common whiting (carbonate of lime) mixed with one part of carbolic acid in four parts of boiled linseed oil, so as to form a firm putty....So long as any discharge continues, the paste should be changed daily and, in order to prevent the chance of mischief occurring during the process, a piece of rag dipped in the solution of carbolic acid in oil is put on next to the skin, and maintained there permanently'.

It seems incredible that this treatment did not do more harm than good. The reason for its success undoubtedly must be sought in unacknowledged changes in management, perhaps the most important of which was that the contaminated hands of the attendants no longer came into contact with the wound. It was indeed fortunate that others, notably William Macewan, abandoned the antiseptic method and introduced aseptic techniques. Lister himself was gradually weaned away from antiseptics, so that by 1896 he was able to report to the British Association for the Advancement of Science that 'The irritation of the wound by antiseptic irrigation and washing may therefore now be avoided, and nature left quite undisturbed to carry out her best methods of repair.'

The normal method of auditing one's clinical results towards the end of the nineteenth century was by giving testimonials. There were, of course, people who wanted to see more accurate descriptions of the outcome of diseases and operations, and annual reports of mortality were produced in many hospitals. An exceptional piece of original clinical research was by Henry Burdett (1882), who gave a paper to the Statistical Society on *The relative mortality, after amputations, of large and small hospitals, and the influence of the antiseptic (Listerian) system upon such mortality*. He personally collected statistics on amputations for injury and disease from 61 cottage hospitals with a total of 553 beds, from 1858 to 1878. There were 326 such cases and 58 deaths (18%). He compared this figure with published figures from large hospitals in London (38%), Paris (60%), Zurich (46%), Edinburgh (43%), and Glasgow – up to 1868 – (39%). He drew attention to the work of Sir James Simpson who had written about a disease he called 'hospitalism'. He also noted that Dr Schede of Hamburg had adopted aseptic practices and published a 3% mortality after 234 amputations.

In the early twentieth century hospitals were in the process of change and 'the pesthouse [was] transformed into a compartmentalised repair shop' (Illich, 1976). People became concerned about the outcome of operations, and James Rigby of Preston published an article in a lay journal, *The Independent Review*, pleading for the establishment of independent enquiries into postoperative deaths. He proposed that 'in the interests of the people at large, it is time the power of life and death should be seriously inquired into'. This suggestion went down extremely badly with the establishment, and in 1907 and again in 1908 the *British Medical Journal* published editorial articles complaining that Rigby was proposing a 'Star Chamber of Surgery'.

The first serious attempts to introduce national audits of outcome were made in Britain by Ernest Hey Groves (1908) and in 1910 in the United States by Ernest Amory Codman (Reverby, 1981).

Ernest Hey Groves

Groves gave a paper at the 76th annual meeting of the British Medical Association in Sheffield in 1908 in which he complained that the methods of compilation of statistics by individual surgeons were 'very inadequate' and represented 'the best and not the average results'. He estimated that in the 15 737 beds available in Britain some 73 000 major operations were performed each year, and wrote that 'the question which I would like to propose today is whether it would not be worthwhile making a systematic effort to collect these records in a uniform way, so as to constitute an annual standard of reference and index of progress....In this way the profession would be afforded each year an absolutely authoritative and impartial report of the results of all the major operations performed in the United Kingdom. From this could be derived the most valuable knowledge as to the prognosis after operations, the increase or decrease of various diseases, and the different operations performed for their relief. And the improvement in results could be noted in each procedure by the comparison of one year's results with another.'

Groves sent a circular letter to the surgical registrars at 50 large hospitals, asking 'what the practice was at each institution with regard to the keeping and publishing of operation statistics in relation to the immediate and remote mortality, and what was the opinion of each registrar as to the advisability and feasibility of adopting a uniform system of registration throughout the country'. Replies were received from only 27 of the 50 hospitals, and only 17 claimed to publish details showing operative mortality. None of the hospitals recorded remote results of operations. From the limited figures available to him, Hey Groves estimated that the operative mortality for cancer of the stomach was 44%, for cancer of the rectum 24%, for prostatectomy 24%, and for appendicitis 9%.

He put forward six points for consideration and action:

1. There should be a central authority (he suggested the British Medical Association) to collect and publish statistics from all hospitals.
2. There should be an organising committee to draw up details of nomenclature and registration.
3. There should be a uniform system of nomenclature of diseases and operations.
4. The late outcome of patients operated on for cancer should be recorded.
5. The data should be recorded under the supervision of the registrar at each hospital.
6. Data should be sent to a central registrar at the end of each year and 'he would put them together and present the combined figures as a collective report.'

One would have thought that Groves's revolutionary ideas would have generated a lot of correspondence, but the publication of his paper was greeted by a stony silence. Neither in the correspondence column of the *British Medical Journal*, nor in the editorial column, was the slightest reference made to his paper, and the suggestion was not acted on.

Ernest Amory Codman

Codman was appointed assistant surgeon to outpatients at Massachusetts General Hospital in 1898, at a time when the status of hospitals was gradually being transformed from that of hospices towards the present-day concept that they are factories for the treatment of diseases. He became interested in evaluating the practice of surgery scientifically, and as early as 1900 he and his chief, F.B. Harrington, started recording the outcome of the treatment of patients under their care. This remained a personal programme for many years, but by 1910 he had formulated the End Result System, which he claimed 'was merely the common sense notion that every hospital should follow every patient it treats long enough to determine whether or not the treatment has been successful and then to enquire 'if not, why not?' with a view to preventing similar failures in future'. In a privately published monograph entitled *A study in hospital efficiency as demonstrated by the case reports of the first five years of a private hospital* he enumerated the causes following which 'all results of surgical treatment which lack perfection may be explained....These should be acknowledged to ourselves and to the public, and study directed to their prevention'. They were:

- Errors due to lack of technical knowledge or skill
- Errors due to lack of surgical judgement
- Errors due to lack of care or equipment
- Errors due to lack of diagnostic skill
- The patient's enfeebled condition
- The patient's unconquerable disease
- The patient's refusal of treatment
- The calamities of surgery or those accidents and complications over which we have no known control

Codman required hospital trustees and administrators to take part in audit and wrote to surgeons all over the United States urging them to introduce his system. He made one of the earliest attempts to define the product of a hospital – analogous to the product of a manufacturer (Codman, 1914). He defined the product of the Massachusetts General Hospital in terms of the numbers of patients treated, of students trained, of nurses graduated, and of scientific papers published. The concept of the products of hospitals was revived in the 1960s and culminated in 1983 in the introduction of Diagnosis Related Groups as a mechanism for justly rewarding hospitals for their care of patients under the Medicare scheme in the United States.

In 1913 at the Clinical Congress of Surgeons (the forerunner of the American College of Surgeons) Codman was appointed chairman of the Committee on Hospital Standardisation. The other members of this committee were W. J. Mayo (Rochester, Minnesota), W.W. Chipman (Montreal), J.G. Clarke (Philadelphia), and A.B. Kanavel (Chicago). The committee produced reports in 1914 and 1916 (Codman, 1916). In the second report Codman, who had an abrasive personality, made sure that he irritated as many people as possible when he wrote: 'This [the prevailing system of hospital appointments] drives every doctor to care more for his reputation than his efficiency and tempts him to spend his time in concealing his ignorance rather than increasing his knowledge.'

Codman's 'End Result System' had no more success than Groves's Uniform Registration of Operation Results. His abrasive manner seems to have mellowed as he got older, and he was reinstated as a consultant surgeon by the Massachusetts General Hospital in 1929 at the age of 60, where he devoted his time to the establishment of the Registry of Bone Sarcoma. He died in 1940 at the age of 71 years.

The next step towards an audit of surgery was the establishment of the Hospital Standardization Program by the American College of Surgeons. This resulted from the work of Abraham Flexner.

Abraham Flexner

Flexner was commissioned by the Carnegie Foundation to produce a report on the state of the medical schools in the United States (Flexner 1910). Most of the 165 medical schools were profit-making institutions that accepted poorly prepared students, some without a high school education. After 2 or 3 years of tuition, in some cases without even being allowed to see hospital patients, these students were given diplomas, and no less than 5200 new doctors a year were poured out into a profession that was already overcrowded (Lembcke, 1956). Flexner recommended a shift to scientifically based professional education that would exclude other approaches to treatment, thereafter stigmatised as quackery. The basis of good treatment was to be the intelligent use of drugs, and all medical schools were required to have departments of pharmacology. They were also to be associated with universities.

Mainly as a result of Flexner's report the newly formed American College of Surgeons established the Hospital Standardization Program in 1917. The scope of the programme was limited to assessment of aspects of structure and process. These embraced qualifications for membership of the medical staff, rules and policies governing professional work in hospitals, medical records, and diagnostic and therapeutic facilities. The College began inspecting all hospitals with more than 100 beds in 1918, but only 89 of 692 hospitals came up to their 'minimum standards' (Roberts, Coale and Redman, 1987). This figure was made public, but the names of the hospitals that failed to meet the requirements are forever lost because the College burned the list of hospitals in the furnace of the Waldorf Astoria hotel in New York.

Joint Commission on Accreditation of Hospitals

The Hospital Standardization Program became increasingly accepted by hospitals in the United States. It accomplished a tremendous amount of good and ensured that the quality of hospitals and medical schools came to match the best in the world. It remained in existence until 1951 when, in cooperation with the American Medical Association, the American College of Physicians, and the American Hospital Association, the American College of Surgeons established the Joint Commission on Accreditation of Hospitals. For the next 35 years the Commission used criteria of structure and process to audit the acceptability of hospitals throughout the United States. It laid stress on two aspects: the establishment of tissue committees to review operative specimens and to pronounce whether the organs or tissues had been justifiably removed or not, and the establishment of mechanisms for peer review.

As time went on the standards of the Joint Commission became more detailed, and its 'agenda for change' in the 1990s will require accredited hospitals and other health care organisations to show not only that they have the potential for providing high quality medical care, but also that they actually do provide care of a standard that results in an acceptable outcome. As a result of its acceptance of accreditation programmes for hospice care and home care it became necessary for the Commission to change its name and it is now known as the Joint Commission on Accreditation of Healthcare Organizations.

The Joint Commission is not a statutory body and it does not have any powers of sanction. Nevertheless, many purchasers of health care will deal only with hospitals that are accredited. Other organisations have emerged, some with statutory powers. These include the Health Care Financing Administration and the Peer Review Organization. New York State has accepted the standards of the Joint Commission and conducts periodic inspections of accredited hospitals. It has the power to close down without notice any hospital that fails to comply with those standards.

Relman (1988) wrote that we are now in the midst of a third revolution in medical care. The first was the expansion of hospital technology and scientific medicine, the second the era of cost containment, and the third he calls the 'era of assessment and accountability'.

Joint Committee on Higher Surgical Training

The function of this British committee is to investigate whether the structure and process of surgery in British hospitals are adequate to allow them to train surgeons. It requires that hospitals have the necessary operating theatres and staff, that libraries and other educational facilities are adequate, and that morbidity and mortality meetings are held. No attempt has been made to audit outcome although, as we will discuss in Chapter 14, the Association of Surgeons of Great Britain and Ireland, together with the Association of Anaesthetists of Great Britain and Ireland conducted a pilot study on a Confidential Enquiry into Perioperative Deaths in 1985, and this has been expanded into a national study.

Medical audit in Britain, 1991

In 1989 the government published a working paper, which recommended the setting up in each district in Britain of a district medical audit advisory committee. These committees are to be chaired by senior clinicians and include representatives of the major medical specialties including general practice. Their role is to plan and monitor a comprehensive programme of medical audit, to produce annual forward programmes and annual reports. These reports will detail the procedures used, the services covered, the results of audits carried out (with suitable precautions to preserve confidentiality), and to recommend actions to remedy defects in effectiveness or efficiency that have been disclosed by the audits.

Australian Council on Healthcare Standards

Founded in 1974, the Council adopted its present name in 1988 to reflect its interest in all aspects of health care, not only in hospitals. The chairman is a surgeon, Brian Collopy, and the Council, which is an independent non-profit making organisation, has the following objectives (ACHS Accreditation Guide, 1990):

- To establish optimal standards relating to administration, quality of care, essential services, and safety, for Australian hospitals and other health care facilities.
- To conduct a national programme of voluntary accreditation of health care facilities by survey and issuance of an appropriate certificate.
- To assist in achievement of accreditation by educational activities.
- To encourage the development and evaluation of systems for assessment of patient care.
- To liaise with government, professional bodies, and other associations in regard to the standard requirements of health care facilities and the community.
- To promote the above objectives through public information.
- To conduct such other activities as are compatible with the achievement of optimal standards.

The Council issues accreditation guides at frequent intervals, and hospitals and other facilities are invited to seek accreditation after being surveyed by a visiting team of three people – a doctor, a nurse, and an administrator – who enquire chiefly into the structure and processes of the places that they visit. In 1990 the Council took the further step of setting up a Care Evaluation Programme and issued draft indicators of clinical care to evaluate the quality of the outcome of interventions. We consider these and other indicators in Chapter 10.

Accreditation is for limited periods, after which reaccreditation is required. The key elements that are required of all facilities are 'a commitment to quality patient care, efficiency, safety, and evaluation of the services provided'.

The eighth edition of the Guide, which occupies 300 pages, lays down standards for the following services: accident and emergency, allied health professional, anaesthetic, day procedure, environmental (including safety procedures, engineering and building, disaster plans, infection control, and central sterilising), governing body and management (including patients' rights and special needs), laboratory, library, medical records, medical and surgical (including rigorous quality assurance programmes), nursing, operating suite, pharmacy, radiology, rehabilitation, social work, special care, maternal and neonatal, nuclear medicine, psychiatry, psychology, and community health.

Conclusion

The last 150 years have seen great progress in the collection of national statistics, although those of the causes of death remain inaccurate because most deaths are not followed by necropsies. Audits of structure and process are well established and probably effective, but audits of outcome are essentially parochial, often confined to the results of a single doctor's practice, or at most to that of a few doctors. There is a lot of work to be done, and a lot of opinions to be changed, before anything approaching national audits of outcome can be produced.

References

ACHS Accreditation Guide (1990) Standards for health care facilities, 8th edn. ACHS, Melbourne

Burdett, H.C. (1882) The relative mortality, after amputations, of large and small hospitals, and the influence of the antiseptic (Listerian) system upon such mortality. *Journal of the Statistical Society*, **45**, 444–483

Codman, E.A. (1914) The product of a hospital. *Surgery, Gynecology and Obstetrics*, **18**, 491–496

Codman, E.A. (1916) Report of Committee on Hospital Standardization. *Surgery, Gynecology and Obstetrics*, **22**, 119–120

Flexner, A. (1910) *Medical Education in United States and Canada: report to Carnegie Foundation for Advancement of Teaching*. DP Updike, the Merrymount Press., New York

Groves, E.W. Hey (1908) Surgical statistics: a plea for a uniform registration of operation results. *British Medical Journal*, **2**, 1008–1009

Illich, I. (1976) Limits to medicine. *Medical Nemesis: The Expropriation of Health*. London, Marion Boyars, p. 163

Lembcke, P.A. (1956) Medical auditing by scientific methods. Illustrated by major female pelvic surgery. *Journal of the American Medical Association*, **162**, 646–655

Lister, J. (1867) On the antiseptic principle in the practice of surgery. *British Medical Journal*, **2**, 246–248

Pope, A. (1733). *An Essay on Man*, second epistle, lines 43–44

Relman, A.S. (1988) Assessment and accountability: the third revolution. *New England Journal of Medicine*, **319**, 1220–1222

Reverby, S. (1981) Stealing the golden egg: Ernest Amory Codman and the science and management of medicine. *Bulletin of the History of Medicine*, **55**, 156–171

Roberts, J.S., Coale, J.G. and Redman, R.R. (1987) A history of the Joint Commission on Accreditation of Hospitals. *Journal of the American Medical Association*, **258**, 936–940

The components of audit

Chapter 3

What is audit?

*Know then thyself, presume not God to scan. The proper study of
mankind is man.* Alexander Pope (1733)

*Good medical practice requires a high level of professional knowledge,
personal dedication, the ability to communicate, and – most of all – the
ability to make time. It also demands a difficult balance between self-
confidence and self-questioning. Too much of the former leads to
arrogance, too much of the latter to indecision.* Black (1981)

'Clinical audit' is a time honoured term. Most people would, however, be
happier with the term 'quality assurance'. The main reason for undertaking clinical audit is to assure the quality of care.

What is quality?

Maxwell (1984) wrote about the six dimensions of health care quality.
They are:

- Access to services
- Relevance to need (for the whole community)
- Effectiveness (for individual patients)
- Equity (fairness)
- Social acceptability
- Efficiency and economy

Donabedian (1989) required three components: good technical care, good
interpersonal relationships, and good amenities. The four aims of good
practice are that it should be effective, safe, efficient, and that it should
satisfy patients.

Effectiveness implies that the correct steps are taken in the correct
order to restore health and to minimise suffering and the risk of death. It
must be distinguished from efficacy, which implies that a certain treatment
works under ideal circumstances (such as a random control clinical trial).

Safety includes the avoidance of iatrogenic, drug-induced, and nosocomial complications.

Efficiency (cost effectiveness) includes not only consideration of the cost of a particular service, but also the distribution of resources in accordance with need: resources are finite and if too many are poured into one division of care, others will be deprived. The Committee of Enquiry into Competence to Practise (Alment, 1981) reported that 'resources ... used for one patient may be denied to another. This conflict of interests ... involves the doctor in consciously rationing his time and often amending an ideal course of treatment for one of his patients so that others may benefit'.

If patients are to be satisfied – and this is probably the most important of all the aspects of quality assurance – they must be satisfied not only with the availability, appropriateness, and accessibility of health care, but also with the continuity, reasonable cost, and satisfactory outcome of that care. Communication and compassion are equally important, as is the patient's awareness that he or she is a partner in the process of care, not merely a dumb recipient. As Stokes (1971) wrote: 'Most patients when they are ill are more interested in kindliness than creatinine clearance, in understanding rather than iron binding capacity'.

The components of audit

Audit has three components: structure, process, and outcome. Sheldon (1982) defined clinical audit as 'A study of some part of the structure, process, and outcome of medical care, carried out by those personally engaged in the activity concerned, to measure whether set objectives have been attained, and thus assess the quality of care delivered.' He published the five steps of clinical audit, of which the following is a modified version:

1. Set clinical obectives after discussion with peers, reading journals, and attending meetings. *What am I trying to achieve? How should I go about it?*
2. Collect and analyse information. *What do I actually do?*
3. Evaluate the process and outcome of care. *Have my original objectives been achieved?*
4. Review objectives and clinical care. *Were the original objectives realistic? What changes should I make?*
5. Repeat the process to monitor changes.

This is a sort of private audit and most doctors follow some such scheme, whether consciously or unconsciously. Dr K. Carnegie-Smith (personal communication) wrote that 'The anticipated future funding of the National Health Service will allow very little growth unless from efficiency savings made from within the existing services. This is where the concept of medical audit is useful .... Doctors [must] ask:
Am I doing what I think I am doing?
Am I providing services to the right people?
Am I providing services at the right time?
Am I providing services in the right place?
Is there any way I could achieve comparable results using fewer resources?

Are patients getting the service they require?
What services ought I to be providing?'

The Royal College of Physicians of London (1989) suggested that certain factors should be common to all systems of audit:

- Purpose: should be educational and relevant to patient care
- Control: should be by clinical peers with voluntary participation
- Standards: should be set locally by participating clinicians
- Method: should be non-threatening, interesting, objective, and repeatable
- Resources: should be cheap, simple, and cause minimal disturbance
- Records: should contain adequate clinical content and be easily retrieved.

Audit of structure

The audit of structure is essentially administrative. Are there enough hospitals, enough doctors, enough nurses? Are educational standards satisfactory? Are there adequate facilities for treating old people, and mentally ill people, and patients in need of joint replacements? Are there enough operating theatres and is the equipment up to date? Are the facilities for diagnostic imaging adequate?

In all these cases the collection of accurate figures is essential, and it is up to individual doctors to make sure that the data collected by administrators are accurate and valid, and to help administrators and politicians to make balanced decisions about priorities in the allocation of resources. We must never lose sight of the fact that doctors are responsible for nearly all the spending on health care, and it is up to them to see that the resources are used wisely and justly.

Audit of process

Process is a word borrowed from industry, where it serves well: if the correct steps are taken in the correct order, the outcome be it measured in goods or services will be satisfactory. In medicine the audit of process is so much easier than the audit of outcome that it tends to be carried out with greater assiduity.

Audit of outcome

Difficulties arise when it comes to peer audit of the outcome of the practice of individual doctors. Sir Karl Popper (1980) wrote that 'The wrong view of science betrays itself in the craving to be right.' Doctors are not primarily scientists, and opposition to external audit is strong. Doctors do not like admitting that they make errors, nor do they like being criticised. As Gorowitz and MacIntyre (1976) wrote: 'The physician's propensity for damaging error is widely denied, perhaps because they themselves hold ... that error arises either from their or their colleagues' ignorance or ineptitude.'

There are other reasons for the resistance to external audit: in the first place a good doctor considers his patients and their welfare first, and he feels that the revelation of errors could undermine the paternalistic relationship between him and his patients. Secondly, doctors, once they have passed their training years, are independent practitioners and dislike anybody prying into their affairs. Thirdly, faced with an unfortunate outcome of treatment they are likely to adopt an attitude of nonchalance, claiming that it was not their error but the patient's constitution, the severity of the disease, or social factors, that determined the poor outcome (Nelson, 1976). Hilfiker (1984) wrote a moving account of how a general practitioner in northern Minnesota, 110 miles from the nearest ultrasound facilities, was misled by four negative pregnancy tests into doing a dilatation and curettage for a friend's wife who was 13 weeks' pregnant. He discussed medical mistakes, how serious they can be, and how it is impossible to deal with them in a psychological healthy fashion by confession, restitution, and absolution. He regretted that there is no place in medical practice for real confession – for the doctor to say 'this is the mistake I made; I'm sorry'.

Finally, there are fears that an audit may uncover an error, may not remain confidential, and may lead to legal action by an injured patient or his family. A friend of ours, newly appointed to an academic post, set up a weekly 'Deaths and complications' meeting and, to set the right tone, spoke of an error that he had made. An envious colleague disclosed details of the case to the press and to the family of the patient, and litigation followed.

The assumption by some doctors that they do not make mistakes has led to the accusation that the profession is arrogant. Ingelfinger (1980) disputed this, holding that bioscientists show no more hubris than other groups, that a certain amount of authoritarianism, paternalism, and domination are essential to good medical care, and that 'arrogant' is the wrong word; that adjective should apply rather to those who reach conclusions on the basis of inadequate data and refuse to admit that their evidence is inadequate. If a doctor is to help his patients they must believe in him. Having put forward all alternatives the doctor must give his advice – it is then up to the patient to make up his own mind. After having a gastrectomy for cancer, Dr Ingelfinger himself became increasingly confused and emotionally distraught by the conflicting advice he was given about chemotherapy or radiotherapy until a friend said 'What you need is a doctor.' He pleaded for more empathy and complained that nowadays a patient is first 'processed' through a battery of questionnaires or computer terminals, then interrogated and examined by ancillary personnel; he finally gets to see the doctor who delivers his verdict. How, asked Ingelfinger, can a doctor get to know his patients like that?

The establishment of standards

Structure

In America the structure of medical care has grown haphazardly, fuelled by no more compelling reasons than local demand and the willingness of local inhabitants to pay for new hospitals and for all the paraphernalia of modern medical technology. This has resulted in the supply of far too many hospital beds and is partly responsible for the astronomical cost of health care in the United States.

Rosenthal (1964) outlined the history of the establishment of hospitals in the United States. 'Prior to the enactment of the Hospital Survey and Construction (Hill Burton) Act in 1946, any discussion of the allocation of facilities among the states would have been merely an academic exercise. Until the 1930s the construction and expansion of general hospital facilities were the responsibility of the local community. The decision to locate facilities in any particular community was the result of local interest and the availability of local financing .... The economic depression of the 1930s was responsible for an almost complete halt in new hospital construction .... More than 700 hospitals were closed ... because of inadequate funds. During this period the first federal grants in aid for hospital construction were made as part of the government public works program. However, no attempt was made to allocate the hospital facilities according to a plan, since the primary value of the program was held to be its effect on income and employment .... Another program of federal assistance was introduced during World War II under the *Lanham Act*. This emergency program provided funds ... for the construction of health facilities in communities where increases in population had occurred as a result of the expansion of production for defense purposes.'

The *Lanham Act* required comprehensive planning in each state, starting with an inventory and including minimum standards of design for functional adequacy and safety. There had to be local demand and local money before federal support was forthcoming. The number of beds regarded as adequate was fixed at 4.5 per 1000 population in those states in which there were more than 12 people per square mile, 5.0 in states with 6 to 12 people per square mile, and 5.5 when the population density was less than 6 per square mile. There was no provision for other indicators of need, and no way of ensuring that the facilities would be used. Two communities of identical size seldom need the same number of hospital beds. Such need varies widely with the cultural characteristics of the area, the age distribution, the quality of preventive care, the effectiveness of outpatient and home care, and the adequacy of social welfare services. It is necessary also to take into account the acceptability of shorter stays in hospital, the emergence of new operations to treat previously untreatable conditions, and the number of 'cross border' and tertiary referrals.

Nearly all hospitals need to keep a certain number of beds for emergencies, but the calculation of the number required is difficult. The formula suggested in 1928 by the United States Committee on the Costs of Medical Care was that the number should be three times the square root of the mean daily occupancy. This means that the proportion of beds kept empty for emergencies needs to be less in a large hospital than in a small one.

The structure of medical care in Britain has been equally unorganised, depending as it does on the continued existence of the old charity and municipal hospitals that were established before the start of the National Health Service in 1948. The inequalities in structure are illustrated by an analysis of the number of acute beds per 1000 resident population in different districts. For example, among districts with teaching hospitals, this ranged from 2.65 (Leicestershire) to 16.08 (Bloomsbury), and among districts without teaching hospitals from 1.85 (North Derbyshire) to 4.37 (Haringey) (Performance Indicator Group, 1987).

Process: the collection of data

In the United States the Joint Commission of Accreditation of Hospitals was established in 1951 by the American College of Surgeons in cooperation with the American Medical Association, the American College of Physicians, and the American Hospital Association. At first the criteria for accreditation were the existence of a Tissue Committee to report on the proportion of normal tissues removed, and of a Credentials Committee to monitor staff appointments. In the 1960s federal money was used to establish 'utilisation reviews', the functions of which were to ensure that admissions were necessary and that duration of hospital stay was not unduly long. This kind of review was not cost effective and 'its continued survival for 16 years ... is a tribute to the durability of bureaucracy' (McSherry, 1982).

In 1979 the report of a Royal Commission on the National Health Service in Britain (the *Merrison report*) was scathing on the subject of data gathering: 'The information available to assist decision-makers in the NHS leaves much to be desired. Relevant information may not be available at all, or in the wrong form. Information that is produced is often too late to assist decisions or may be of dubious accuracy.' The Hospital Activity Analysis programme in Britain was not only inaccurate, but also the figures were produced far too late to have any influence on medical or surgical practice.

In 1980 the Department of Health and Social Security announced that Mrs Edith Körner was to chair a Steering Group on Health Services Information, the duties of which were 'to agree, implement, and keep under review principles and procedures to guide the future development of health service information systems; to identify and resolve health services information issues requiring a coordinated approach; to review existing health services information systems; and to consider proposals for changes to, or developments in, health services information systems arising elsewhere and, if acceptable, to assess priorities for their development and implementation.'

There were seven main Körner reports published between 1982 and 1984, the purposes of which were the identification of minimum data sets that were 'desirable, feasible, and affordable' (Körner 1982). The Körner reports did not address the question of retrieval and analysis of clinical data in individual doctors' practices for auditing the outcome of treatment.

The purpose of gathering information in industry is to guide management to maintain the profitability of the business: the basic requirements are a knowledge of throughput, of stock, and of manpower to measure the surplus value produced. In health care, however, there is scant correlation between measurements of process and of outcome. McAuliffe (1978) tried to show that outcome is dependent on process. He found methodological defects in many of the studies purporting to show that measures of process and of outcome were unrelated. He claimed that many writers failed to recognise contributory causes, other than the quality of process, of poor (or of good) outcome. He gave the example of two patients with fractured femurs – one an athlete aged 21, the other a lady of 90. Given the same quality of care, the outcome is likely to be better for the young man. McAuliffe suggested that audit of process could be improved if medical procedures were evaluated by controlled trials and if records – for research at least – were better than they are in casenotes. He concluded that 'we know very little regarding the validity of methods being used to assess quality of care. Recent policies and pronouncements strongly favouring outcome measurements should therefore be reconsidered'.

There have recently been attempts to evolve measurements of 'quality assurance' both in the United States (Performance Evaluation Procedure) and in Britain (Performance Indicators).

Performance evaluation procedure
The procedure was devised by the Joint Commission on Accreditation of Hospitals in the USA to 'predict what the results of intervention should be for a patient with a particular problem, if the health care team is doing the job it can and should do'. The procedure relies mainly on Tissue Committees to confirm the clinical diagnoses of disease in organs removed, and the use of simple outcome criteria.

Performance indicators
In Britain the Department of Health and Social Security started working on Performance Indicators in 1981 (James and Roberts, 1987). The latest package contains about 450 indicators derived from data generated by hospital and community administrators and, starting in 1988, from those required in order to conform with the recommendations in the Körner report. These indicators of quality assurance require ranking of health districts from 1 to 100, the higher the value the 'better' the service. Data were originally stored on floppy disks and analysed in a BBC microcomputer. More recently analysis of data was transferred to the Lotus Symphony software program running on IBM compatible microcomputers. An 'expert system' has been constructed around the software program Crystal that allows rapid analysis of data, the ranking of performance among districts, the selection of high and low scores, and the answers to such questions as: what management steps are appropriate IF waiting lists for non-urgent operations are high AND operating theatres are underused AND numbers of nursing staff are low. The complete expert system is available to health authorities for £566 (Payling, Bowen and Briggs, 1987).

The Performance Indicator Group (1987) produced nine *Consultation Papers* dealing with manpower, acute hospital services, performance indicators with a financial component, support services, services for mentally handicapped people, community services, services for the mentally ill, services for the elderly, and maternity and children's services.

Among the Performance Indicators for acute hospital services recommended by this group are the following:

1. Measurements designed to judge equality of access to health care among districts.
2. Comparison among regions of the numbers of joint replacements, cataract operations, coronary artery bypass grafts, services for patients with end stage renal failure, and bone marrow transplants.
3. The following measurements of activity for up to 10 major conditions within each specialty: length of hospital stay, expected length of stay, throughput per bed, lost opportunity to admit patients, percentage of day cases, expected percentage of day cases, lost opportunity to admit patients as day cases, percentage of immediate admissions, percentage of patients not operated on, and length of stay before and after operation.
4. Operating theatre usage is enquired into – information is required about the number of operations per session, cancelled sessions, and the proportion of cases operated on outside scheduled sessions.
5. Finally, the group required details of 'avoidable deaths' and total mortality standardised for age, sex, and operation or International Classification of Diseases code.

Outcome

The evaluation of the outcome of health care comprises the establishment of standards by consensus, followed by the assessment of the effectiveness (a measure of outcome), efficiency (a measure of cost), and acceptability of an intervention (Holland, 1983). It is much more difficult than the evaluation of process and is not popular with planners: it is demanding and the objectives must be clearly stated beforehand; these objectives must be measurable – they may be the prevention of disease, or reduction in mortality, or the altering of the natural course of the disease, or the relief of symptoms. Evaluation of outcome puts an absolute value on the programme of intervention, a value that may not be applicable in every case, and it requires a complex design. Sometimes the events studied are easy to assess, such as death or survival. Sometimes they are much more difficult and the prolongation of life must be judged against the quality of life – the degree of self-sufficiency, satisfaction, and personal fulfilment. Sometimes there is a long time between the intervention and the outcome, and the evaluation of the process of care in preference to its outcome will then be out of date.

Research

There is a second compelling reason to undertake clinical audit. If full details of every patient with a particular condition are available for retrieval and analysis, valuable information about the outcome of particular methods of treatment can be extracted. Among the most influential research publications in medicine are those that are based on accurate and complete records of patients who have had a certain disease or operation.

We studied all the papers reporting original work in the 12 issues of the *British Journal of Surgery* in each of the years 1965, 1975, 1985, and 1990. Table 3.1 shows that the number of those reporting audits of the outcomes of interventions was greater than of all other categories (except in 1965 when there were more case reports).

Table 3.1 Number of original papers in four volumes of *British Journal of Surgery*. Figures in parentheses are percentages of total original papers in that year.

	1965	1975	1985	1990
Clinical audit	59(32)	67(32)	88(29)	130(42)
Prospective human research	14(8)	44(21)	52(17)	36(12)
Laboratory research	12(7)	9(4)	16(5)	32(10)
Case reports	67(36)	44(21)	68(22)	29(9)
New techniques	4(2)	12(6)	18(6)	27(9)
Random controlled trials	0	14(7)	28(9)	23(7)
Animal research	23(12)	13(6)	22(7)	23(7)
Epidemiology	5(3)	4(2)	11(4)	11(4)

Accurate reports of audits of outcome are valuable not only because they document the natural history of diseases, but because they prompt clinical trials. Random control trials are the 'gold standard' of clinical research, but there are some diseases and treatments in which random control clinical trials cannot be done for ethical or other reasons, and then a complete audit is particularly useful.

A central research and development committee for the National Health Service was established in Britain in 1991 (Peckham, 1991). It has a broad mandate, being concerned with clinical trials, case control and other epidemiological studies, and the clarification of the relation between audit, algorithms, expert systems, and information technology. It will work closely with universities and with industry and it is expected that its coordination of research efforts will lead to greater dissemination of cost effective methods of treatment.

Education

The Royal College of Physicians and the Royal College of Surgeons have both emphasised the educational value of medical audit. Batstone (1990) pointed out that audit is effective in several ways:

- Small group work, which is effective in modifying attitudes and management of clinical conditions.
- Critical review of current practice, which encourages learning about new techniques and treatments and when to use them.
- Review of current practice, leading to reinforcement of agreed procedures and thus making teaching junior doctors more explicit and practice based.
- Observation of practice, which may indicate gaps in knowledge and skills for which appropriate educational programmes may be developed.

Conclusions

The purposes of clinical audit are to improve the standard of delivery of health care, and to provide data for clinical research. It must address aspects of the structure and process of delivery of that care, but it must also include evaluations of the outcome of treatments and there is little evidence that the three aspects can be closely correlated. We shall go into more detail of each of the three components in later chapters.

References

Alment, A. (1981) Looking back on *Competence to Practice*. In *Reviewing Practice in Medical Care. Steps to Quality Assurance*, edited by G. McLachlan.Nuffield Provincial Hospitals Trust, London, pp. 3–8

Batstone, G.F. (1990) Educational aspects of medical audit. *British Medical Journal*, **301**, 326–328

Black, D. (1981) Preface to McLachlan, G. (ed). *Reviewing Practice in Medical Care. Steps to Quality Assurance*. Nuffield Provincial Hospitals Trust, London

Donabedian, A. (1989) Institutional and professional responsibilities in quality assurance. *Quality Assurance in Health Care*, **1**, 3–11

Gorowitz, S. and MacIntyre, A. (1976) Towards a theory of medical fallibility. *Journal of Medical Philosophy*, **1**, 51–71

Hilfiker, D. (1984) Facing our mistakes. *New England Journal of Medicine*, **310**, 118–122

Holland, W.W. (1983) *Evaluation of Health Care.*Oxford University Press, Oxford

Ingelfinger, F.J. (1980) Arrogance. *New England Journal of Medicine*, **303**, 1507–1511

James, M. and Roberts, A. (1987) Performance Indicators for the National Health Service. *Health Trends*, **19**, 12–13

Körner, E. (1982) *Steering Group on Health Services Information. First Report to the Secretary of State.*Her Majesty's Stationery Office, London

McAuliffe, W.E. (1978) Studies of process-outcome correlations in medical care evaluations: a critique. *Medical Care*, **16**, 907–930

McSherry, C.K. (1982) Quality assurance and surgical practice. *Surgical Clinics of North America*, **62**, 751–759

Maxwell, R.J. (1984) Quality assessment in health. *British Medical Journal*, **288**, 1470–1472

Nelson, A.R. (1976) Orphan data and the unclosed loop: a dilemma in PRSO and medical audit. *New England Journal of Medicine*, **295**, 617–619

Payling, L., Bowen, T. and Briggs, I. (1987) PIs become crystal clear. *The Health Service Journal*, **97**, 502–503

Peckham, M. (1991) Research and development for the National Health Service. *Lancet*, **338**, 367–371

Performance Indicator Group (1987) *Acute Hospital Services. Consultation Paper No 2.*Department of Health and Social Security, London

Pope, A. (1733) *An essay on man.* II, 1

Popper, K. (1980) *The Logic of Scientific Discovery.*Hutchinson, London, p. 281

Rosenthal, G.D. (1964) *The Demand for General Hospital Facilities.* American Hospital Association, Chicago

Royal College of Physicians of London (1989) *Medical Audit. A First Report. What, Why, and How?* Royal College of Physicians, London

Sheldon, M.G. (1982) *Medical Audit in General Practice.* Royal College of General Practitioners occasional paper 20, pp. 1–21

Stokes, J.F. (1971) Aims of evaluation. In Gilbert, J.A.L. (Ed). *Proceedings of Conference on Evaluation in Medical Education.*Bulletin-Commercial Printers, Edmonton, pp. 9–17

Audit of structure and process

Chapter 4

How do you start an audit?

I see you standing like greyhounds in the slips, straining upon the start.
Shakespeare (1598–9)

We have often been asked for advice by surgeons who are keen to start an audit. They are confused, and probably a little frightened, by all the information they have been sent about computers and the seemingly endless flow of software packages, all with strange acronyms, that come their way. In this chapter we are going to try to simplify the process.

The first thing you have got to decide is whether you are going to audit all your work or only selected topics, and then whether it is only your own work, or whether it is to include that of your colleagues in the same department or practice, or in the same hospital. The borderline between audit for improvement of clinical practice and audit for research is a fine one; many surgeons start auditing their practices and then find a deficiency which encourages them to look for different ways of doing things – research.

There is seldom any point in trying to find common grounds among numerous disciplines: surgeons are mainly interested in incorrect diagnoses, inappropriate or incompetent operations, and postoperative complications; internists in incorrect diagnoses, inappropriate treatment, and in the outcome of medical treatment; radiologists in unnecessary imaging investigations and incorrect reports; pathologists in quality assurance by reference to standard specimens, and clinical feedback. All disciplines are interested in high quality note keeping, and all are (or should be) interested in making the best use of resources.

We are going to assume that your data wil be entered into and retrieved from a microcomputer with a database program. As we indicated in Chapter 5, this is not essential and it may not even be cost effective if you are going to audit only a small topic. Nevertheless, most of this chapter applies whether you are going to use a computer or not.

Audit costs time and money, and a cheap audit – which is likely to be incomplete – can result in the wrong decisions being taken. The costs of audit of structure and process are less than those of outcome, because an accurate audit of outcome must take account of late complications and of the quality of life.

The audit cycle

The Royal College of Physicians in London (1989) recommended that clinical audit should follow a cycle. It should start with choosing a topic. Then follows the setting of target standards (preferably by local consensus rather than by imposition from above), observing of practice, comparing performance with targets, implementing change, and returning to the same topic later to verify improvement in care as a result of the changes.

Audit in the department of pathology

For many years the departments of pathology in hospitals in Britain have participated in a voluntary system of quality assurance. The scheme is funded by the Department of Health. For example, all 442 National Health Service laboratories that practise microbiology are sent three simulated clinical specimens each month; these are distinguished only by numbers (Gardner, 1983). The answers are marked – a minus mark is given for a report that could endanger a patient – and every six months the marks are averaged and any laboratory that is more than 1.96 standard deviations below the mean of all laboratories is regarded as a poor performer. If the poor performance persists, that department is offered help.

Audit in other spheres of laboratory activity is more haphazard. Van der Walt, Baithun and Berry (1983) analysed 176 histological reports on mastectomy specimens from two hospitals. They found that tumour size was not recorded in one third, contour in 4/5, and completeness of excision in two thirds. In half the histological grade was not assessed, and in 4/5 the lymphocyte reaction. Invasion of blood and lymph vessels was seldom recorded. Audits such as this are essential for improving standards.

Incident and critical incident reporting

It is more important to audit failures than successes, and in many departments – notably anaesthetics – systems are in place that require the reporting in confidence of any deviation from the expected, and particularly of any 'critical' incident. This is defined as a deviation that was not immediately discovered and corrected and which could adversely affect outcome.

The spontaneous reporting of adverse drug reactions is encouraged in many countries, but there is a serious degree of underreporting – as much as 98% according to Fletcher (1991). He recommended its replacement by event monitoring by doctors who prescribe drugs, so that clusters of adverse events can be discovered, each of which individually might not have encouraged the doctor to report the reaction.

Apart from reporting of critical incidents, which are by definition individual cases, it is essential that accurate and honest information about *every* patient is available. We strongly advise, therefore, that you take the data for your database from specially designed forms and not from casenotes. Casenotes get lost.

Constructing an audit form

Whatever you put in the form that you design you can be quite sure of two things: that some items are superfluous and will never be used, and that you have not put in something you will discover later to be essential. The best thing to do is to design a form but do not spend a lot of money on having it printed: do a pilot study with, say, 20, find out the defects, and then alter it accordingly. Never ask a question that is unlikely to be answered, and put your questions in temporal order so that the people filling in the form do not have to search for questions. It is always better to phrase a question so that it can be answered by marking 'yes' or 'no', or ticking a box, because it is more likely to be answered than one that requires a written answer.

Make up your mind what you want

A clinical audit can result in changes in your practice only if you produce periodic reports. These reports are of little value when they are produced annually and contain no more information than, for example:

> 'I did 50 cholecystectomies last year. The patients' mean age was 56 years. There were 40 women and 10 men. One patient died, and there were 6 complications. The patients stayed in hospital a mean of 5 days, range 2 to 30.'

I suggest that a monthly summary should be produced of number of patients admitted; number operated on and by whom; number not operated on; number of deaths and their causes; and number of major and minor complications and their nature. At each year's end a more detailed breakdown should be produced. It might be embellished with charts, and each aspect should be cross correlated with name of surgeon operating, case mix, and assessment of fitness scores. It should be accompanied by a commentary containing suggestions for improvements. An example of such a report is:

> 'I did 50 cholecystectomies last year. The mean age of the patients was 56 years, range 35 to 80. There were 40 women and 10 men. 30 were admitted as emergencies and operated on within 5 days (mean 3, range 1–5). The other 20 were elective. In addition, 5 patients admitted as emergencies were not operated on; their mean fitness score was 7; they all settled and will be reassessed for operation. The mean fitness score of those operated on was 2 (range 0–6). Preoperative liver function tests were abnormal in 10, 5 of whom had raised serum bilirubin concentrations.
>
> Antibiotic prophylaxis was by preoperative intraincisional Augmentin in all cases, and prophylaxis of thrombosis by subcutaneous low dose heparin. 35 operations were done by me, 10 by registrar A, and 5 by registrar B. Peroperative cholangiography was done in 30 cases: it showed normal ducts in 25 and stones in 5. These five had supraduodenal choledochotomies and were drained with T tubes.
>
> Peroperative complications: none.
>
> Postoperative course: 5 patients had pyrexial scores of >10; the median stay was 5 days, range 2 to 30. The mean postoperative pain

score was 5 on day 1, range 2 to 8. Postoperative analgesia was by intra-muscular pethidine as required.

Postoperative complications: major, lethal: 1 death: a woman aged 80 admitted as an emergency, fitness score 6; operation by me; congestive cardiac failure treated; died 6th day; necropsy showed congestive cardiac failure, clean abdomen. Major, non-lethal: 1 man aged 75, cigarette smoker, fitness score 6, developed *H. influenzae* pneumonia on third day; stayed 30 days. 1 woman aged 55 had wound infection with fever. Minor: 2 women had wound infections without fever; 1 man had temporary retention of urine – catheterised; 1 man had exacerbation of chronic bronchitis.

Comments: I should not have operated on the woman who died. I am disturbed by the high postoperative pain score: liaise with anaesthetists and introduce other measures: ? patient controlled analgesia, ? epidural analgesia.'

In Chapter 5 we give an example of a form that suited our surgical interests. When, however, we were conducting clinical trials we designed other forms that were much more detailed. Above all in designing your form, make sure that no question is ambiguous. Get one of your friends to check it for sense and readability, and to suggest things that you may have left out.

Ensure that every patient is recorded

Whether you are starting an individual audit or one that includes other members of your specialty, it is essential that you make sure that you have a record of every patient who comes under your care with the condition that you are auditing; it is only in this way that you can calculate the incidence of whatever aspect of process or outcome you are interested in. Without complete records your denominator cannot be relied on. It must become a habit to make sure that every set of casenotes is scrutinised and an audit form filled in as soon as a patient leaves the hospital. We stress the urgency of this – casenotes have a habit of disappearing to other hospitals, to the department of pathology if there has been a necropsy, or to the records department. Or they may simply disappear. Shaw (1990) reported that of 94 sets of casenotes recently requested by a teaching hospital for audit, only 30 could be found. Except when you are auditing the quality of note keeping – a worthy exercise – do not rely on hospital casenotes for your audit.

We have found that it is effective for the nurse in charge of each of our admission wards to have a supply of audit forms, to one of which is attached an adhesive label with personal details of every patient as soon as the patient is admitted. These forms are not filed in the casenotes but sent straight to the office, where they are filed alphabetically until the patient is discharged and the casenotes are sent to the office. In this way we can be quite sure that we are dealing with a consecutive series of patients. It is essential that the form is filled in from the information in the casenotes by a member of the team, and that the accuracy of the data is checked by the consultant. Coding clerks are valuable, but they cannot be expected to pick out salient points from a complicated case history. These may be insignificant from the administrative point of view, but essential for audit.

Fixing priorities

The next step is to decide what it is that you want to audit – in other words to fix priorities. You cannot expect to audit more than 10 topics a year, however big your department, and it is essential to choose topics that have a chance of bringing to light data that can lead to improvements in the quality of care.

About one third of 1400 priority topics chosen by 46 hospitals in The Netherlands concerned effectiveness of treatment, one third concerned efficiency – the best use of resources – and one third concerned communication, patient satisfaction, and interpersonal conflicts (Reerink, 1991).

The topics that you select will probably be brought to your attention by a failure somewhere along the line. It may be that a patient has written complaining of an unacceptable time of waiting for a consultation in the outpatient department. It may be that you or one of your colleagues has detected an unacceptable deficiency in the structure of your hospital – an essential piece of apparatus not available, or no arrangements for daycase surgery. It may be that there has been an unexplained burst abdomen or an unexpected death. Any of these topics is suitable for audit. You will not have far to seek.

Hopkins (1990) suggested the following examples of conditions that it is desirable to audit, the occurrence of which may indicate low quality of care:

Perioperative deaths
Perioperative cardiopulmonary arrest
Deaths from potentially remediable conditions
    status epilepticus
    diabetic ketoacidosis
    extradural haematoma
Unplanned removal or injury to tissues during operation
Unplanned return to operating theatre
Hospital acquired infections
Problems with drugs
    error in prescribing
    inappropriate use of antibiotics
    inadequate supervision when using aminoglycosides
    prescription of drugs with adverse interactions
Problems with infusions
    inadequate calculation of fluid and electrolyte needs
    unnecessary infusions
    tissue infiltration
Problems with transfusions
    unnecessary transfusions
    transfusion reactions
Abnormal result of investigation, no appropriate action

Pressure sores
Falls and other injuries to patients
Complaints by patients and their relatives
Litigation
Delays in giving lytic treatment to patients with myocardial infarction
Failures of emergency pacemaking
Failure to intubate comatose patients during transport
Inappropriate admission of, or failure to discharge, patients
Unnecessary X rays of skull, chest, and cervical spine
Missing X rays in orthopaedic clinics
Extensive and unnecessary 'screening' biochemical investigations.

Hopkins gave further examples of subjects suitable for prospective audit, including accuracy of diagnostic coding, waiting times, delays in communication, inadequate control of anticoagulant treatment, use of psychotropic medication in the elderly, and inadequate follow up of detected hypertension.

Criterion based audit

Explicit criteria can be agreed for many aspects of the structure, process, and outcome of care. For example, the maximum tolerable delay between referral of a patient with an urgent problem can be defined and referral times that exceed this can be brought to light, their cause investigated, and solutions suggested. Criteria of clinical note keeping – adequate history taking, physical examination, and appropriate special investigations – can be laid down. Finally, expected outcomes of common diseases or interventions, and target levels of compliance, can be agreed.

These criteria – whether they are derived from consensus statements, Delphic pronouncements, or meta-analyses – must be accepted by those taking part in the audit. It is rare for externally imposed criteria to be acted upon. Kosecoff *et al.* (1987) reviewed the medical records of 2770 patients treated in 10 hospitals in Washington State to see whether the quality of care had improved after the publication of 12 recommendations by four consensus panels concerning surgery for breast cancer, estimation of steroid receptors in breast cancer specimens, caesarean section, and coronary artery bypass operations. Care was assessed 2 years before, and 13 to 24 months after, the publications. They found little impact and suggested that guidelines had to be evolved and accepted locally.

In the United States the Council on Medical Services (1986) advised that guidelines about the scope and process of quality assessment activity should be incorporated into peer review systems. The guidelines should include the following:

- Criteria must be agreed by the doctors being reviewed
- Criteria can relate to structure, process, or outcome, and should preferably be interrelated
- Those elements of structure and process that are related to favourable outcomes should be defined

- Outcome studies should be prospective as well as retrospective
- Intermediate outcome is easier to assess than late outcome
- Reviews should concentrate on specific targets, or on samples
- Both explicit and implicit criteria can be useful
- Prior consultation, concurrent peer review, and retrospective peer review can all be valid
- The results of quality assessment should be used to improve the quality of care
- The quality assessment process itself needs continued evaluation and modification

It is important that an audit that has shown up deficiencies in any part of care should be repeated after a decent interval to verify improvements. The cliche is 'closing the audit loop'.

Recording and retrieval of data

We are not going to repeat what we have written in Chapter 15, but we emphasise once again that the log book is an excellent way of starting an audit, even if the retrieval of information is so much more difficult than if the data were entered in a suitable database in a computer. If you are going to use a computer program you must decide whether it should produce letters to referring general practitioners as a byproduct of the audit. This is usually not a good idea, because you need a great deal more information in your audit than the general practitioner needs.

Presentation of audit

There is no point in accumulating a large database if you are not going to use it to bring out aspects of practice that can be improved. We suggest that there should be a weekly meeting of all the members of each team – including senior nurses – at which all deaths and discharges during that week are examined critically; that the standard of note keeping should be monitored at these meetings; that there should be a monthly *Mortality and Morbidity* meeting at which selected cases are presented and discussed; and that an annual report should be produced, with commentaries and comparison with regional or national figures. Once again we stress the necessity for confidentiality: the minutes of these meetings must not mention names.

References

Council on Medical Services (1986) Quality of care. *Journal of the American Medical Association*, **256**, 1030–1032

Fletcher, A.P. (1991) Spontaneous adverse drug reaction reporting vs event monitoring: a comparison. *Journal of the Royal Society of Medicine*, **84**, 341–344

Gardner, P.S. (1983) Microbiological quality assessment and the clinician. *British Medical Journal*, **287**, 1493–1494

Hopkins, A. (1990) *Measuring the Quality of Medical Care.*Royal College of Physicians, London

Kosecoff, J., Kanouse, D.E., Rogers, W.H., McCloskey, L., Winslow, C.M. and Brook, R.H. (1987) Effects of the National Institutes of Health consensus development program on physician practice. *Journal of the American Medical Association*, **258**, 2708–2713

Reerink, E. (1991) Arcadia revisited: quality assurance in hospitals in The Netherlands. *British Medical Journal*, **302**, 1443–1445

Royal College of Physicians (1989) *Medical Audit: a first report*. RCP, London

Shakespeare, W. (1598) *Henry V* III, i, 31

Shaw, C.D. (1990). Criterion based audit. *British Medical Journal*, **300**, 649–651

Van der Walt, J.D., Baithun, S. and Berry, C.L. (1983) Histopathology reporting of mastectomy specimens – an assessment of inter-hospital variations. *Journal of Clinical Pathology*, **36**, 1276–1280

Chapter 5

Recording, retrieval, and analysis of clinical data

I must create a system or be enslaved by another man's.

William Blake (1804)

If you can't measure it you can't manage it.　　　Anonymous

We have discussed the audit of structure and process and concluded that these essential activities are not too difficult to monitor. To individual surgeons, however, the audit of outcome is more important, whether they are interested in monitoring the quality of their own performance and that of members of their team, or whether they want to use the results of the audit for research. In either case surgeons must keep constantly in mind the four fundamental rules of audit of outcome: audit must never be a witch hunt; audit must be complete – every patient must be recorded; audit must be honest and accurate; and finally it must be confidential to avoid any possibility of the use of data or opinions in legal proceedings. This is usually done by erasing the names of patients after the data have been analysed and presented.

Four methods of recording data

We must remember that patients have the right of access to data held about them and their illnesses, whether these data are written or in a computer. It is essential that the information that is recorded is neither offensive to the patient nor exposes the doctor or any other health care worker to the danger of unwarranted and mischievous litigation.

There are four ways in which clinical data can be recorded. The simplest form of self audit is the 'log book' kept by some surgeons in training, in which they write the names of all patients whom they have treated, what they did for them, and what the outcome was. This is unquestionably salutary and can satisfy all of the four requirements of audit of outcome. The retrieval and analysis of such data, however, is tiresome and usually inaccurate, although it may be the best method of recording for the purposes of regular 'Deaths and Complications' meetings.

The second method makes retrieval of information much easier, but only a small amount of information can be recorded about each patient, and more detailed information has to be obtained from the casenotes. This comprises writing or typing on cards headed with diagnoses, operations, and complications the names and hospital numbers of patients who have that diagnosis, that operation, and that complication.

The third way of recording clinical information is to allot a numbered edge-punched card to each patient. These cards can store a great deal of information, which can be retrieved and analysed by inserting a steel welding rod – this is stronger than a knitting needle – through each hole and counting the cards that fall out. As soon as a patient leaves the hospital the details are written on the card (most hospitals issue sheets of adhesive labels bearing the patient's name and address, and one of these labels can be attached to each card). The numbers round the edges of the cards are given meanings that include personal details, details of the diagnosis, of the operation, and of any complications; these are ringed and punched out. The lexicon is stored with the cards and the cards are filed alphabetically until you are ready to analyse the data. Men, for example, might be allotted the number 1, women 2. Additional explanations and comments can be written on the cards. This method is accurate and informative, but exceedingly tedious when there are more than a few hundred cards. It was, however, the way we organised our surgical audit for 12 years before we acquired a personal computer and the appropriate software.

Computers in clinical practice

Personal computers are used for several purposes: guidance in diagnosis and treatment, word processing, statistical analysis, and recording, retrieval, and analysis of data. This last use is invaluable for infection control and hospital epidemiology on the one hand, and clinical quality assurance and research on the other.

Computer aided diagnosis

Weed (1990) was the originator of the Problem-Knowledge Coupler. This is essentially a memory jogger that generates an appropriate differential diagnosis. It works by linking every possible diagnosis with the history, examination, and tests, and presents a ranked list of possible diagnoses. It does not predict probabilities.

The most successful use of the computer for diagnosis has been in patients with acute abdominal pain. A Bayesian algorithm to simulate good clinical practice was used to generate a conditional probability matrix by actuarial techniques (de Dombal *et al.*, 1972). Using modifications of the database, Edwards and Davies (1984) and Adams *et al.* (1986) found evidence of an increase in the proportion of correct diagnoses in patients with acute abdominal pain, particularly in those in whom the differential diagnosis included acute appendicitis. The probable reason for improvement in diagnostic ability lies in the use of structured forms, which demand attention by the clinician to all aspects of the patient's illness (Sutton, 1989). Feedback of information may also be a factor.

de Dombal, Dallos and McAdam (1991) conducted a survey in two hospitals of the accuracy of diagnosis of acute abdominal pain by senior house officers (interns). They took as their end points the overall accuracy, the rates of appendicular perforation, of negative laparotomy, and of surgical diagnoses missed. Before the introduction of structured forms the rates (as percentages of 2060 patients) were 48.5, 27.0, 22.0, and 4.6, respectively. The use of forms alone improved the overall accuracy in one hospital to 57.5%, but the greatest improvement was found when, in addition to the forms, each participant was given either feedback after a computer aided diagnosis, or a teaching package. The teaching package, which was on a computer, comprised multiple choice questions, case histories for diagnosis, simulation studies, and Delphic teaching, and it occupied between 5 and 6 hours of the young doctor's time. The figures for overall accuracy when forms and feedback were used were 65–66%, and when forms and teaching were used were 73–76%.

An alternative approach using techniques evolved to give computers 'artificial intelligence' is being developed (Spiegelhalter, 1984), but there are enormous problems to be overcome. Schwartz, Patil and Szolovits (1987) described the program INTERNIST, which depends on collecting a database and then giving greater or lesser weighting to each symptom, sign, and test. It cannot, however, recognise deviations from the normal presentations of diseases, and may have to be modified by incorporation of pathophysiological knowledge into the database: the more information that is stored in the database, the slower and more complex the program becomes. The substitution of compact disks for floppy disks or Winchester (hard) disks allows a more extensive database. Nimbus Records have introduced a system which they call CD-PEDIA, run with CD-ROM.

Computers as aids to therapeutic decisions

It is relatively easy to devise a program that will, in response to the entry of observations or investigations, suggest appropriate treatment. An example is the 'audit in action' that is used in some neonatal units to remind those who are caring for very low birthweight infants to add sodium phosphate to the diet of the infants from the age of 10 days to prevent rickets, and to check the effectiveness of this treatment by X-raying their bones every 6 weeks. The computer will remind carers to give immunoglobulin intravenously for a month, and to start routine immunisation a month after the last dose. It will also remind them to check for retinopathy of prematurity when the baby is 7 weeks old.

There is no limit to the possibilities once a computer is accepted as an essential tool in clinical practice.

Computers for word processing and statistics

The outstanding achievements of computers in word processing and in statistical analysis of data are well known, and many different software systems are available. We will not comment any further on these applications.

Computers for recording, retrieval, and analysis of data

In departments of microbiology, data that are recorded on computer are an enormous help to an infection control team (Feldman and Ridgway, 1988). At University College Hospital in London a DEC 11/70 minicomputer was installed with the Massachusetts General Hospital Multi-user Programming System (MUMPS). The computer not only generates reports on individual specimens, but can also produce reports on the geographical location of infections in the hospital, the organs or tissues from which the specimens came, the names of the organisms isolated and their clustering, and the antibiotic sensitivity of the organisms. There is a facility for 'flagging' organisms such as methicillin-resistant staphylococci. Daily, weekly, and monthly summaries are produced that warn the infection control team of unusual problems related to specific areas or units. Epidemiological research is simplified and problems of cross infection rapidly identified.

In many hospitals in the USA laboratory results can be accessed speedily in the wards by summoning the data on satellite computers. Charing Cross Hospital in London was one of the first hospitals in Britain to introduce this time- and cost-saving method (Benson, 1991).

Numerical classification of diseases

Data cannot be analysed by a computer unless they are recorded in digital form. This implies that diseases and procedures must be classified and coded and that each disease, each procedure, and each complication must have a unique number (or combination of numbers and letters). It is, of course, essential that the coding should be accurate. Many believe that doctors should do their own coding, rather than rely on coding clerks. If, however, the casenotes are clearly written and comprehensive, a coding clerk will probably do a better job. There are three systems which automatically produce codes when they are fed with clinical information. Two of these are American and do not produce Read codes, whereas the third is British and does; it is known as the Medicode.

The best known of the classifications of disease is the *International Classification of Diseases*, the ninth edition of which was published by the World Health Organisation in 1975. It is improved by the addition of the *Clinical Modification* in the United States, which includes a classification of operations. There are grave objections to using these codes for the purposes of audit, mainly because they are single axis systems and each disease has a unique four digit number. It is, therefore, difficult to produce tables or graphs that show for example, all diseases of the heart, or all injuries, and then to classify them further. For the same reasons the *Classification of operations* published by the Office of Population Censuses and Surveys in Britain does not allow easy retrieval; even the fourth edition of 1987 retains the single axis.

The tenth edition of ICD, renamed *The international classification of diseases and related health problems*, was published in 1991 and will come into effect in 1993. It adopts for the first time an alphanumeric coding –

for example, A 99.9. It creates categories in most chapters for postoperative disorders and complications. In addition to the standard classification for mortality and morbidity statistics there are three other classifications: information support for primary health care; specialty-based adaptations; and the *International Nomenclature of Disease*.

For both administrative and research purposes it is preferable to have lexicons that allow multiaxial or hierarchical coding. Most workers interested in computer audit systems have therefore designed their own lexicons and these are not interchangeable. They do, however, have the merit of allowing recording and retrieval of data that are relevant to the clinician using the system.

Multiaxial and hierarchical clinical classifications

There are two main contenders as replacements for the *International Classification of Diseases*. In the United States SNOMED has attracted considerable attention and a lot of hostile comment, whereas in Britain the Department of Health has bought the right to use the Read classification.

The American College of Pathologists introduced a multiaxial coding system called SNOP (systematised nomenclature of pathology). The principle of a multiaxial nomenclature was then extended to the systematised nomenclature of medicine (SNOMED) in 1979 (Cote and Robboy, 1980, Earlam, 1988). The seven axes of this system refer to occupation, anatomical site, morphology, aetiology, signs and symptoms, procedure, and (when possible) disease. These are represented by different fields in the computer and allow much more flexibility and greater accuracy in retrieval of cohorts of patients with similar conditions.

SNOMED is acceptable to pathologists, but most clinicians have found the terminology too complicated and the system has failed to gain wide acceptance even in the United States.

The *Read Clinical Classification* uses terms that are in common use by doctors and aims to describe each illness as comprehensively as possible by using a hierarchical uniaxial structure. Chapters include occupations, history/symptoms, examination/signs, results of imaging and laboratory diagnostic tests, preventive procedures, operations, other therapeutic procedures, administration, drugs/appliances, health state measurements, diagnosis, drugs and appliances, and diagnosis related groups (DRGs). The nomenclature is cross referenced to ICD9 and OPCS4.

Out of a possible total of over 656 million different codes the present nomenclature contains 70 000 terms, and a synonym list of 130 000 terms. The synonyms make it much easier for the user. For example, calling up 'pile' will produce the code for 'haemorrhoid'. The codes are alphabetical (upper and lower case) and numerical; there are five levels in the hierarchy. Thus any level can be summoned to produce data for both administrative and clinical needs. For example, 7 is *operations and procedures*, and the number of these may be all that is needed for national statistics. An orthopaedic surgeon may be satisfied with 7K1 (bone operations), whereas for detailed audit and research all five steps may be needed: 7K1E4, for example, is primary open reduction of a fracture of the ankle.

Clinical audit on computers

Nowadays any serious surgical audit system must be run with the help of a personal computer. The systems based on hospitals, districts, regions, or whole countries suffer from several disadvantages. Yates and Davidge (1984) wrote that 'Data routinely collected from hospitals are neither accurate, nor complete, nor relevant, nor timely.' A vicious circle exists: information is not used because it is inaccurate, and it is inaccurate because it is not used. Firstly, data are inaccurate because doctors fail to record all the diagnoses and complications of every patient who is discharged and fail to record the causes of death accurately on death certificates. Secondly, errors can easily arise when lay people have the responsibility for coding these data using the *International Classification of Diseases* so that they can be recorded in a computer (Sunderland, 1985). A third disadvantage of these impersonal systems is that the information generated by the analysis of the data takes such a long time to reach the surgeon that it no longer has any meaning for him. Finally, the purpose of the collection of data for administrative audit is the containment of costs. What an opportunity for epidemiological research over 40 years has been lost because the data collected by the National Health Service in Britain have not been related to the problems of diseases and their treatment. Computerised clinical databases can have an enormous impact on our understanding of the natural history of diseases, and of the effects of treatment. There are many conditions the treatment of which cannot be validated by random control clinical trials. In such cases, complete, accurate, and honest collection of data in computers will have great influence on improving the care of patients.

In *The Lancet* the following personal view appeared (Anonymous, 1991):

'For many years before audit came into vogue I kept a record of the annual numbers of admissions, discharges, and deaths at a psychiatric hospital to which I provide consultant cover. The task was always easy because in the hospital general office were two obliging and mature gentlemen who, among their various duties, meticulously entered in massive leather-bound registers each admission, discharge, and death as it occurred. It was easy to tell at a glance whether a discharge was 'to home', a 'self-discharge', or to other accommodation. Each month's total was neatly pencilled in. It was possible to check back on the records over many years.

Then the system was 'improved', 'brought up to date' and 'computerised' in a medical records office, the gentlemen and their registers having been retired. I naively supposed that this change would enable information to be obtained in an instant. I was taken aback when at my usual yearly inquiry I was greeted with blank and startled looks in the office. It would take some time to produce the data. Eventually I was given rolls of computer printout, totalling 20 feet (616 cm) in length, of lists of patients' names, dates, wards, and addresses. An accurate interpretation of these could be made only by someone with the knowledge, which fortunately I possessed, of particular patients and the hospital and the changes in the wards that had taken place over the year, because the computer had not distinguished new admissions from inter-ward transfers – they were all 'admissions'.

My experience prompts the thought of who or what audits or monitors computerised information, increasingly regarded as essential in future resource management, to ensure that it is not GIGO – garbage in, garbage out.'

Medical informatics

This new discipline has been introduced into a few academic units in the United States (Greenes and Shortliffe, 1990), its purpose being to support education, decision making, communication, research, and other aspects of professional activity. The aim is to provide both vertical and horizontal integration, and so increase efficiency and effectiveness. Other countries, notably Australia and France, have set up departments of medical informatics.

There is no doubt that in future there will have to be some sort of vertical integration of computer records within hospitals, and that data of concern to both administrators and clinicians must be in a form that can be integrated in one master record for each patient. As Benson (1991) wrote: 'The facility to reuse data is the key to many of the improvements in clerical and managerial productivity which have benefited other industries'.

Information technology advances all the time, and there are many ways of implementing hospital information support systems. They are notable chiefly for their prolific use of abbreviations and acronyms, and many of those that are useful for management are no use for clinical audit or research because they do not store enough clinical information.

One such system, comprising interfacing modules, was introduced in Australia by McDonnell Douglas and, with modifications, has been installed in Bangour General Hospital in Scotland (Jack, 1988). Known as HOMER, this system promises to eliminate the wasteful duplication of data for administrative and clinical audit.

A similar concept underlies the introduction by the Huddersfield Health Authority of an integrated database known as the Clinical Information System (CIS) (Steele, 1989). This uses the Read clinical coding system and IBM hardware and software. The main object of the CIS is to improve patient care by giving clinicians access to a comprehensive range of information about patients in both clinical and administrative terms. The database contains useful information for clinical research, and much of the information given to clinicians is in the form of comparisons between 'expected' and 'actual'. The expected length of stay after, for example, cholecystectomy, is established by consensus and outlying values are easy to detect.

A new computer software system called PATS (Patient Analysis and Tracking System) was introduced in 1991 by the International Hospitals Group Consultancy Services, Stoke Poges SL2 4NS. It has been used by the UK National Heart Valve Registry to track the long term progress and outcome of cardiac procedures in hospitals throughout the country; it is a powerful flexible system that allows clinicians to construct their own databases, which can then be downloaded into regional or national databases.

Designing forms for computerised audit

It is usually necessary to design a form that is filled in for every patient. This form must be in plain language, and most programs require that against each entry there should be a number or combination of numbers and letters that can be entered into the audit disk and subsequently retrieved and classified. The questions that have to be answered on the form depend on the work that is being audited.

Table 5.1 Surgical audit form

Patient identification	11. Treatment 1=no operation 2=minor operation 3=intermediate operation 4=major laparotomy 5=other major operation
Date of admission...	12. Postop stay, days
1. Sex 1=male, 2=female	13. If 10 or more, cause? 1=nature of disease 2=complications 3=social reasons
2. Age or birth date	
3. Date of admission	14. Postop complications 1=none
4. Admission procedure 1=emergency, 2=elective	2=minor 3=major
5. Preoperative assessment of fitness score	15. Patient satisfied? 1=yes
6. APACHE score (sepsis)	2=no
7. TRISS score (trauma)	*Now add codes from lexicon*
8. Days in hospital before operation	Diagnoses... ....
9. Surgeon operating 1=consultant, 2=senior registrar, 3=registrar	....
10. Diagnosis 1=symptoms only	Operations.. ....
2=benign tumour or cyst	....
3=malignant, no metastases	....
4=malignant, metastases	Complications..
5=inflammatory	....
6=endocrine	....
7=traumatic, blunt	....
8=traumatic, penetrating	Comments..
9=congenital	....
10=degenerative	....
11=other	....

The form for a psychiatric unit or a medical unit naturally differs from one that is useful in a department of general surgery, and when the range of information is small – in recording operative anaesthesia, for example – it is quite easy to produce a form that can be read by an optical mark reader and so avoid having to key the data into the computer. The Southern Derbyshire Health Authority has produced such a form, the software being provided by Kendata Peripherals of Southampton SO4 3NB. The Medical Audit Information System produced by Compucorp also allows this facility.

An example of a form for use by general surgeons is given in Table 5.1.

A few years ago it was impossible to buy software that would allow sensible storage and retrieval of such data, and each surgeon had to devise his own program. Now, however, there are several commercial programs available. The cheapest of these are the database programs that are widely used in commercial management. They can be adapted to store information about patients, allow selection and classification of data, interrogation of the data by clinicians, and the production of printed tables or graphs. The best known is dBase IV, which can be built on to suit specific requirements. A dedicated medical audit information system (MAISY) has been produced by Computext of Kenton, Middlesex, HA3 9ED, which is claimed to be flexible and adaptable to all specialties.

An early system for computer auditing was in use at the Royal Army Medical College in London in 1978; the form comprised four pages and included identification of the 'hostile action casualty', the cause of the injury, the part of the body and the structure(s) injured, the treatment given, and the early and late complications including residual disabilities.

An audit system that is not confined to one unit but takes in all the surgeons in the Lothian district (Edinburgh) has been running for 30 years, and 10 years ago data that previously had been entered on 'feature cards' was entered into BBC (subsequently IBM-compatible, using dBase IV as a template) microcomputers in each of 12 units, and collated centrally. The organisers discarded the *International Classification of Diseases* coding in favour of their own three-part coding, comprising an organ code, a disease code, and an operation code. The onus is on individual surgeons to complete the operation form and to check the outcome form. Until recently no data were available on preoperative assessment of fitness or postoperative complications, but these are now an integral part of the program. Postoperative deaths were at first merely reported, but their causes are now enquired into.

Each year an annual report is produced and circulated to all surgeons in the district. Each surgeon is informed of his mortality from all diseases and operations, expressed as a percentage of the mean mortality in the whole district for that disease and that operation. One of the principal values of these reports lies in the commentaries that are written by senior registrars who have studied the analyses of data relating to specific diseases and operations.

A more ambitious integrated computerised hospital information system (ICHIS) has been installed at the Hammersmith and associated hospitals in London. Data about patients are recorded in diagnosis related groups on a master disk and can be accessed by each of 300 terminals. The computer creates a total picture of the services provided for each individual and simplifies the job of management. Its place as a tool of clinical research, however, has not yet been established.

Multifunctional audit programs

Three computer programs that cost between £4500 and £6000 each, are available and will perform many functions including the generation of discharge letters to referring doctors. The first of these is the Oxford Surgical Departmental System (Sifo Ltd). This evolved from an interest in clinical audit extending over many years (Gough *et al.*, 1980). The system 'is designed to enable relatively inexperienced medical secretaries to enter the data during their normal work routine...from the patient's casenotes'. If this is indeed what happens, the data are not much more valid than those entered into regional based Hospital Activity Analyses (Whates, Birgzalis and Irvine, 1982).

The second comprehensive computer audit system was developed by D.C. Dunn in Cambridge, and is marketed under the name of Dunnfile (Perthcrest Ltd). It runs on an ICL DRS 300 computer with a 40 megabyte hard disk and three terminals. It uses two lexicons for diagnoses and one each for operations and complications (Dunn, 1988). Data are collected on forms by the surgical house officer and verified by the consultant. To ensure that every patient admitted is included in the audit, names are kept in a register and ticked off as each form is received. From the form the secretary enters the data on to the computer and at the same time generates a discharge summary.

The third comprehensive system was devised by B.W. Ellis in Ashford, Middlesex (Ellis *et al.*, 1987). It is marketed as MicroMed General Surgery System (Medical Systems Ltd). Data are entered on cards by doctors and verified by senior doctors before being entered into the computer by non-medical staff, using lexicons for diagnoses, operations, and complications. These are not standard *International Classification of Diseases* classifications of diagnoses, nor *Office of Population Censuses and Surveys* classification of operations, but these can be deduced from the entries. The system supports practice administration, general management, and ad hoc enquiries, as well as formal analyses of the incidence of diseases, operations, complications, and deaths. It is more useful for administration and quality assurance than for research, but the research application can be extended by bringing in one or two unused fields.

Many other systems are in process of being developed and we advise surgeons to shop around and find a program that suits their needs. Some systems claim to integrate with administrative records, but at present it is probably better to retain personal control over clinical computer records so as to guarantee that they are complete, accurate, and honest. Crombie and Davies (1991) argued that 'microcomputer based audit packages, far from offering solutions to audit problems, are more akin to the Sirens luring the unwary auditor to disaster'. Audit is not finished when data are collected; it is not finished when they are retrieved and analysed. It is necessary then to compare the analysis with a standard and to plan and implement changes. Computers can store vast quantities of information, but most of it is of no value for audit.

The Derby surgical audit system

This program was written for the Apple Macintosh computer. It requires little input from the keyboard, most of the data being selected by using a 'mouse' to point to variables that appear on the screen. The program was developed by David Thomas, a general surgeon at Derby, and Paul Whitby, a computer programmer. It is written in 'Fourth Dimension', a modern database program developed by Laurent Ribardière and produced by Analyses Conseils Information (ACI). The program is large (30 megabytes) because it incorporates the whole of the Read codes and cross refers to the ICD9 and OPCS4 numbers.

Besides producing records of patients for audit it also generates abbreviated and edited discharge letters and lists of patients' codes to compare with those assigned by hospital clerks.

The start-up screen has a menu that gives access to the three main parts of the program: PATIENT (for data input); LIBRARY (for maintaining an internal dictionary of doctors and codes and for configuring the system to the user); and REPORTS (for selecting a standard report or the custom report editor).

The most useful feature of this system is the extensive use of embedded choice lists. These lists are easily activated and the appropriate item is selected by pressing a button on the 'mouse'. No typing is needed and the user can be certain that the item chosen is correctly coded.

A new patient (either inpatient or outpatient) is entered first into the Patient Identity section, which comprises three clearly labelled screens. Page 1 contains the usual identification details. Page 2 contains optional fields for comments in free text and medical history. Page 3 is a tabular summary of all admissions of the patient. This is filled in automatically and allows a secretary to answer telephone queries with minimal delay.

After the identification section, a new inpatient record is opened by pressing a button. Six screens are displayed:

Screen 1. Dates of admission and discharge, where the patient came from and went to, a provisional diagnosis and up to three final diagnoses from an embedded list, which automatically generates the Read and ICD9 codes.

Screen 2. A number of check boxes – for example, for conservative management, blood transfusion, admission to intensive care unit, day case, and American Society of Anesthesiologists fitness grade.

Screen 3. Investigations. The type and details of the investigation are selected from lists that appear on the screen, and the dates and results are typed in.

Screen 4. Operations. The operation is selected from a list of the 20 operations that the user does most often (previously entered manually). This automatically generates a Read and an OPCS code. If the operation is not on the list, OTHER is requested and the unusual operation is selected.

Screen 5. Complications. There is a list of check boxes and these can be added to by the clinician.

Screen 6. Advice given to the patient on discharge.

Retrieval of data in the Derby surgical audit

The file can be searched systematically, level by level, choosing from the display at each level as follows (using ruptured aortic aneurysm as an example):

- level 1: Circulatory system disorders (Read code G, ICD 390-459)
- level 2: Artery/arteriolar/capillary disease (Read G7, ICD 440-448)
- level 3: Aortic aneurysm (Read G71, ICD 441)
- level 4: Abdominal aortic aneurysm + rupture (Read G713, ICD 441.3)

Conclusions

It is practically impossible to conduct a useful clinical audit without using a computer. Doctors must decide whether they want to use a system for management and budgeting as well as for audit of outcome before buying the software to suit their computer. They must also decide how much detail they would like to have recorded about each patient. All the systems that we have described are valuable for administration and for quality assurance, but their value as tools of research is limited by the amount of information entered for each patient. Above all, and irrespective of what system they are using, doctors must ensure that the data are complete, accurate, and honest.

References

Adams, I.D., Chan, M., Clifford, P.C. *et al.* (1986) Computer aided diagnosis of acute abdominal pain: a multicentre study. *British Medical Journal*, **293**, 800–804

Anonymous (1991) Personal view. *Lancet*, **337**, 848

Benson, T. (1991) *Medical Informatics*. Longman, Harlow

Blake, W. (1804) *Jerusalem* 10, 20

Cote, R.A. and Robboy, S. (1980) Progress in medical information management systematized nomenclature of medicine (SNOMED). *Journal of the American Medical Association*, **243**, 756–762

Crombie, I.K. and Davies, H.T.O. (1991) Computers in audit: servants or sirens? *British Medical Journal*, **303**, 403–404

de Dombal, F.T., Leaper, D.J., Staniland, J.R. *et al.* (1972) Computer-aided diagnosis of acute abdominal pain. *British Medical Journal*, **2**, 9–13

de Dombal, F.T., Dallos, V. and McAdam, W.A.F. (1991) Can computer aided teaching packages improve clinical care in patients with acute abdominal pain? *British Medical Journal*, **302**, 1495–1497

Dunn, D.C. (1988) Audit of a surgical firm by microcomputer: five years' experience. *British Medical Journal*, **296**, 687–691

Earlam, R. (1988) Körner, nomenclature, and SNOMED. *British Medical Journal*, **296**, 903–905

Edwards, F.H. and Davies, R.S. (1984) Use of a Bayesian algorithm in the computer-assisted diagnosis of appendicitis. *Surgery, Gynecology and Obstetrics*, **158**, 219–222

Ellis, B.W., Michie, H.R., Esufali, S.T., Pyper, R.J.D. and Dudley, H.A.F. (1987) Development of a microcomputer-based system for surgical audit and patient administration: a review. *Journal of the Royal Society of Medicine*, **80**, 157–161

Feldman, R.G. and Ridgway, G..L (1988) Database handling for infection control and hospital epidemiology. *Journal of Hospital Infection*, **11** (supplement A), 37–42

Gough, M.H., Kettlewell, M.G.W., Marks, C.G., Holmes, S.J.K. and Holderness, J. (1980) Audit: an annual assessment of the work and performance of a surgical firm in a regional teaching hospital. *British Medical Journal*, **281**, 913–920

Greenes, R.A. and Shortliffe, E.H. (1990) Medical informatics: an emerging academic discipline and institutional priority. *Journal of the American Medical Association*, **263**, 1114–1120

Jack, J. (1988) HOMER at Bangour. *British Journal of Healthcare Computing*, January, 14–15

Schwartz, W.B., Patil, R.S. and Szolovits, P. (1987) Artificial intelligence in medicine: where do we stand? *New England Journal of Medicine*, **316**, 685–688

Spiegelhalter, D.J. (1984) Computer aided decision making in medicine. *British Medical Journal*, **289**, 567–568

Steele, R. (1989) Clinical information systems. *British Journal of Healthcare Computing*, May, 25–26

Sunderland, R. (1985) Inaccurate coding corrupts medical information. *Archives of Disease in Childhood*, **60**, 593–594

Sutton, G.C. (1989) Computer-aided diagnosis: a review. *British Journal of Surgery*, **76**, 82–85

Weed, L.L. (1990) The premises and tools of medical care and medical education: perspectives over 40 years. In Blum, B.I. and Duncan, K. (eds). *A History of Medical Informatics*. ACM, New York

Whates, P.D., Birgzalis, A.R. and Irvine, M. (1982) Accuracy of hospital activity analysis operation codes. *British Medical Journal*, **284**, 1857–1858

Yates, J.M. and Davidge, M.G. (1984) Can you measure performance? *British Medical Journal*, **288**, 1935–1936

Chapter 6

Audit as a tool of clinical research

Human knowledge does not stay put, it evolves by what we call trial and error, or as is more usually the sequence, error and trial.

Attrib: Lewis Thomas

The proper conduct of a programme of audit or quality assurance requires the acquisition, recording, and retrieval of complete, accurate, and honest data. These data can then be used to evaluate the cost effectiveness of interventions. They can be used to compare the performance of one doctor or one hospital with that of others or with accepted guidelines. But one of the most important things that an audit can do is to provide data for the comparison of the results of an intervention, either medical or surgical, with the results of a control group. This is clinical research.

It is beyond question that such comparisons are best made between groups that have been treated during the same time period, and that the groups have been allocated to 'new' or 'old' treatment at random. This is the basis of the random control clinical trial.

It seems remarkable that the adoption of the techniques of the random control trial in surgery was delayed until the 1950s and that even now it is exceptional for a journal to contain more than 10% of papers reporting random control trials. What is so special about these trials? The obvious answer is that a properly conducted and analysed random control trial eliminates the possibility of bias. But does it? I think the answer to that must be in our definition of the word 'properly'.

When Ronald Fisher was appointed statistician to Rothamsted Experimental Agricultural Station in 1919 his task was to examine 'by modern statistical methods' the mass of data that had accumulated from field trials dating as far back as 1843. He later described this as 'raking over the muck heap'. Ideas on the errors of experimental results were confused, and Fisher perceived that analysis of variance provided the best means of separation of the sources of variation in agricultural field trials. It was not, however, until several years later that he realised that only randomisation can do away with bias and provide valid data for tests of significance (Fisher, 1925).

He conceived the idea of randomisation to eliminate the bias attached to comparing the yields of crops in different seasons or in fields of differing fertility. In 1923 he used the word random for the first time in a paper published in the *Journal of Agricultural Science* (1923; **13**, 311–320) entitled 'Studies in crop variation. The manurial response of different potato varieties'. His aim was to eliminate bias by dividing a field into numerous plots, half of which would be treated in one way and the other half (selected at random) in another. In this way all variables except the one being studied were equalised and any differences in yield could be confidently ascribed to the treatment being studied.

In medicine the importance of randomisation was not appreciated until much later. The first edition of Sir Austin Bradford Hill's *Principles of Medical Statistics* (Hill, 1937) specified allocation of *alternate* patients to experimental and control treatments, and it was not until the trial of streptomycin for the treatment of pulmonary tuberculosis that the bias inherent in the allocation of alternate patients was recognised and central randomisation was introduced (Medical Research Council, 1948).

People are not plots of land. Patients have first of all to attend the hospital or practice where the random control trial is being carried out. They then have to agree to take part in the trial; the investigators have to remember to allocate patients at random and not because they think that one or other regimen would be in a patient's best interests.

The assessment of the outcome of the intervention in agriculture is easy: all you need do is to weigh or count the crop. The outcome of a medical regimen is much more difficult to estimate. In trials of chemotherapy for relatively unresponsive disseminated cancers, how do you estimate outcome? By response? What do you mean by a partial reponse or even a complete response? Do you mean the same as other workers?

Tonkin, Tritchler and Tannock (1985) studied 61 published reports of 62 trials of cancer chemotherapy for recurrent or metastatic colorectal cancer, squamous cell cancer of head and neck, and non-small-cell lung cancer, all of which are relatively resistant to chemotherapy. They found that reported rates of tumour response varied from 0 to 52% and that higher rates of response and longer duration of response tended to be reported in studies that were smaller, assessed patients less frequently, and withdrew more patients. They pointed out that overgenerous definitions of response, coupled with 10% or more of withdrawals, could allow some workers to claim a 75% response to treatment. Other workers who used stricter criteria of response and withdrew no patients, might report a response with the same regimen of 20%.

Clinical investigators of the results of surgical treatments were even slower to adopt the discipline of the random control trial, but during the last 30 years it has come to be accepted as the 'gold standard' of clinical research. There are, however, barriers against its use to settle all the controversies in surgery.

Firstly, the concept of randomisation is difficult to put across to patients. Most patients expect a reasoned diagnosis, an account of all therapeutic options, and finally a recommendation by the surgeon that a particular line of treatment be adopted. They do not expect their surgeon to be ignorant of the respective merits of two or more regimens, nor do they expect their treatment to be decided at random. For this reason in any large multicentre trial, in which the options are clearly of interest to patients, there are bound to be a large number of exclusions of eligible patients.

Secondly, the population eligible to be entered into a random control trial is not a random sample of the whole population with the disease that is being studied. This applies particularly to trials in patients presenting themselves to hospitals, as Berkson (1946) pointed out: this is the 'Berkson fallacy'.

Thirdly, clinicians taking part in a random control trial may, either from forgetfulness or for other reasons, fail to enter eligible patients. This is particularly so when the treatment options are operative versus conservative treatment. In 1976 the National Surgical Adjuvant Project for Breast and Bowel Cancers (NSABP) set up a trial of segmental mastectomy, segmental mastectomy with radiotherapy, and total mastectomy in 94 institutions, estimating that the total number required would be about 2500 and the accrual 75 per month. After 44 months only 519 patients had been entered, 16% of the expected rate. Taylor, Margolese and Soskolne (1984) mailed questionnaires to each centre and 97% responded. The explanations for not entering eligible patients were:

- Concern that the doctor–patient relationship would be affected (73%).
- Difficulty with informed consent (38%).
- Dislike of open discussion involving uncertainty (22%).
- Perceived conflict between the roles of scientist and clinician (18%).
- Practical difficulties in following the protocol (9%).
- Feelings of personal responsibility if the treatments were found to be unequal (5%).

The Scottish breast conservation trial fared no better (Jack, Chetty and Rodger, 1990). In 1988, 147 of 324 patients with breast cancer were eligible for conservative operations, but only 40 were finally recruited into one of two protocols. Patients who are fully informed of the options are unlikely to accept that the treatment that they are given is going to be decided by chance.

A multicentre international trial of extracranial–intracranial bypass against medical treatment of symptomatic inoperable extracranial arterial disease recruited 71 centres and 1377 randomised patients (EC–IC Bypass Study Group, 1985). The conclusion of this study was that the operation offered no advantage. Subsequent investigation, however, showed that a large number – probably between 50% and 70% – of eligible patients had not been entered, and the results in the selected group studied could not be generalised to all patients with the disease (Dudley, 1987a). In a subsequent letter Dudley (1987b) concluded that 'much more open and less adversarial debate is needed about how we acquire new, and particularly treatment related, information ... we must actively seek alternative ways of getting at a form of the truth that is acceptable'.

Finally, many trials recruit too few patients (their 'power' is too low) to provide valid conclusions. This defect can sometimes be annulled by analysing the results of many clinical trials together – meta-analysis – but trials often have different criteria both of eligibility and of the events studied, and the results of one trial may contradict those of another. Some trials are badly designed and executed, and there is an additional bias that arises from the unwillingness of many editors to publish papers that report negative results. There have been many publications about the proper design and analysis of random control clinical trials (Evans and Pollock, 1985; Koes *et al.*, 1991), and a meta-analysis must take account of the adequacy of the trials that are being reviewed. Thompson and Pocock (1991) concluded:

> '... meta-analysis is not an exact statistical science that provides defini- tive simple answers to complex clinical problems. It is more appropri- ately viewed as a valuable objective descriptive technique, which often furnishes clear qualitative conclusions about broad treatment policies, but whose quantitative results have to be interpreted cautiously'.

The value of meta-analysis is exemplified by an analysis of the place of adjuvant tamoxifen and cytotoxic treatment in patients with early breast cancer (Early Breast Cancer Trialists' Collaborative Group, 1988).

The conclusions of this analysis were that tamoxifen improved disease- free survival by 11.4% in women over the age of 50; it was no more effec- tive in doses greater than 20 mg/day than in doses of 20 mg/day; it was effective in oestrogen receptor negative cancers; and it was no more effec- tive when it was given in addition to chemotherapy. Chemotherapy improved disease-free survival by 12.8% in women under the age of 50; the combination of cyclophosphamide, methotrexate, and 5-fluorouracil was as effective as any other regimen; and it was no more effective if it was continued for more than 6 months.

This meta-analysis was updated in 1992 (Early Breast Cancer Trialists' Collaborative Group, 1992). The group reported data on about 75 000 women and found that recurrence-free survival and 5 and 10 year overall survival were highly significantly improved by tamoxifen, by ovarian ablation in premenopausal women, and by polychemotherapy.

Another important oncological meta-analysis concerned chemotherapy of advanced ovarian cancer (Advanced Ovarian Cancer Trialists Group, 1991). This group studied 45 published and unpublished trials in 8139 patients, 6408 of whom had died. They concluded that platinum was better than no platinum (relative risk 0.93, 95% confidence interval 0.83 to 1.05), that platinum in combination with other chemotherapeutic drugs was better than platinum as a single agent (0.85, 0.72 to 1.0), and that there was nothing to choose between carboplatin and cisplatin (1.05, 0.94 to 1.18).

Audit as a substitute for random control trials

It is obvious that many problems cannot be solved by the technique of the random control trial. What are the alternatives? Controls there must be, but bias is introduced by using the wrong controls. The results of the Japanese extended gastrectomy and lymphadenectomy for cancer of the stomach (the R 2 gastrectomy) are outstandingly better in Japan, in terms of the length of survival, than those of the standard radical gastrectomy practised in Western countries. Is this because the operation is so much better, or because cancers are diagnosed earlier in Japan, or because gastric cancer in the Japanese is different biologically?

Historical controls can be used only if the new treatment is immeasurably better than the old, and then only if the sample of the population is similar in the old series and the new. The variations in outcome from one decade, even in the absence of changes in specific treatment, can be considerable. There is still controversy about the extent to which postoperative infection rates were influenced by the adoption of Listerian practices and how much by improvements in the nutrition of patients and the adoption of public health measures such as the isolation of infectious patients from those having operations.

On the other hand, new treatments that are capable of curing previously incurable conditions are sometimes introduced, and require nothing more than historical controls for validation. This was the case when penicillin was first produced in sufficient quantities to allow the treatment of patients with group B streptococcal endocarditis, which was previously uniformly fatal. It does not need a random control trial to validate the relief of pain and disability by total arthroplasty in patients with severe arthritis of the hip. In these and many other cases historical controls were not only sufficient, but also the only controls that were ethically justified.

The advent of fibreoptic endoscopes has encouraged the emergence of 'minimally invasive' surgery. Transurethral resection of the prostate took the place of retropubic prostatectomy for most patients with adenomatous enlargement of the prostate many years ago, and nobody compared the two operations in a formal random control clinical trial. Roos *et al.* (1989) published an audit of 54 077 patients in Denmark, Canada, and England who had had prostatectomies by either the incisional or the transurethral route. The patients were followed up for as long as 8 years and, after adjusting for differences in comorbidities, they reported that the cumulative percentage requiring a second prostatectomy was substantially higher after transurethral resection (12–15%) than after open prostatectomy (2–4%). Even more surprising was the finding that the long-term age-specific mortality was significantly higher after transurethral than after open operation, the 95% confidence interval for the relative risk being 1.15 to 1.84.

Among newer minimally invasive operations are hysteroscopic ablation of the endometrium for menorrhagia, percutaneous nephrolithotomy, and laparoscopic cholecystectomy. A random control trial is being conducted in Bristol to compare hysteroscopic ablation with hysterectomy (Stirrat, Dwyer and Browning, 1990), but the place of most of these procedures will be established not by formal trials but by accurate audit of the results.

For every innovation that produces dramatic improvement over previous results, however, there are many whose benefits and particularly risk–benefit ratios are less obvious. If these innovations cannot, for ethical or logistic reasons, be subjected to the discipline of the random control trial, there are other options. One is to randomise surgeons instead of patients. Surgeon A will treat patients with a certain disease in the standard way, while surgeon B treats all similar patients in the new way. This suggestion has never had much success, but in retrospective studies it may be a valid way of controlling the results of a new treatment.

Horwitz and Feinstein (1981) suggested that where random control trials are impossible for ethical or practical reasons cohort studies should be undertaken. They illustrated this by analysing 151 deaths and 151 survivors matched for age and other risk factors among 1463 patients who had been admitted to hospital with myocardial infarction. In each cohort they enquired about the use or non-use of prophylactic lidocaine (lignocaine). They calculated the odds ratio, chi square, and 95% confidence interval and stratified patients according to the New York Heart Association (1979) classification. They divided deaths into those caused by pump failure and those caused by arrhythmias. Overall there was no significant advantage attributable to the use of lidocaine, but in the subgroup of deaths from arrhythmia there was strong support for the prophylactic use of lidocaine. On 136 survivors, 35% were given lidocaine, whereas of the 35 deaths from arrhythmia, only 14% were given lidocaine. In the poor risk patients (Killip classes 2 to 4) the odds ratio was 4.03, chi square 4.65, 95% confidence interval of the odds ratio 1.14 to 14.17.

Closely related to the technique of the cohort study is the establishment of national registers of specific diseases (Thompson, 1989). These must be complete, and follow up information must be meticulously collected, documented, and analysed.

Another way of estimating the benefit (and the cost) of a new treatment is by conducting a detailed, complete, and honest audit of the results of a single doctor's practice. This audit should comprise all patients with the disease being studied, including if necessary the patient first discovered to have the disease at necropsy.

Sometimes data that are taken from a database reveal unexpected and unpalatable results. Tunis, Bass and Steinberg (1991) analysed 10 years of data from the Maryland Health Services Cost Review Commission. They reported that the rate of percutaneous transluminal angioplasty for vascular disease of the lower limbs rose during those 10 years from 1/100 000 to 24/100 000, and of bypass operations from 32/100 000 to 65/100 000; the total hospital costs rose from $14.7m to $30.5m. The rate of major amputations of the lower limbs remained at 30.5/100 000. The apparent lesson from this audit is that treating patients with peripheral vascular disease by angioplasty or bypass surgery has no effect on the eventual rate of amputation of ischaemic legs.

Audit exists for research as much as for quality assurance. It is only by recognising this that surgeons can be encouraged to ensure that all patients are completely and honestly recorded, and that the method of retrieval allows analysis of risk factors as well as outcome. The measures of outcome must include the immediate postoperative complications and deaths as well as the long term quality and duration of life.

Biased and false claims can result from incomplete data and selection of patients, and many operations that were fashionable at one time have been shown to be useless after being tested in controlled clinical trials.

Conclusions

Complete, accurate, and honest audit of surgical interventions plays an important part in clinical research and the advancement of knowledge.

References

Advanced Ovarian Cancer Trialists Group (1991) Chemotherapy in advanced ovarian cancer: an overview of randomised clinical trials. *British Medical Journal*, **303**, 884–893

Berkson, J. (1946) Limitations of the application of fourfold table analysis to hospital data. *Biometrics Bulletin*, **2**, 47–53

Dudley, H.A.F. (1987a) Extracranial-intracranial bypass one; clinical trials nil. *British Medical Journal*, **294**, 1501–1502

Dudley, H.A.F. (1987b) Extracranial-intracranial bypass one; clinical trials nil. *British Medical Journal*, **295**, 389

Early Breast Cancer Trialists' Collaborative Group (1988) Effects of adjuvant and of cytotoxic therapy on mortality in early breast cancer: an overview of 61 randomized trials among 28 896 women. *New England Journal of Medicine*, **319**, 1681–1692

Early Breast Cancer Trialists' Collaborative Group (1992) Systemic treatment of early breast cancer by hormonal, cytotoxic, or immune therapy. *Lancet*, **339**, 1–15 and 71–85

EC-IC Bypass Study Group (1985) Failure of extracranial-intracranial bypass to reduce the risk of ischaemic stroke: results of an international randomized trial. *New England Journal of Medicine*, **313**, 1191–1200

Evans, M. and Pollock, A.V. (1985) A score system for evaluating random control clinical trials of prophylaxis of abdominal surgical wound infection. *British Journal of Surgery*, **72**, 256–260

Fisher, R.A. (1925) *Statistical Methods for Research Workers.* Oliver and Boyd, Edinburgh

Hill, A.B. (1937) *Principles of Medical Statistics.* The Lancet, London

Horwitz, R.I. and Feinstein, A.R. (1981) Improved observational method for studying therapeutic efficacy. *Journal of the American Medical Association*, **246**, 2455–2459

Jack, W.J.L., Chetty, U. and Rodger, A. (1990) Recruitment to a prospective breast conservation trial: why are so few patients randomised? *British Medical Journal*, **301**, 83–85

Koes, B.W., Assendelft, W.J.J., van der Heijden, G.J.M.G., Bouter, L.M. and Knipschild, P.G. (1991) Spinal manipulation and mobilisation for back and neck pain: a blinded review. *British Medical Journal*, **303**, 1298–1303

Medical Research Council (1948) Streptomycin treatment of pulmonary tuberculosis. *British Medical Journal*, **2**, 769–782

New York Heart Association (1979) *Nomenclature and Criteria for Diagnosis of Diseases of the Heart and Great Vessels.* (8th edn).New York Heart Association Inc, New York

Roos, N.P.,Wennberg, J.E., Malenka, D.J. *et al.* (1989) Mortality and reoperation after open and transurethral resection of the prostate for benign prostatic hyperplasia. *New England Journal of Medicine*, **320**, 1120–1124

Stirrat, G.M., Dwyer, N. and Browning, J. (1990) Planned trial of transcervical resection of the endometrium versus hysterectomy. *British Journal of Obstetrics and Gynaecology*, **97**, 459

Taylor, K.M., Margolese, R.G. and Soskolne, C.L. (1984) Physicians' reasons for not entering eligible patients in a randomized clinical trial of surgery for breast cancer. *New England Journal of Medicine*, **310**, 1363–1367

Thompson, J.R. (1989) The role of registers in epidemiology: discussion paper. *Journal of the Royal Society of Medicine*, **82**, 151–152

Thompson, S.G. and Pocock, S.J. (1991) Can meta-analysis be trusted? *Lancet*, **338**, 1127–1130

Tonkin, K., Tritchler, D. and Tannock, I. (1985) Criteria of tumor response used in clinical trials of chemotherapy. *Journal of Clinical Oncology*, **3**, 870–875

Tunis, S.R., Bass, E.B. and Steinberg, E.P. (1991) The use of angioplasty, bypass surgery, and amputation in the management of peripheral vascular disease. *New England Journal of Medicine*, **325**, 556–562

Chapter 7

The presentation of audit

We come not to offend, but with good will. Shakespeare (1596)

It is easy to collect a vast quantity of information and then store it away in a computer or filing cabinet, where it never again sees the light of day. An immense amount of time, effort, and money can be wasted if data are not properly presented. It is necessary to present them so that they are absolutely truthful and yet not so boring that they remain unread. It is no good dumping a pile of computer print-outs on a busy surgeon's desk and expecting him to make sense of columns of anonymous figures.

Data can be presented formally or informally, but it is essential that the interest of the audience is maintained. People who are bored are not going to be influenced to improve their practice. Among the informal ways are regular meetings to review casenotes, regular morbidity and mortality conferences, weekly grand rounds, meetings to discuss reports of incidents and critical incidents, and journal clubs. Formal presentation of data in the form of monthly, quarterly, half yearly, or yearly reports must also be undertaken.

Review of casenotes

This system was introduced in the departments of medicine and clinical pharmacology in Birmingham in 1978, and still flourishes (Heath, 1990). Weekly meetings are held at which a random selection of the casenotes of patients admitted under the care of one consultant are reviewed by doctors attached to another consultant. It has the merit of simplicity and does not need access to data held on computer. The notes are assessed for their quality at admission and at follow up, the appropriateness of investigations and drug treatment, the timeliness and quality of discharge summaries, and the quality of communication among doctors and between doctors and patients. Heath commented that 'audit could be practised in a friendly, non-confrontational manner in a form that was enjoyed by all who participated .... Most weeks it is considered that at least one important problem that warrants attention is unearthed'.

Morbidity and mortality conferences

These are usually more structured than reviews of casenotes, but in a large hospital it is impossible to deal with all deaths and all complications, and the selection of those that are to be presented can be arbitrary. Nevertheless, they can be interesting and valuable. They encourage those presenting the cases to be completely honest – indeed if they are not the whole purpose of the exercise is lost. Secondly, they encourage free (but polite) criticism, comments, and questions from the audience that should engender lively and constructive debate. Thirdly, they are educational in that they teach the junior staff not only about acceptable differences in clinical practice, but also to be self-critical and not to become complacent. The more honest a presentation, the kinder will be the criticism, as it will be in the forefront of everybody's minds 'There but for the grace of God....'

Case presentations are best done by the junior staff, not only because they are the ones most concerned in the day-to-day care of the patients but also because they may be particularly conscious of gaps in their knowledge that their seniors may be unaware of, and discussion of particular cases may help to fill these gaps.

This is not the sort of audit that is published, unless as a report of a case or a series in a learned journal, and then with the full permission of all concerned. Confidentiality is vital if honesty is to be preserved.

Grand rounds

If these are to have any relevance to audit they must include presentation and discussion not only of the 'fascinoma of the week', but also of the error of the week. They have not, in our experience, been of any great value for the improvement of clinical practice.

Dissemination of reports of incidents and critical incidents

Within a department this can be a valuable method of bringing to the attention of the staff what things can go wrong and why, thereby putting them on their guard against recurrence of the same problems.

Journal clubs

Each member of the surgical team is asked to review recently published papers on a particular topic and then make these relevant to local experience by concluding with a review of practice in that firm or that hospital. This is followed by general discussion of the topic. Linzer *et al.* (1988) studied the impact of a journal club on reading habits, knowledge, and critical abilities. They concluded that journal clubs do develop the critical reading habits of participants.

To make the best use of the data generated by audit, all the methods of presentation should be used. In that way the entire surgical firm is involved in monitoring standards of practice.

Formal presentation of audit data

The method of presenting audits of structure and process is different from that of outcome, and in some ways easier. The purpose of the Körner data set – and of the ways in which data are analysed and presented – is to bring to the attention of clinicians variations from national standards in such matters as length of stay in hospital. These data suffer from the drawbacks of incompleteness, inaccuracy, and untimeliness. Barrie and Marsh (1992) found that Hospital Activity Analysis data about orthopaedic work in Manchester was 90% complete, but only 70% accurate.

When we consider the presentation of audits of outcome, the simplest is an overall statement of numbers and types of operations, together with morbidity and mortality figures. This can be a useful statement of a surgeon's workload, efficiency, and effectiveness, when set against national or regional figures. It is easily achieved using computer data processing and graphics.

The question of who should do the analysis and presentation of audits of outcome (which are not covered by the Körner requirements) can be difficult. Perhaps the district medical officers (consultants in public health medicine) should be responsible. These doctors have been trained in epidemiology, have extensive knowledge of differences in case mix, and are able to comment without bias. An additional advantage of their doing the job is that they have ready access to the computer facilities necessary to make analysis and presentation easier.

One of the most valuable aspects of the Lothian surgical audit is the commentary written by senior registrars. It was the disclosure that mortality after replacement of aortic aneurysms was higher when the operations were done by general surgeons than when they were done by surgeons with a special interest in vascular surgery that resulted in the policy of all patients with aneurysms being transferred to vascular surgeons for treatment. Most district hospitals, however, do not have senior registrars, and it would not be appropriate to leave the task of commenting to anybody more junior.

What information should be presented? This will depend on the use to which the audit is being put. Of course any figures must be presented alongside adequate controls, either historical or contemporary. The computer can be programmed to convert masses of indigestible figures into histograms, bar charts, pie charts, or graphs. For example, wound infection rates among surgeons or among hospitals, or from year to year, may be compared in the same way as audits of process – such as lengths of stay in hospital for particular operations, use of theatre time, and so on, which are covered by reports published by the Department of Health, the Office of Population Censuses and Surveys, and by regional statistical units.

Correct statistical analysis has a part to play. Take the example of a surgeon whose infection rate after clean operations was 5%, compared with a national figure of 2%. If he had done 200 such operations and 10 wounds had become infected, whereas 20 000 had been done nationally with 400 infections, the difference was unlikely to have arisen by chance

(p = 0.006). The 95% confidence interval of the difference (3%) is 0 to 6% in favour of the national figure. It is therefore important that that surgeon, 10 of whose patients' wounds became infected, should not be misled into thinking that his poor figures were a chance occurrence. Such a presentation should encourage him to set up an enquiry into his technique and investigate possible breaks in asepsis in his operating theatre.

The presentation of the results of audit can be carried out quarterly, or half yearly, or only once a year, and are best accompanied by a short analytical commentary by the director of public health. Each surgeon should be given a copy only of his own results and those of his juniors, together with a copy of the district, regional, or national figures, and with his own for the previous 6 months or a year, or for the same period in the previous year, for comparison. In this way confidentiality is maintained while still making sure that the surgeon can put his results in the context of others.

Conclusion

There are many ways of presenting the results of audit, but they all have certain things in common. They must be completely honest and accurate while not being too detailed for a busy surgeon to absorb. They must be confidential and they must be unbiased. Under no circumstances should any element of the witch hunt enter into them. If they fulfil all these requirements, then they have the potential for improving clinical practice and the lot of the patient.

References

Barrie, J.L. and Marsh, D.R. (1992) Quality of data in the Manchester orthopaedic database. *British Medical Journal*, **304**, 159–162

Heath, D.A. (1990) Random review of hospital patient records. *British Medical Journal*, **300**, 651–652

Linzer, M., Trig Brown, J., Frazier, L.M., DeLong, E.R. and Siegel, W.C. (1988) Impact of a medical journal club on house staff reading habits, knowledge, and critical appraisal skills. *Journal of the American Medical Association*, **260**, 2537–2541

Shakespeare, W. (1596) *Midsummer Night's Dream*. V.i.109.

Chapter 8

Economic audit: introduction

What we must decide is perhaps how we are valuable rather than how valuable we are.   Edgar Friedenberg (1959)

When the National Health Service was introduced in Britain 44 years ago, its principal architect, Aneurin Bevan, told the House of Commons that the provision of 'free' health care would have such a profound influence on the health of the population that the share of the national resources devoted to health care would, after a few years, be able to be reduced. What nobody realised was that the demand for better health care is limitless, and that the elimination of most of the infectious diseases and the diseases of deprivation has led, not to a reduction in demand, but to a change in the nature of that demand. In the real world one cannot do everything for everybody. The best you can do is to put the resources that you have to good use. The decision about allocation of these resources between, for example, a working man with a troublesome hernia and a psychogeriatric service is not one that can be made by doctors. It is a political matter and has to be made by the general public. It is, however, up to the profession to offer suggestions about priorities, particularly concerning innovations.

Evaluation of innovations

St Leger, Allen and Rowsell (1989) suggested that any new investigation or treatment should be explicitly evaluated so as to guide decision making. They put forward a checklist, a brief version of which is as follows:

- Who, and how many, will benefit?
- Quantify the expected outcome.
- Quantify the costs and savings.
- Were the results of pilot studies favourable?
- Should further trials be done?
- How are outcome and cost effectiveness to be evaluated?

If you use resources in one way they will not be available for use in another way. The cost of a resource is equal to the benefits that would have been generated by its best alternative use. It is obvious, therefore, that people who make decisions about the allocation of health care resources must place explicit weights on the relative benefits of different courses of action.   One of the problems is that statistics about costs do not necessarily reflect professional standards.   Lower costs can mean more efficiency or lower standards, and higher costs can mean higher standards or less efficiency (Klein, 1982).

Escalation of costs of health care

People's rising expectations of the sort of health care they would like, together with the increasing number of elderly people, the development of operations and investigations that were undreamed of 50 years ago, the emergence of new diseases and new treatments for old diseases, and the demand for screening of healthy people, have produced demands that continue to rise every year in all countries.

Prevention of diseases is both cheaper and more effective than cure, and much of the recent resurgence of the importance of family practice in Britain depends on the application of preventive medicine. One of the cheapest ways of preventing premature death is by advising people not to smoke cigarettes. This is widely practised by general practitioners. Many infectious diseases can be prevented by immunisation, and here again the role of the primary care doctor is paramount.

Holland and Stewart (1990) listed the objectives of the United States Public Health Service and of the British Health Education Council for the coming decade. Curiously enough the American objectives do not mention control of firearms or eradication of inequalities of health caused by poverty and race, and the British list mentions adequate income and safe housing only at the end. Prevention of accidents features in both lists, and it is important to realise that accidents are the leading cause of death among people under the age of 30 and account for more years of life lost than heart disease and cancer combined.

Screening

Antenatal, neonatal, and childhood screening are cost effective and are part of good preventive medicine. Holland and Stewart (1990) gave a list of desirable and undesirable screening methods for preconception, antenatal, and neonatal screening:

Desirable antenatal investigations:
- Blood pressure and urine albumin
- Blood group
- Haemoglobin
- Haemoglobinopathies in selected groups
- Serology for syphilis
- Serology for toxoplasmosis in high prevalence countries
- Serum α fetoprotein (neural tube defects)

- Ultrasonography when there are clinical indications
- Amniocentesis or villus sampling to exclude Down's syndrome if indicated by maternal age or other investigations.

Unnecessary or undesirable antenatal investigations:
- Vaginal examination
- Fundal height
- Breast examination
- Weight

Desirable neonatal investigations:
- Congenital dislocation of the hip
- Congenital heart disease
- Undescended testes
- Phenylketonuria
- Thyroid function tests
- Haemoglobinopathies
- Weighing
- Measuring head circumference
- Congenital cataract and other causes of blindness
- Hearing loss (not earlier than 7 months)

Doubtful or unhelpful neonatal investigations:
- Biochemical tests for inborn errors of metabolism
- Stool trypsin for cystic fibrosis
- Serum cholesterol
- Blood pressure
- Cover test for squint
- Neurodevelopmental tests

Screening of adults

Diseases are more effectively treated if they are detected early, and the purpose of screening is to detect diseases in people who have no symptoms. To be cost effective, however, a cohort of people who are likely to have the disease has to be identified (Holland and Stewart, 1990). There is no point in screening for breast cancer in young women, or for cervical cancer in nuns. On the other hand, screening of the entire population for glycosuria and hypertension should be a normal event in regular medical care.

Screening of adults who have no symptoms is much more widely practised in the United States and in some European countries than in Britain.   The cost effectiveness of regular surveillance of the health of workers, particularly in the dye and rubber industries, is recognised, as is advice about cigarette smoking, screening for and treatment of hypertension, and periodic testing of the urine for sugar.

Mass screening with mammography has resulted in the detection of more women with 'early' (node negative) cancer of the breast, and presumably enhanced chances of cure. Eddy (1989) projected that if 25% of women aged 40–70 years were screened every year by mammography and physical examination, there would be 51 000 deaths instead of 55 000 in the year 2000, at an annual cost of $1.3 billion. Gray, Vessey and Patnick (1991) combined random control and case control studies to do a meta-analysis of the benefits of mammography. They rejected the negative results of the Malmö and Edinburgh trials and concluded that regular mammography does save lives. Skrabanek (1988) emphasised the importance of telling women who are invited to have a mammogram about the expected benefits and about the potential harm, in terms of the number of unnecessary mammograms, false positive mammograms, unnecessary biopsies, and unnecessary mastectomies for each life saved. The issue is still open to question.

Screening of women for preinvasive carcinoma of the cervix allows less radical operations and greater chance of cure than if one waits for women to complain of vaginal bleeding on intercourse. There is disquiet in the minds of some women about cervical cytology, and particularly the attitude taken by some doctors – that they are not prepared to prescribe oral contraceptives or hormone replacement medication unless the woman has had a cervical smear examined.

Ransohoff and Lang (1991) reported that there is no convincing evidence that annual screening by faecal occult blood testing of all people over the age of 50 years reduces the mortality from colorectal cancer. They suggested that a possibly better bet would be a single colonoscopy at the age of 60–65 years. The risk of cancer developing from a small adenomatous polyp is probably less than the risk of colonoscopy, which costs up to £250 for each examination. It is only large polyps, and especially villous adenomas with severe dysplasia, that are clinically important (Pollock and Quirke, 1991). Regular colonoscopy of people who have family histories of colonic carcinoma is probably cost effective, as is that of blood relatives of patients with familial adenomatous polyposis. Patients who have had a carcinoma of the colon or rectum successfully treated should be followed up indefinitely and examined regularly by double contrast barium enemas or colonoscopy.

Friedman *et al.* (1991) set out to establish the value of routine rectal examinations for the detection of carcinoma of the prostate, but in a cohort of 139 men with metastatic prostatic cancer they found that the relative risk of cancer in men who had had one or more rectal examinations within the previous 10 years was 0.9 (95% confidence interval 0.5 to 1.7), and concluded that no benefit was to be derived from routine rectal examinations.

Efficiency

Culyer (1991) identified three essentials for the efficient use of resources in health care:

- Services should be provided only if they have been shown to promote better health than if they were not provided
- Services should be provided at the least cost
- Resources should be concentrated on providing those services that offer the biggest benefit to health.

The British government in the name of the Secretary of State for Health (1991) published a document entitled *The Health of the Nation*, in which 'key areas' are suggested on the basis of their being big health problems, of their being amenable to correction, and of their being amenable to setting objectives and targets. The foreword states that 'It must be right to redouble our efforts to reduce avoidable disease and premature death. This must not, however, be at the expense of caring for ill people....' As in most proposals about health care, there are more words than actions.

There are, however, what Light (1991) called 'embedded inefficiencies' in all health care systems. He drew attention to the work that is done in hospitals that should be done in the community at lower cost; to the high staff turnover in hospitals; to professional pride that demands that operating theatres are kept empty when the consultant has to cancel a list; to unscheduled absences of consultants; to 'job demarcation' – senior nurses who instruct that no nurse, however well qualified, shall give an intravenous injection; and to underfunding, which means that wards, or sometimes whole hospitals, cannot accept patients because the funds have run out.

Variations in referral rates to hospitals

One of the main economic strengths of the National Health Service in Britain is the flourishing state of primary care in the community. There are, however, wide variations from doctor to doctor in the rates of referral to hospitals, but no relation has been found between quality of care and either higher or lower than average rates of referral. Both random variation and differences in case mix are likely to explain much of the variation, but it is proper that a primary care physician should be aware of his or her referral rate to each specialty in comparison with the mean rate (Roland *et al.*, 1990).

A Royal College of Radiologists Working Party (1991) found that rates of referral for radiological investigation varied among firms in the same specialty by as much as 13-fold for outpatients, and 25-fold for inpatients, and concluded that the previously announced figure of 20% of radiological investigations being of no clinical benefit was correct.

Inappropriate requests for investigations in the department of pathology are common. Those for cross matching of blood were investigated by Baraka *et al.* (1991) at the Amiri Teaching Hospital in Kuwait. During 6 months, 713 units of blood were cross matched, but 511 were never used; 271 were thrown away when they became outdated, and the annual cost of the wasteful cross matching was estimated to be \$US25 000.

The Audit Commission (1991) examined the pathology service in Britain and recommended establishment of protocols for requesting tests, measurement and costing of work, and cooperation among districts to use expensive equipment more effectively. Many departments are finding themselves so overworked that research and even routine necropsies tend to get put aside.

Inefficient use of operating theatres

An operating theatre costs about £150 an hour to run, whether it is used or not. Planned lists that are cancelled reflect inefficiency in management as much as shortages of staff, beds, or other resources. The Comptroller and Auditor General (1991) reported that the efficiency of operating theatres in England had improved since the last report three years before, when only 50% of scheduled available time was used. The report found that use varied from 67% to 100%, and was critical about the lack of information technology, particularly computers, in many operating departments.

Another aspect of inefficient use of medical staff in relation to operating theatres is the unacceptable number of operations that are done at night. McKee *et al.* (1991) examined the records in four hospitals in four non-consecutive months. They found that 'dirty' operations like appendicectomies were left until last and accounted for 53% of operations that were done after midnight. They concluded that at least 30% of evening operations and nearly all those done after midnight should have been done the previous day or left until the following morning. They advised having one fully staffed theatre reserved for emergencies only.

Containment of costs in hospitals

The hospital services take about two thirds of the total money allocated to the National Health Service in Britain. In 1989–90 government spending on health was £26 461 million. This compared with £20 630 million on defence, £52 020 million on social benefits, and over £20 000 million on education.   The estimated spending on health care in Britain in 1989–90 was 5.19% of gross domestic product, compared with 11.9% of gross domestic product in the United States, and it is rising from year to year.

No activity in a hospital is more expensive than that of the intensive care unit. Many patients are treated there who in the past would have been allowed to die quietly in their beds. Knaus (1987) suggested that some people are too old and sick for intensive care. It has been suggested that a patient should not be denied access to the intensive care unit purely on the grounds that he or she has an APACHE II (Acute Physiology And Chronic Health Evaulation) score above 30 (which reflects such serious disease that survival is unlikely). If, however, the score fails to improve during the first two days in the unit, further invasive monitoring and treatment should cease.

A Report (1989) from the King's Fund Panel considered guidelines for the admission of patients to intensive care units. They assigned them to four categories, from 'expected to survive', through 'prognosis uncertain', to 'death probable shortly whatever is done' and 'death apparently imminent'. The panel recommended that only the first two categories should be admitted to intensive care units, but stressed the absence of reliable clinical and economic data about these units and suggested that more data should be collected to allow proper audit.

Coupled with the higher expectations of health is the common fallacy accepted by many people that medical science can cure everything, and that the failure of an operation to cure a patient must be a failure of the surgeon's judgement or technique.

The unrestrained use of expensive special investigations is a feature of much modern surgical and medical practice. Hampton *et al.* (1975) studied

80 new referrals to a medical clinic.   The physician recorded his diagnosis and the predicted management after reading the primary care doctor's referral letter, again after taking a history, and again after the physical examination. Two months later the final diagnosis and management were compared with the provisional opinions.   In 66 of the 80 cases the diagnosis that was made after reading the referral letter and taking a history was correct, physical examination was useful in only seven, and laboratory and other special investigations in only seven more. We shall have more to say about 'defensive' investigations and treatments when we discuss the increase in malpractice suits against doctors.

Containment of administrative costs

More information technology means more money being spent for non-medical purposes. The costs of administration are crippling the health service in France, and in the United States Reinhardt is quoted by Lee and Etheridge (1989) as having found that overall health care expenditure increased by 85% between 1980 and 1986, but that during that period administrative costs rose by 186% from $9200 million to $24 500 million. Most of the increase was in the administrative costs of private health insurance, which more than tripled from $5100 million in 1980 to $17 800 million in 1986. It appears that competition in the market for health care does not reduce costs.

The 'formidable and frustrating' (Rue, 1991) task of introducing resource management into hospitals is going slowly and has yet to prove that it results in more efficiency and lower costs for comparable treatment.

Containment of costs by rationing

If demand is limitless and resources are limited, two things follow: firstly, that providers of resources must demand cost effectiveness, and secondly that shortages and rationing must result. In most countries demand (as opposed to need) is curbed by economic forces – the more demands you make the more you have to pay, whether directly to the health providers, or in the form of higher insurance premiums, or in higher supplements to what is guaranteed by the insurance agencies. In Britain the fact that the average annual cost of health care is £1600 for each family is obscured by the way in which the health service is funded by the central government. The result is that rationing is by two other methods: firstly, surgeons in Britain operate on patients only when they perceive a need (Jennett, 1987), and not when the patient demands an operation, and secondly, by the mechanism of the waiting list (Mozes et al., 1987).

Klein (1984) wrote that the British National Health Service provides a comprehensive system of health care at the lowest cost, measured by the proportion of the national income devoted to it. He asked how the appropriateness of any particular level of care can be assessed. In Britain there is a humane clinical conservatism, whereas in the United States there is a heroic aggressive style of medicine. In Britain, he claimed, doctors rationalise scarce resources (like renal dialysis) by classifying patients as suitable or unsuitable for treatment, whereas in the United States doctors maximise their incomes by maximising treatment, irrespective of the outcome for patients.

Justice requires that scarce resources should not be withheld from people suffering from curable diseases or from programmes to prevent diseases, to be diverted to such activities as in vitro fertilisation or cosmetic surgery. Who, however, is going to decide priorities among such interventions as joint replacements, care of the elderly, care of the mentally ill, cytotoxic drugs for inoperable cancer of the lung, or organ transplantation? An attempt has been made at the University of York to quantify benefits of alternative treatments by the use of Quality Adjusted Life Years (QALYs), but the calculation of these is inaccurate because of our relative ignorance of the natural history of many diseases.

In 1991 the North East Thames Regional Health Authority in Britain announced that treatment in its hospitals would not be offered under the National Health Service for uncomplicated varicose veins, benign 'lumps and bumps', wisdom teeth, and tattoos. These decisions were acclaimed by the Chief Executive of the National Health Service, who has encouraged other regions to follow suit. The conditions that would not be treated were decided without consultation with the general public, and such implicit rationing has always been practised. It is, however, the right of all the people in a country to make the decisions about what is and what is not a proper use of limited resources. In the United States the state of Oregon has taken a much more far-sighted view and has introduced explicit criteria.

The Oregon experiment

The Oregon Medicaid plan, properly titled the Oregon Medicaid Demonstration Project, was designed to extend health care coverage to all citizens of that state who are defined as poor (those with incomes below about $12 000 for a family of four). At present the Medicaid roll accounts for only about half the population below the official poverty line, and the solution was either to raise state taxes or to ration health care. Federal regulations, however, do not allow exclusion of services, and Oregon has asked the Health Care Financing Administration to waive this requirement. In February 1991 the state published a list of 714 condition-treatment pairs, ranked in order of priority. A cutoff point will be announced (provisionally item 587), and conditions with ranks higher than that point (indicating lower priority) will not be funded by Medicaid (Dixon and Welch, 1991). The list was compiled by a community-based organisation called Oregon Health Decisions, under the guidance of Dr John Kitzhaber, the president of the Oregon State Senate. Residents in the state were asked, both by telephone and in public meetings, to take three aspects into consideration:

- The cost of treatment
- The improvement in the quality of life that was likely
- The likely duration of life

The organisation then distilled the replies from the public into 13 values and incorporated data and opinions from professional sources. The cutoff point has not yet been finally decided, and its position on the list will doubtless reflect the amount of money available when the scheme is introduced (perhaps in 1992).

One of the main criticisms of the Oregon Health Decisions organisation was that the data about quality of life, and even about the likely duration of life, were inadequate. Nevertheless, Oregon has set a precedent for ensuring that guidelines are explicit and this is surely the way forward for the rest of the world. The Oregon Health Services Commission has strongly recommended strict audit of the outcome of all health services and periodic technical adjustment of the guidelines (Kirk, 1991). The difficulties surrounding the setting of explicit priorities were exemplified by a conference in Southampton (Cochrane *et al.*, 1991), in which not only the pragmatic and social issues were aired, but attention was also directed to moral and ethical matters – have we the right to refuse treatment to anyone?

Business administration in health care

Cost effectiveness is the aim of all providers of resources. In industry skilled managers use operational research techniques to plan their business. They ask three questions: Is our work well done? Is it worth doing? Does it pay its way? The result of bad management is bankruptcy. Translated into the management of health care resources these three questions require assessment of the standard of care, the effectiveness of care, and the efficiency of care – does it make the best use of limited resources? Operational research techniques are, however, applicable only to aspects of the problem, and not to the whole (Luck *et al.*, 1971).

Kaizen

The Japanese introduced the word 'kaizen'. It means continual improvement in quality. It is achieved by identifying deficiencies in the process (of the manufacture of motor cars, or electronic gadgets, or of medical care) and by taking steps to remedy that deficiency before going on to find and remedy other defects. It is represented in Western countries by the expression 'total quality management' (TQM), the essence of which is 'getting it right first time' (Koch, 1991).

Total quality management

Continuous improvement in quality was taught largely by American experts sent to Japan to help in the rebuilding of that country in the 1950s (Berwick, Enthoven and Bunker, 1992). It relies on four principles:

- Organisational success depends on meeting the needs of customers
- Quality is an effect caused by the processes of production
- Most people who work are motivated to try hard and do well
- Simple statistical methods, linked with careful collection and analysis of data on work processes, can yield insights into the processes and lead to their improvement

The practitioner of TQM says: 'They are already trying, so how much can be gained by imploring them to try harder?' All the workers in a factory, or an office, or a health service, must be invited to discover and make suggestions for overcoming deficiencies in processes. People should not have the attitude of 'Did I pass inspection?' but rather 'How could I do this better?' Guidelines and standards may indicate to people that those minimal standards are also the best ones, instead of trying for continuous improvement.

The Griffiths report

In 1983 the British government asked a man who had considerable experience of management in business, Sir Roy Griffiths, to make recommendations for the more efficient use of manpower and other resources in the National Health Service. Griffiths saw the main defect as a lack of proper management, and recommended that responsibility at national, regional, and local levels should be on the shoulders of a single general manager in each case. He argued that effective management could provide the same service at lower cost, or a superior service at the same cost. One of the essential parts of the structure of the new management system would have to be the availability of accurate and timely statistics, and his initiative coincided with the reports of the Körner group.

Griffiths emphasised that it is the duty of a health service, in common with all other service industries, to regard the wishes of the consumer as paramount. He suggested that market research should be undertaken with this in mind. He also foresaw the introduction of patient administration systems, and stressed the importance of management budgeting: that clinicians and nurse managers should be responsible for budgets to cover the resources that they use. In this way he envisaged a more cost-effective service.

The search for efficiency

In insurance-based health care systems the insurance companies bring pressure to bear on uneconomic hospitals to ensure that they use their funds efficiently, and the Department of Health, Education, and Welfare in the United States has introduced payment by diagnosis related groups (DRGs) for patients covered by Medicare. Some insurance companies retain the services of expert medical auditors to monitor hospital costs, and there has been a spectacular growth in Health Maintenance Organisations, the object of which is to prevent diseases and to seek the most economical way of treating them. We shall have more to say about cost effectiveness when we discuss short stay and day case operations.

In Britain the National Health Service is funded by a monolithic government bureaucracy; this means that in spite of (or because of) repeated reorganisations there are few incentives to better management and greater efficiency, and hardly any to greater effectiveness.

The Department of Health and Social Security published a statistical bulletin in 1987 that showed an increase of 16% in inpatient activity between 1974 and 1984 (West, 1987). This, however, did not distinguish between the number of patients admitted and the number of patients readmitted, and the increase in numbers treated could even be a reflection of worse treatment because more people needed readmission. Quantity cannot be equated with quality.

Quality is best shown by comparative trials or by honest and complete clinical audit of outcome. If the National Health Service were a private business it would by now either have had to put its finances, staffing, and administrative structure on to a cost effective footing, or have gone out of business. Everybody knows that the National Health Service will not be allowed to go out of business, so there is not the same incentive to try and rationalise administration to give better service for less money.

A lot of attention is now paid to the concept of competition, but there are some suggestions – such as hotel charges for patients in hospital – that attract little support. The curious thing is that in Britain the only people who pay for their beds in health service hospitals are old age pensioners, whose pensions are reduced after they have been inpatients for 8 weeks.

The Centre for Policy Studies (1987) suggested that hospitals should be allowed to make a profit from selling services not essential to the treatment of sick people, and that contracts for certain services should be put out to competitive tender. These services should include not only the housekeeping ones such as cleaning, but also the supply of special investigations.

Klein (1988) examined three ways of raising more money for health care in Britain. He considered the introduction of hotel charges for hospital inpatients and concluded that it had 'some worrying elements of rough justice'. At present prescription charges are levied, but so many groups of patients are exempted that fewer than one fifth actually pay them. If the same applied to hotel charges – the exemption of children, the elderly, those on social security, and the mentally and physically handicapped – the weekly hotel charge would need to be in the region of £40 to raise another £280 million a year. Injustices would arise because working men and women whose incomes were just above the poverty line would have to pay, and conversely many wealthy elderly people would not be expected to pay.

The second choice that Klein examined was the financing of the National Health Service by a payroll tax – an extension of the existing National Insurance contributions (which fund pensions and welfare payments as well as the National Health Service).   These contributions are levied on both employers and employees. On earnings above £52 ($86) a week or £226 ($375) a month the employee pays 2% of earnings on the first £52 a week and 9% on the rest. The employer pays 4.6% of the employee's earnings if they are between £52 and £85 a week, 6.6% if they are between £85 and £130 a week, 8.6% if they are between £130 and £185 a week, and 10.4% on earnings above £185 a week. Above the upper limit of income of £390 ($647) a week or £1690 ($2805) a month employees pay no more than 9% of earnings up to £390 a week, but employers pay 10.4%

of the total wage. A rich employed person, therefore, pays no more than a moderately well-off one. Self employed people also contribute to National Insurance, but retired people do not, and there seems to be some injustice in making only wage earners pay for the National Health Service, particularly as the number of retired people continues to rise.

Klein's third option is that the government funded health service should offer its services in competition with health maintenance organisations funded by private insurance. He concluded that none of the three strategies is wholly just, and that more money is not the main answer.

In any other industry one of the most important guides to efficiency is productivity – the amount of output per employee. In a market economy resources are allocated to the most highly valued wants and inefficient production processes are eliminated. Health care differs from all other industries, and the evaluation of efficiency is much more difficult.

When surgeons are paid by item of service rendered rather than by sessions worked, there is a greater temptation for the less scrupulous to arrange superfluous investigations and undertake unnecessary operations. The result can be that the poor do not get the treatment they need and the well-off get treatment they do not need. In hospitals increased productivity usually means increased throughput of patients and increased costs, and during the current restrictions on spending the only way that many hospitals have of reducing their expenditure is by closing wards and not treating patients. The National Association of Health Authorities (1988) claimed that the National Health Service should be seeking not a new formula for funding, but a change in the system of allocating and using available funds to relate income to service activities more efficiently and more effectively. We consider this more fully in the chapter on Performance Indicators, which shows that there are considerable variations in efficiency among hospitals.

References

Audit Commission (1991) *The Pathology Services: a management review.* HMSO, London

Baraka, A., Juma, T., Asfar, S.K. and Al-Sayer, H. (1991) Conserving blood in preparation for elective surgery. *Journal of the Royal Society of Medicine*, **84**, 600–601

Berwick, D.M., Enthoven, A. and Bunker, J.P. (1992) Quality management in the NHS: the doctor's role – I. *British Medical Journal*, **304**, 235–239

Centre for Policy Studies (1987) *Healthy Competition: how to improve the NHS.* Centre for Policy Studies, London

Cochrane, M., Ham, C., Heginbotham, C. and Smith, R. (1991) Rationing: at the cutting edge. *British Medical Journal*, **303**, 1039–1042

Comptroller and Auditor General (1991) *Use of NHS Operating Theatres in England: a progress report.* National Audit Office, London

Culyer, A.J. (1991) The promise of a reformed NHS: an economist's angle. *British Medical Journal*, **302**, 1253–1256

Dixon, J. and Welch, H.G. (1991). Priority setting: lessons from Oregon. *Lancet*, **337**, 891–894

Eddy, D.M. (1989) Screening for breast cancer. *Annals of Internal Medicine*, **111**, 389–399

Friedenberg, E.Z. (1959) Quoted in *The International Thesaurus of Quotations.* Tripp, R.T. (ed). Penguin Books, New York, p. 671

Friedman, G.D., Hiatt, R.A., Quesenberry, C.P. Jr and Selby, J.V. (1991) Case-control study of screening for prostatic cancer by digital rectal examination. *Lancet*, **337**, 1526–1529

Gray, J.A.L.M., Vessey, M.P. and Patnick, J. (1991) Breast cancer screening: the current position. *British Medical Journal*, **302**, 1084

Hampton, J.R., Harrison, M.J.G., Mitchell, J.R.A., Prichard, J.S. and Seymour, C. (1975) Relative contributions of history-taking, physical examination, and laboratory investigation to diagnosis and management of medical outpatients. *British Medical Journal*, **2**, 486–489

Holland, W.W. and Stewart, S. (1990) *Screening in Health Care.* Nuffield Provincial Hospitals Trust, London

Jennett, B. (1987) Waiting lists: a surgeon's response. *Lancet*, **i**, 796–797

Kirk, E.P. (1991) Oregon revises health care priorities. *British Medical Journal*, **302**, 1020

Klein, R (1982) Performance evaluation and the NHS: a case study in conceptual perplexity and organisational complexity. *Public Administration*, **60**, 385–407

Klein, R. (1984) Rationing health care. *British Medical Journal*, **289**, 143–144

Klein, R. (1988) Financing health care: the three options. British Medical Journal, **296**, 734–736

Knaus, W.A. (1987) Too old and sick for intensive care. *British Journal of Hospital Medicine*, **13**, 381

Koch, H. (1991) *Total Quality Management.* Longman, Harlow

Lee, P.R. and Etheridge, L. (1989) Clinical freedom: two lessons for the UK from US experience with privatisation of health care. *Lancet*, **i**, 263–265

Light, D.W. (1991) Embedded inefficiencies in health care. *Lancet*, **338**, 102–104

Luck, G.M., Luckman, J., Smith, B.W. and Stringer, J. (1971) *Patients, Hospitals, and Operational Research.* Tavistock Publications, London

McKee, M., Ginzler, M., Priest, P. and Black, N. (1991) Which general surgical operations must be done at night? *Annals of the Royal College of Surgeons of England*, **73**, 295–302

Mozes, B., Halkin, H., Katz, A., Schiff, E. and Modan, B. (1987) Reduction of redundant hospital stay through controlled intervention. *Lancet*, **i**, 968–969

National Association of Health Authorities (1988) *Funding the NHS.* NAHA, Birmingham

Pollock, A.M. and Quirke, P. (1991) Adenoma screening and colorectal cancer. *British Medical Journal*, **303**, 3–4

Ransohoff, D.F. and Lang, C.A. (1991) Screening for colorectal cancer. *New England Journal of Medicine*, **325**, 37–41

Report from the King's Fund Panel (1989) Intensive care in the United Kingdom. *Anaesthesia*, **44**, 428–431

Roland, M.O., Bartholomew, J., Morrell, D.C., McDermott, A. and Paul, E. (1990) Understanding hospital referral rates: a user's guide. *British Medical Journal*, **301**, 98–102

Royal College of Radiologists Working Party (1991) A multicentre audit of hospital referral for radiological investigation in England and Wales. *British Medical Journal*, **303**, 809–812

Rue, R. (1991) Evaluation of resource management. *British Medical Journal*, **302**, 1291–1292

Secretary of State for Health (1991) *The Health of the Nation.* HMSO, London

Skrabanek P (1988). The physician's responsibility to the patient. *Lancet*, **i**, 1155–1157

St Leger, A.S., Allen, D. and Rowsell, K.V. (1989) Procedures for evaluating innovatory proposals. *British Medical Journal*, **299**, 1017–1018

West, R.R. (1987) Interpreting government statistics on acute hospital care. *British Medical Journal*, **295**, 509–510

Chapter 9

Economic audit – reducing hospital stay

Hospital: a house or hostel for the reception of pilgrims, travellers, and strangers; a hospice. Oxford English Dictionary

The functions of hospitals have changed radically during the last 50 years. They now bear little relation to the original definition or to its derivatives – hotel, hostel, hospice, and hospitality. They have become factories or workshops for the diagnosis and treatment of serious illnesses. It is natural, therefore, that good management requires that patients be kept in expensive hospitals for as short a time as possible. In 1974 patients stayed an average of 7.3 days after repair of inguinal hernias in England and Wales, and 5.8 days in the United States (McPherson, 1984). Six years later these figures were 5.8 and 5.0, respectively. The Office of Technology Assessment of the United States Congress published a paper entitled *Variations in hospital length of stay: their relationship to health outcomes*, in which it was recorded that patients stayed longer in hospital in the North East than in the West of the United States. The difference could not be accounted for by seriousness of disease or operation but the report could not be certain that the length of stay was correlated with outcome.

In a hospital in Tel Aviv, Israel, criteria for duration of inpatient care were set for a medical ward, resulting in the mean length of stay declining from 6.3 to 4.6 days. There was no significant change in a control ward. At follow up after one month no differences between the wards were found in readmission rates, death rates, or patient satisfaction (Mozes *et al.*, 1987).

The Audit Commission, an independent organisation in Britain, has investigated aspects of the delivery of health care. In January 1992 it published a report that showed that if all medical (as opposed to surgical) beds were used in all hospitals as efficiently as in the top 25%, the number of beds could be reduced by 30% (Audit Commission, 1992).

Hospital at home

This scheme has been set up in a number of places and, provided the home care (by doctors, nurses, physiotherapists, and others) is of a high standard, it has resulted in significant saving of hospital beds. Parenteral nutrition, haemodialysis, and peritoneal dialysis are complex procedures, but most patients can be trained to give them at home. Success of the scheme depends primarily on dedication on the part of the hospital staff, the general practitioner, and the district nurse. The largest single group of users are those with recurrent or terminal cancer and strokes. The King Edward's Fund Centre (1990) reported that in Peterborough and Oldchurch the number of days patients stayed in hospital after hip replacement was halved after setting up the hospital at home service, that patients found it much to their liking, and that their rehabilitation was not jeopardised. There is a considerable economic problem of expensive acute hospital beds that are blocked by patients who need nursing but have not the necessary support to be nursed at home. It is for such patients that well staffed nursing homes and hospices are so valuable.

Care of the dying

We have commented before on the disproportionate expenditure on the care of the terminally ill. Bayer *et al.* (1983) showed that 20% of all payments for Medicare in the United States are for people who die, and wrote: 'We believe ... that the relation between the economic and the moral dimensions of care for the terminally ill is a subject that can be addressed openly, without embracing a crude calculus that trades life for dollars.' They proposed three things: better criteria for admitting patients to intensive care units; promoting the autonomy of patients and their families; and promoting alternative institutions like hospices. 'The position that the dying have a greater right to economic resources runs the double risk of doing an injustice to other patients and using scarce resources without reflection.'

St Christopher's Hospice was opened by Dame Cicely Saunders in Sydenham, England, in 1967 (Saunders, Summers and Teller, 1981), and hospices have been established all over the country since then. The movement is complementary to hospital and home care and is an antidote to too much reliance on technology. As well as developing new techniques of pain control, hospices offer 'compassionate care for the dying'. In the United States the first modern hospice movement began in New Haven, Connecticut in 1971, and the National Hospice Organization was established in Washington DC in 1978. Unfortunately many of the services offered by the hospice movement are not reimbursed by conventional health insurance programmes.

Early discharge after operations

During the first half of the twentieth century it was customary to keep people in bed for anything up to three weeks after hernia repairs and similar operations, presumably on the grounds that it took at least as long as that for healing to be complete. This was obviously inefficient as far as hospital resources were concerned; it was also ineffective in that the final recovery was greatly delayed by the prolonged immobilisation. Doctors slowly came to realise that the sooner a patient is got up and moving the sooner he recovers (Asher, 1972), and that, barring complications, most people are happier, better fed, and sleep better at home than they do in hospital.

During the last decade surgeons have gradually extended the use of day case and overnight stay facilities. Many general surgical, orthopaedic, urological, and gynaecological operations can safely be done as day cases (Royal College of Surgeons of England, 1985), with the proviso that patients are carefully selected beforehand and that they are admitted, possibly only overnight, if there is an indication to do so. The two operations that have attracted most attention are herniorrhaphy and excision of varicose veins. The Shouldice Clinic in Toronto popularised the use of local anaesthesia and short stays for hernia repairs, and prolonged follow up has shown a commendably low rate of recurrence. The use of local anaesthesia has obvious attractions particularly for elderly people who are in most danger if their hernias strangulate.

Cross and Johnston (1987) reported that, of 113 patients operated on for small bowel obstruction in the west of Ireland in the five years 1977–1982, strangulated hernias accounted for 57%. This compares with 78% in Ghana, 65% in Nigeria, and only 8% in the United States. There seems little doubt that older people in the west of Ireland are not being advised about the dangers of hernias, and that a policy of short stay repair of hernias under local anaesthesia would be an effective way of reducing the rate of strangulation.

A World Congress on Surgical Efficiency and Economy was held in Lund, Sweden, in 1987. At that congress Dr R.C. Hall of Indianapolis reported that 'Admission two hours before and discharge two days after elective cholecystectomy is safe and feasible.' He claimed that paralytic ileus is rare, that oral analgesics are sufficient, that home is the best place to recover, and that adequate preparation relieves fear.

Any programme of short stay operating must take into account not only proper preparation of patients, including investigation of any complicating diseases, but also the wishes of patients. When 36 women were questioned after they had had laparoscopic sterilisation done as day cases (at their own request), 11 wished they had stayed in hospital (Thomas and Hare, 1987).

Another aspect of the cost benefit equation that is sometimes overlooked is that though day case operations are decidedly cheaper for the hospital, it is doubtful if they really save so much money when the total cost of the illness is considered, including the time off work. John and Potthoff (1987) examined the workings of the 'Bavarian Contract'. This was introduced in 1979 after negotiations between office based doctors and Bavarian sick funds and aimed to increase ambulatory medical care and reduce hospital inpatient care. Examination of the working of the scheme from 1979 to 1985 showed that it had resulted in a certain amount of substitution, but that there was no evidence that expansion of outpatient care helped to contain total expenditure on health care.

Encouraging uptake of daycase operations

The proportion of operations considered suitable for day care was established by a 'Delphi study' (Gabbay and Francis, 1989). This they defined as 'a method of obtaining a collective view of a small group of experts by using repeated rounds of questionnaires and giving anonymous feedback of the responses of colleagues from earlier rounds'. The indications for day care of 83 operations were agreed, and the proportion was then compared with that actually achieved in one district. The prediction was that many more daycase operations could have been done. In the United States particularly the impact of 'ambulatory care' has been considerable, and there is little doubt that other countries could benefit by extension of the indications.

Minimally invasive surgery

The most efficient way of treating many conditions is not to operate on them at all. Rates of admission to hospital for operation are remarkably variable, not only among countries, but also among different centres in the same country. Rates are substantially higher in those countries in which surgeons get paid by item of service rendered, rather than by salary – suggesting that some procedures are overused when the indications for operation are financial rather than clinical. This applies particularly to cholecystectomy, hysterectomy, tonsillectomy, and prostatectomy.

As a result of the issuing of guidelines and audits of the outcome of conservative rather than operative treatment, there has been a shift of opinion towards non-operative treatment for tonsillitis, menorrhagia, and asymptomatic gall stones discovered incidentally during radiographic or ultrasonographic examinations. The long term outlook for patients with silent gall stones has long been debated, but the probability is that not more than 18% will develop symptoms within 20 years, and that survival is not increased by cholecystectomy (Bouchier, 1983).

Advances in urology

The history of minimally invasive surgery goes back not much more than a decade (Wickham, 1991). It was in 1979 that surgeons in London and in Mainz developed the technique of percutaneous nephrolithotomy: a fine needle is introduced into the renal pelvis and the track is dilated until it accommodates an endoscope, through which the stone or stones can be removed with or without first being fragmented with ultrasound or other probes. This was followed in 1982 by the introduction of extracorporeal shockwave lithotripsy, which required general anaesthesia, and then by piezoelectric shockwave lithotripsy, which requires no anaesthesia and can be done as a day case procedure.

It soon became apparent to surgeons that the trauma of classic incisional surgery was greater than they had appreciated – the trauma of anaesthesia and analgesia, of surgical access, of blood loss, and psychological trauma – and the Society of Minimally Invasive Surgery was founded in 1989. Laparoscopic cholecystectomy caught the attention of the surgical world in 1990 (Dubois *et al.*, 1990).

Advances in abdominal surgery

Pure cholesterol gall stones can be dissolved by prolonged oral administration of bile salts, but the economic advantages are slender, and there are few indications for this treatment nowadays. On the other hand, lithotripsy – which has proved to be so effective in the treatment of renal stones – has a reasonable chance of success, and many minimally invasive techniques have been used for the treatment of symptomatic gall stone disease. Refinements of endoscopes and endoscopic technique have encouraged more surgeons to clear stones from the common bile duct by endoscopic papillotomy and retrieval by stone baskets or Fogarty catheters.

Transhepatic drainage of the obstructed bile duct had a vogue, but the morbidity and mortality turned out to be unacceptable. On the other hand, endoscopic drainage and the use of stents have reduced the necessity for laparotomy and internal drainage for malignant obstructions. Acute cholecystitis associated with obstruction of the cystic duct can be treated satisfactorily by 'minilaparotomy' with endoscopic evacuation of the stones – possibly aided by laser or ultrasonic disintegration. The important development, however, was the refinement of laparoscopic instruments, which has allowed surgeons to remove nearly all gall bladders without subjecting the patient to a laparotomy (Dubois *et al.*, 1990).

One of the attractions of laparoscopic cholecystectomy (and other 'minimally invasive' operations) is that patients can go home within a day or two of their operation.

References

Asher, R. (1972) The danger of going to bed. In *Richard Asher Talking Sense*. Pitman Medical, London, pp. 119–123

Audit Commission (1992) *Lying in Wait: the use of medical beds in acute hospitals.* HMSO, London

Bayer, R., Callahan, D., Fletcher, J. *et al.* (1983) The care of the terminally ill: morality and economics. *New England Journal of Medicine*, **309**, 1490–1494

Bouchier, I.A.D. (1983) Brides of quietness: silent gall stones. *British Medical Journal*, **286**, 415–416

Cross, K.S.H. and Johnston, J.G. (1987) Small bowel obstruction. A review of 456 cases in a West of Ireland region. *Journal of the Royal Society of Medicine*, **80**, 149–150

Dubois, F., Icard, P., Berthelot, G. and Levard, H. (1990) Coelioscopic cholecystectomy. Preliminary report of 36 cases. *Annals Surgery*, **211**, 60–62

Gabbay, J. and Francis, L. (1989) How much day surgery? Delphic predictions. *British Medical Journal*, **297**, 1249–1252

John, J. and Potthoff, P. (1987) Cost containment in a statutory insurance scheme by substitution of outpatient for inpatient care? The case of the Bavarian Contract. *Health Policy, Amsterdam* **8**, 153–169

King Edward's Fund Centre (1990) *Hospital at Home – the coming revolution.* King Edward's Fund Centre, London

McPherson, K. (1984) Length of stay and health outcome. *British Medical Journal*, **288**, 1854–1855

Mozes, B., Halkin, H., Katz, A., Schiff, E. and Modan, B. (1987) Reduction of redundant hospital stay through controlled intervention. *Lancet*, **i**, 968–969

Royal College of Surgeons of England (1985) *Guidelines For Day Case Surgery*. Royal College of Surgeons, London

Saunders, C., Summers, D.H. and Teller, N. (eds) (1981) *Hospice: the living idea*. Edward Arnold, London

Thomas, H. and Hare, M.J. (1987) Day case laparoscopic sterilization – time for a rethink? *British Journal of Obstetrics and Gynaecology*, **94**, 445–448

Wickham, J. (1991) Minimally invasive therapy. *Health Trends*, **23**, 6 9

Chapter 10

Diagnosis-related groups and performance indicators

The protection of our rights can endure no longer than the performance of our responsibilities.	John F. Kennedy (1963)

In almost any other sphere of human activity the providers of goods and services can specify the quality of the raw material that they are working with. Even farmers, although they are at the mercy of the weather, can at least be assured that the seeds, fertilisers, and feedstuffs that they use are of a standard quality. It is only health workers who have to take their raw material, their patients, as they come, and one of the difficulties of auditing the performance of these people is that the outcome of an intervention is likely to depend not only on the effectiveness of that intervention, but also on the ability of the patient to withstand the disease and the treatment.

The British National Health Service employs nearly a million people, more than any other organisation in Europe. In 1988 this number was exceeded only by the numbers employed by the Indian Railways and the Red Army (Bowden and Gumpert, 1988). Until recently, however, there was no way in which the government could assess whether sick people were getting value for money. The 1948 legacy of voluntary hospitals, which were supported partly by fees paid by patients and partly by donations from charitable sources, meant that these hospitals continued their previous style of management – largely based on the assumption that if you needed more money you asked for it, and that the most successful hospitals, in terms of their treatment of patients, were bankrupt.

At the inception of the National Health Service there were, however, a number of hospitals that did not rely on voluntary subscriptions. These were the municipal hospitals and those set up during the Second World War as Emergency Medical Services hospitals. In 1948 all hospitals in Britain were taken over by the National Health Service and the process of levelling out the allocation of resources has continued ever since then.

Diagnosis-related groups

When Medicare was introduced in the United States in 1965 to pay for the treatment of people over the age of 65, hospitals and doctors were reimbursed for 'reasonable' costs and charges. During the following decade, however, spending on Medicare was in danger of getting out of control. The concept of diagnosis related groups (DRGs) arose from work at Yale University in the 1960s (Fetter, 1987). This attempt to classify people according to how ill they were, and how much of a hospital's resources they would consume, was seized upon by the United States Federal government as a method of restraining the costs of the Medicare scheme. The government passed the *Tax Equity and Financial Responsibility Act* in 1982. This took effect in 1983 and authorised a fixed price to be paid per illness for patients covered by the Medicare programme (Bakken and Young, 1984). Its aim is to restrain costs, not to improve the quality of medical care.

The current version contains 467 classes of illness and the variables classified are: principal diagnosis, surgical procedure, additional diagnoses ('comorbidities' and complications), age, sex, and where patients go when they are discharged (Bardsley, 1987). The groups were designed to be clinically coherent – the same amount of resources would be used for every patient in any particular group. The main outcome measure used was the length of hospital stay and each of the 467 diagnostic categories was given a 'relative cost weight' varying from (for example) 0.2457 for DRG 33 (concussion age 0–17) to 2.6801 for DRG 146 (rectal resection age over 69 and/or with comorbidity or complications) and 4.1840 for DRG 302 (kidney transplant).

Diagnosis-related groups offer a more useful classification of diseases for audit of efficiency than the *International Classification of Diseases*, 9th edition, *Clinical Modification*, but still do not accurately distinguish grades of illness within the same category. A patient with complicated diverticular disease of the colon, for example, may present with a local phlegmon, or he may present with faecal peritonitis; the outlook is quite different. From the economic point of view also they have been criticised on several scores: hospitals with advanced diagnostic equipment will spend more on diagnosis than those without such equipment; the adoption of DRGs implies that both the quality of medical care and the outcome remain constant; there is a temptation to transfer to another hospital very ill patients or those with complications that will demand a long stay in hospital; finally, for DRGs concerning operations, it has to be assumed that the operation was necessary.

The Social Security Act, which set up Medicare, contained a section stipulating that hospitals participating in the Medicare programme should be obliged to offer emergency treatment to all comers (Schneider, 1990). The advent of diagnosis-related groups led to widespread 'dumping' of potentially costly patients, and an amending Act was passed in 1985 and strengthened in 1989. There is now a legal requirement for hospitals accepting Medicare payments to:

- Make an appropriate screening examination of anyone attending the hospital, either by a doctor if that is customary in that hospital, or by a nurse
- Having determined that an emergency condition is present, to stabilise that condition before transferring the patient; the patient must be told of the risks and benefits of transfer

- The physician must sign a declaration that the benefits of a transfer outstrip the risks
- The receiving hospital must accept the transfer, and notes and X-rays must accompany the patient.

Zook *et al.* (1980) studied the records of 2238 inpatients in six hospitals in Massachusetts and concluded that more than half of them required repeated admissions, and that this accounted for 60% of hospital costs. These patients were mainly old and had chronic and incurable diseases.

In defence of diagnosis-related groups and prospective payments, LoGerfo (1990), in an editorial commenting on eight papers from Santa Monica that analysed the quality of care – both process and outcome – before and after the introduction of the prospective payments system, concluded that the rate of unplanned readmissions did not rise, and that some deficiencies in the process of care were detected in 17% of admissions.

The acceptance of diagnosis-related groups in Britain is still some way off, but the concept probably comes as near as can be to an acceptable way of defining case mix. The National Case-mix Office, working in the Department of Health's Resource Management Unit, has set out proposals for English Case-mix Groups (Benson, 1991). These will have the same function as diagnosis-related groups, but will be more easily adaptable to circumstances in Britain. There is a prospect that they may be used in future for auditing the work of doctors, comparing the use of resources by one doctor with that of his peers both in the same hospital and in the whole country. The Yale system is likely to be adopted in most European countries as a means of measuring the final output of hospitals in terms of both efficiency and effectiveness (Rodrigues, 1987).

Standardised mortality rates

In Britain a Resource Allocation Working Party was set up in 1976 to try and even out the unjust concentration of resources in the London regions, which had arisen as a result of historical factors that were no longer as applicable as they were before the establishment of the National Health Service. The indicator of need that the Working Party adopted was the standardised mortality rate. This, however, takes no account of the fact that a great deal of medical effort is required to deal with non-lethal conditions like arthritis. Some London hospitals are tertiary referral centres for complicated cases, and the Working Party tried to adjust for this factor, as well as for the age composition and case mix of the population. The Working Party rejected assessment of need by measurement of morbidity, because the data were not available, but the fact that deprived people need more health care was recognised and the standardised mortality rate is weighted for socioeconomic groups and for classification of residential neighbourhoods. It has become clear over the ensuing 10 years, however, that none of these indicators is sufficiently accurate to base allocation policies on them. The more resources are available, the more they are used (Mays, 1987).

Steering Group on Health Services Information

The obvious difficulties in ensuring justice in the availability of medical care, and indeed in the quality of that care, have spawned numerous working parties and commissions, all of which have suffered from the paucity and inaccuracy of data. It has needed the general introduction of computers to produce what promise to be useful tools of management, particularly for allocation of resources, in the health care industry. The Steering Group on Health Services Information was set up in 1979 and met for the first time in February 1980 under the chairmanship of Mrs Edith Körner. This group set out to improve the supply of information for district management; it asked:

- What data should be collected?
- How should the data be collected?
- How should the collected data be analysed?

Over the next five years six reports were issued, and the collection of statistics started in 1987. The first report (Körner 1982) on hospital based services, stated that

> 'The Steering Group's main concern is with information for health services management. Thus we have not tackled specifically the information needed by health professionals to evaluate the results of their care; nor that needed by individual professional bodies to review the resources available to and the professional work of their members.'

Performance Indicators

The measurement of the efficiency of the National Health Service was pioneered by John Yates and his team in Birmingham. He introduced the Inter Authority Comparisons and Consultancy Service. The work has been complemented by that of the Joint Group on Performance Indicators, and relies on the greater accuracy and scope of the Körner statistics. Performance indicators measure some aspects of efficiency, but not of effectiveness – they are audits of structure and process with particular reference to cost effectiveness. Each hospital in England is allocated its own code and can compare its performance with the mean performance of all hospitals in its region and of all hospitals in England.

Performance indicators do not measure outcome. There is still need, both for the assurance of the quality of care and for research, for individual surgical audit programmes. In June 1988, however, a proposal was put forward at a meeting of the National Association of Health Authorities that all deaths in acute hospitals and within 30 days of discharge should be recorded and that the mortality should be related to diagnosis related groups. Each District Health Authority would be required to analyse its case mix by assigning a diagnosis-related group to every patient discharged from hospital.

The History of Performance Indicators

The Department of Health and Social Security set up the initial study on Performance Indicators in 1981 and this was reported in 1983. In that year eight working groups were appointed to cover:

Acute services
Children's services
Services for the elderly
Services for mental illness
Services for the mentally handicapped
Support and diagnostic services
Estate management
Manpower

These groups reported their recommendations in 1985 and the first Performance Indicators were published that year. There are now about 450 indicators covering 12 health care groups. The Department of Health recognised that the production of endless tables and graphs would overwhelm administrators. The result was the production of the statistics on computer disks, at first designed to be used in the BBC model B micro-computer with a Torch Z 80 second processor. Tabulation and graphic printing were achieved by a standard dot matrix printer, usually the Epson FX 80. A more advanced system used the software packages Lotus or Symphony and Lotus 1-2-3 in IBM compatible personal computers. The 1988 issue comprised 12 floppy disks and the rankings can be displayed as figures, scattergrams, histograms, or centile bars (Lowry, 1988).

A recent method of analysing the data generated by Performance Indicators is the 'expert system' developed by the Operational Research Service of the Department of Health and Social Security in association with Coopers and Lybrand (Payling, Bowen and Briggs, 1987) This Performance Indicator Analyst is written on CRYSTAL, a 'shell' program for writing expert systems from Intelligent Environments Ltd, Richmond, TW10 6TP. It uses IBM compatible personal computers and accepts the data stored in ASCII format. It selects high values (over 80) and low values (under 20) for intelligent analysis, display, and cross correlation. It then makes recommendations based on 11 500 rules written into the system. The system does not claim to replace human analysis but it does supplement it by pinpointing extreme values and calling attention to them in a textual report.

Each Performance Indicator for each district is given a rank from 0 to 100 in relation to all other districts, and a high (over 80) or low (under 20) rank in any indicator is singled out by the expert system and correlated with other indicators. Both high and low rankings (which should not necessarily be construed as 'good' or 'bad') direct attention to those indicators, and the 11 500 'rules' in the expert system are based on the IF, AND, OR, THEN approach: IF the waiting list for non-urgent general surgical operations is high, AND the ratio of operating sessions to surgical beds is low, OR the ratio of immediate to waiting list admissions is high, THEN additional operating sessions should be arranged. Indicators are not measures; their purpose is to draw attention to outliers and stimulate local debate on the reasons for extreme values.

The data are derived from those already collected regionally and nationally (including Hospital Activity Analysis) and suffer from both the delay in publication (up to a year), and from the inaccuracies that are inherent in such data – a figure of 20% error for Hospital Activity Analysis has been established by several authors.

For example, Skinner, Riley and Thomas (1988) compared figures from their internal audit of orthopaedic operations with that produced by the health authority from data generated by Hospital Activity Analysis, which relies on coding in accordance with the Office of Population Censuses and Surveys Classification of Operations (1975). They found a 20% underestimate of the 'weighted number of operations' and a 34% underestimate of the 'number of major operations per consultant'. They suggested that operations should be classified into minor (for example, aspiration of joint – mean duration 27 minutes); intermediate (for example, diagnostic arthroscopy – mean duration 53 minutes); major (for example, hemiarthroplasty – mean duration 96 minutes); major plus (for example, total hip replacement – mean duration 152 minutes); and complex major (for example, revision arthroplasty – mean duration 218 minutes).

In future performance indicators will be based on data gathered in accordance with the recommendations of the Information Steering Group (the Körner report), and possibly modified by taking account of case mix determined by diagnosis-related groups.

The data analysed by Performance Indicators

Most of the approximately 450 indicators relate to cost effectiveness and take account of only crude measures of case mix (such as the percentage of children under the age of 5, of the population over the age of 65, and of diagnostic categories). The most important indicators from the standpoint of surgeons concern the efficient use of beds, of outpatient clinics, and of operating theatres. These are correlated with costs and with the ratios of surgeons, nurses, and other workers per 1000 population. The indicators also deal with the number of patients on the inpatient waiting list, the number of urgent cases waiting more than a month, the number of non-urgent cases waiting more than 12 months, and the notional number of days required to clear the waiting list.

The 'first line' performance indicators in general surgery comprise the following:

Actual length of stay
Expected length of stay
Standardised length of stay ratio
Turnover interval
Actual throughput
Expected throughput
Standardised throughput ratio
Percent day cases
Percent cases not operated on
Preoperative stay

Postoperative stay
Theatre sessions per bed
Waiting list per 1000 population
Notional days to clear waiting list
Percent immediate admissions

Length of stay is defined as the product of the number of occupied beds and the number of days in the week, month, or year, divided by the number of patients discharged or dead during that period. The expected length of stay is the average of all hospitals in England, corrected for age, sex, and diagnostic category.

Turnover interval is defined as the number of available beds minus the number of occupied beds, multiplied by the number of days in a period, and divided by the number of discharges in that period. It is a valuable indicator of the efficiency of bed management.

Actual throughput per bed per year is the number of days in the year divided by the length of stay plus the turnover interval. The expected throughput is the average for all hospitals in England, corrected for age, sex, and diagnostic category.

Notional days to clear waiting list is the number of patients on the waiting list at 31 December, multiplied by 365 and divided by the number of patients admitted from the waiting list during the year.

What do Performance indicators not indicate?

This is an easy question: they do not indicate the quality of an individual surgeon's care. Kirk (1988) explained the satisfaction he used to feel when he examined his conscience and knew that he was trying his best. This has been eroded by the data presented by Performance Indicators. He explained that his policy is to save patients return visits to outpatient clinics. At their first visit they are 'given as much time as they need to discuss investigation, treatment, admission, or operation'. The results of investigations are communicated to patients and general practitioners by telephone or letter, and only if he sees the need does he make a further outpatient appointment.

Kirk went on to write that patients discharged home after an operation are given instructions but no routine follow up appointment. He complained that most of his activities are unrecorded and, by the statistical methods used in the National Health Service, he must seem lazy and inefficient. He likened the plethora of information acquired by the National Health Service to the error that Winston Churchill accused the Americans of making when, at a time of crisis, he was being urged to 'do something'. Churchill is said to have replied that they were 'confusing movement with action'.

Indicators of outcome are now being sought in Britain. The Secretary of State for Social Services addressed the Council of the British Medical Association on 2 March 1988 (Report, 1988). He stressed the need for health care workers to be aware of the costs of their work, but he went on to say that there was a gap in the data – information on health outcomes to assess how the health of the nation was developing. Instead of always asking 'How much money are we spending?', the question should be 'How much health are we getting?'

The correlation between the amount spent on health care and the health of the population is by no means linear. Greece, a country that spends less of its gross domestic product on health care than any other European country, also has the highest male life expectancy. Ireland, on the other hand, which is high on the list of spenders on health care, has almost the lowest male life expectancy. The Minister suggested putting together a portfolio of health indicators – a health index that would cover the results not only of the treatment of diseases, but also of preventive and public educational programmes.

Performance Indicators are unique to England and there is no doubt that their intelligent use will encourage the examination by hospital managers of those aspects of their hospitals that fall into the exceptionally high (over 80%) or exceptionally low (below 20%) categories. Cost is to be measured not only in terms of money, but also of the just allocation of scarce resources; the identification of inefficiency is an essential prelude to providing better health care.

References

Bakken, C.L. and Young, D.S. (1984) Changing American medicine. *British Medical Journal*, **288**, 956–957

Bardsley, M. (1987) Case mix. In Bardsley, M. Coles, J. and Jenkins L., eds, *DRGs and Health Care. The management of case mix*, King Edward's Hospital Fund, London, pp. 13-27

Benson, T. (1991) *Medical Informatics.* Longman, Harlow

Bowden, D. and Gumpert, R. (1988) Quality versus quantity in medicine. *Royal Society of Arts Journal*, **136**, 333–346

Fetter, R.B. (1987) Introduction. In Bardsley, M. Coles, J. and Jenkins L., eds, *DRGs and Health Care. The management of case mix*, King Edward's Hospital Fund, London, pp. 5–10

Kennedy, J.F. (1963) Address, Vanderbilt University, Nashville, Tennessee, May 18

Kirk, R.M. (1988). Personal view. *British Medical Journal*, **296**, 999

Körner, E. (1982) *Steering Group on Health Service Information. First Report to the Secretary of State.* HMSO, London

LoGerfo, J.L. (1990) The prospective payment system and quality. No skeletons in the cupboard. *Journal of the American Medical Association*, **264**, 1995–1996.

Lowry, S. (1988) Focus on performance indicators. *British Medical Journal*, **296**, 992–994

Mays, N. (1987) Measuring morbidity for resource allocation. *British Medical Journal*, **295**, 703–706

Payling, L., Bowen, T. and Briggs, I. (1987) PIs become crystal clear. *The Health Service Journal*, **30 April**, 502–503

Report (1988) *British Medical Journal*, **296**, 803

Rodrigues, J.M. (1987) DRGs: the European scene. A general analysis. *Journal of Management in Medicine*, **2**, 139–150

Schneider, K.C. (1990) Medical review and the newly revised emergency care obligations of Medicare hospitals. *Quality Assurance and Utilization Review*, **5**, 74–79

Skinner, P.W., Riley, D. and Thomas, E.M. (1988) Use and abuse of performance indicators. *British Medical Journal*, **297**, 1256–1259

Zook, C.J., Savickis, S.F. and Moore, F.D. (1980) Repeated hospitalization for the same disease: a multiplier of national health costs. *Milbank Memorial Fund Quarterly*, **58**, 454–471

Chapter 11

The containment of costs of health care

Only when therapeutic equality can be demonstrated does cost become a valid component of the physician's decision-making process. Sade (1983)

The point to remember is that what the government gives it must first take away.   John S. Coleman

Every patient who seeks help (and in relation to screening and preventive medicine, every healthy person in the country) deserves nothing but the best that medical science can offer. The unalterable economic fact, however, is that resources spent in one sphere deprive all other spheres of those resources. This means that some limit must be set on the amount of money that a country can afford to save a life or avoid a severe disability (Roberts, Farrow and Charny, 1985). These authors put forward the idea of a 'benefit : premium ratio', which they suggested should be about 200 : 1, a benefit of £40 000 ($68 000) for an annual premium of £200 ($340). They then calculated that £14 000 ($23 800) was the tolerable upper limit of cost for saving a life or preventing permanent disability.

Williams (1985) analysed the effectiveness of coronary artery bypass grafting in terms of its effect on life expectancy adjusted for the quality of life. He concluded that the operation rated well for patients with severe angina and extensive coronary artery disease.

> 'The cost, however, rises sharply for less severe cases. Bypass grafting seems to compare favourably with valve replacement for aortic stenosis and implantation of pacemakers for heart block; it is distinctly better than heart transplantation and the treatment of end stage renal failure but is probably less cost effective than hip replacement.'

He admitted that the data on which these judgements were based are crude and in need of refinement.

Quality adjusted life years

Audit of the quality of life after operations is just as important as audit of outcome and patient satisfaction. We consider some of the ways of measuring the quality of life in Chapter 16.

The concept of quality adjusted life years (QALYs) (Williams, 1985) was introduced to allow for the fact that many patients are willing to sacrifice a measure of life expectancy for a better quality of life. Kind, Rosser, and Williams (1982) defined four degrees of distress: none (A); mild (B); moderate (C); and severe (D); and eight degrees of disability: I, no disability; II, slight social disability; III, severe social disability or slight impairment of performance at work, or both, able to do all housework except heavy tasks; IV, choice of work or performance at work severely limited, housewives and old people able to do only light housework but able to go out shopping; V, unable to undertake any paid employment, unable to continue any education, old people confined to home except for escorted outings and short walks and unable to shop, housewives able to perform only a few tasks; VI, confined to chair or wheelchair or able to move only with support; VII, confined to bed; VIII, unconscious. They then constructed a matrix that gave a fraction to be multiplied by the number of years of life expected from an intervention. For example, an intervention that produced a distress rating of C, a disability rating of VI, and a survival of 2 years would produce 2×0.680 QALYs. The cost of that intervention can then be expressed as a sum of money per QALY. Hospital haemodialysis was estimated to cost £15 000 per QALY, heart transplantation £8000, kidney transplantation £3000, total hip replacement £800, and counselling by primary care physicians to stop smoking £167. As a basis for allocation of resources the use of QALYs is attractive to economists, but as Fallowfield (1990) wrote: 'The quality of life of sick people can be adversely affected by health economists and others if an objective in QALY research is to provide supporting arguments for limiting financial resources in health care for treatments that are effective but expensive.'

Cost containment by prevention

'For most diseases, prevention by control of their origins is cheaper, more humane, and more effective than intervention by treatment after they occur' (McKeown, 1979).

The health of the people of nearly all developed countries has improved immeasurably during the last 100 years, not only because of improved nutrition and housing, but also because of the adoption of public health measures and preventive medicine. McKeown claimed that the predominant influences which led to the improvement of health in the past three centuries were nutritional, environmental (particularly control of the quality of water and food), and behavioural, the last through the changes in reproductive practices that limited population growth. He suggested that misinterpretation of the major influences, particularly personal medical care, on past and future improvements in health has led to misuse of resources and distortion of the role of medicine.

The standardised death rate from tuberculosis in England and Wales has declined from 2901 per million to 10, from other lung diseases from 2309 to 1170, and the neonatal and infant mortality from 1221 to 72. The infectious fevers (cholera, scarlet fever, and diphtheria) which killed 2835 in every million in the year 1850 are now practically unknown, their place being taken by cardiovascular diseases and cancer (Fitzpatrick, 1986).

The aim of the World Health Organisation is to achieve 'health for all by the year 2000'. In response to this call many countries have put forward plans. The United States Public Health Service proposed 22 objectives, and in Britain the Health Education Authority (1989) put forward 16. Table 11.1 compares these programmes.

Table 11.1 Objectives for the year 2000 in USA and Britain

Objective	USA	Britain
Reduce use of tobacco	Yes	Yes
Stop abuse of alcohol	Yes	Yes
Stop abuse of drugs	Yes	Yes
Promote healthy eating	Yes	Yes
Promote physical activity	Yes	Yes
Improve mental health	Yes	No
Reduce environmental pollution	Yes	No
Promote health at work	Yes	Yes
Promote road safety	Yes	Yes
Reduce violence	Yes	No
Improve maternity services	Yes	Yes
Reduce adolescent pregnancy	Yes	No
Promote dental health	Yes	Yes
Reduce sexually transmitted diseases	Yes	Yes
Promote immunisation	Yes	No
Promote child health surveillance	No	Yes
Promote care of the elderly	Yes	Yes
Promote early detection of cancer	Yes	Yes
Prevent other chronic diseases	Yes	No
Detect and treat hypertension	Yes	Yes
Detect and treat hypercholesterolaemia	Yes	No
Improve health education	Yes	No
Improve data collection	Yes	No
Promote adequate income	No	Yes
Promote good housing	No	Yes

The interesting thing about these objectives is not what they include, but what they leave out or relegate to the bottom of the list. The American list omits all mention of the prevention of poverty and unhealthy housing, and the British list puts these last. The American list mentions 'reduction of violence' but avoids confrontation with the gun lobby by not mentioning the appalling toll of young lives claimed by guns. Although both lists specify the need for better road safety, no emphasis is placed on the fact that road traffic accidents cause more deaths below the age of 35 than any disease.

Surgeons can take little credit for the improved health of the people, and even sulphonamides and antibiotics had only a marginal influence on total mortality, though sulphonamides virtually put an end to the ravages of puerperal fever, which is said to have killed between 3000 and 5000 women in England and Wales in 1910 (Loudon, 1987). Lobar pneumonia is no longer necessarily a killing disease, and most surgical operations are safer than they were 50 years ago; nevertheless, prevention is much more cost effective than treatment. As Kaiser (1986) wrote: 'Ample evidence suggests that in a broad range of surgical procedures ... it is more cost effective to administer prophylactic antimicrobials than to treat the infections in patients who have not received these agents.'

Surgeons are sometimes tempted to operate on asymptomatic lesions in the hope of preventing serious disease in the future. This is the case with parathyroid adenomas or hyperplasia discovered accidentally by routine biochemical tests. It is also the case for many arterial stenoses that are causing minimal or no symptoms. In Britain there is a greater conservatism and, for example, carotid endarterectomy is done 27 times less often per head of population than in the United States, and seven times less often than in Canada (Anonymous, 1991a). Two large multicentre random control trials (the European Carotid Surgery Trial, and the North American Symptomatic Carotid Endarterectomy Trial) concluded that endarterectomy (which has a risk of serious stroke or death of 7.5%) should not be done for stenoses of less than 30%, but that it reduces the risk of subsequent stroke by at least sixfold if the stenosis is greater than 70%. If the stenosis is between 30% and 70% no clear cut advantage or disadvantage from the operation could be discerned.

Social influences on health

In 1926 the British Medical Association gave evidence to the Royal Commission on National Health Insurance and argued as follows (Klein, 1991):

'The organisation of a National Health Insurance scheme is not necessarily, or even probably, the best means of utilising limited resources for the promotion of national health. It is more likely that there are a number of other directions in which severally, or collectively, a corresponding expenditure would produce an even more satisfactory return. Such are (1) proper housing, (2) town planning with the proper provision of open spaces and recreation facilities, (3) smoke abatement, (4) a pure milk supply, (5) public house reform and the regulation of the sale of alcoholic beverages, (6) the destruction of vermin, (7) education, (8) the aiding of medical research.'

In 1988 the life expectancy at birth in the United States was 75.5 years for whites and 69.5 years for blacks (Navarro, 1990). Brenner (1979) calculated that a 1% increase in unemployment, sustained for 5 years, was responsible for 37 000 premature deaths in the USA. He attributed this not only to the reduction in the standard of living, but also to the fear, tension, and stress caused by the feeling of not being needed. The United States is the only developed country that does not collect mortality statistics by class, but the figures on chronic diseases support the theory that morbidity is much more closely related to income than to race, and there is evidence that the differential between rich and poor is increasing.

The excess in the proportions of illness and death among the socially and economically deprived has been documented in every country. Nowhere is this more evident than in South Africa, where the infant mortality in 1985 was 61/1000 among blacks compared with 9.3 among whites; life expectancy at birth was 62 years among blacks, 71 years among whites; and the rate of homicide was 23.7/100 000 among blacks, 2.8 among whites (Benatar, 1991).

Deaths and disabilities caused by accidents

Among the avoidable causes of death and illness are accidents on the roads, in the home, at work, and at play. Road traffic accidents alone claim the lives of 5000 to 6000 people in Britain every year; 60 000 to 80 000 are seriously injured, and about 2000 hospital beds are occupied every day by the victims (Butler and Vaile, 1984). In addition, at least as many people are killed or maimed by accidents in the home or at work (Medical Commission on Accident Prevention, 1988). Half of all the deaths in the age group 15–24 are caused by accidents (Raffle, 1991).

The most important causes of road accidents are motor cycles, age under 25 years, and consumption of alcohol (and tranquillising drugs). It is slightly heartening to find that the incidence of both fatal and non-fatal motor vehicle accidents has fallen during the past decade, and that attention is being directed toward the provision of specialist trauma centres.

In the USA the National Highways Administration reported that 47 000 people were killed and 3.5 million injured in road traffic accidents during 1990. Homicide and suicide by hand guns accounted for 62 897 deaths in the two years 1984 and 1985, more than in the entire 8½ year Vietnam war, and it is estimated that five people are injured for every death (Mercy and Houk 1988). Of the 31 566 deaths in 1985, 17 363 were suicide, 11 836 homicide, 1649 accidental, 242 'during altercations with the police', and 476 from undetermined causes. According to the Texas Department of Health, 3443 people were killed by guns in 1990, compared with 3309 in car accidents. This is the first time that gun deaths have outnumbered road traffic deaths. In 1981, 474 teenagers and 156 children under the age of 12 died of gunshot wounds (Schletky, 1985). Gopal and Lipschitz (1988) estimated that in South Africa 'approximately 10 000 people die on our roads each year and about 30 000 people lose their lives from assault'.

Occupational hazards

In many countries there are mechanisms for surveillance and prevention of accidents and other hazards in the work place. In Britain the Health and Safety Commission publishes guidelines for specific industries, and can take offending employers to court if these guidelines are ignored. Among the recent publications of this authority are 'Lighten the load – guidance for employers on musculoskeletal disorders' (September 1991); 'Provision and use of work equipment: draft proposals for regulations' (November 1991); and endorsement of the European Commission's directive entitled 'Minimum safety and health requirements for the manual handling of loads where there is a risk particularly of back injury to workers' (November 1991).

In the United States there is no comprehensive national surveillance of disease, but the US Occupational Safety and Health Administration regulations require that workers be offered medical examinations for a variety of conditions; and employers have a duty to maintain a log of injuries and illnesses among their workers (Baker, 1991). In most countries there are workers' compensation schemes.

Containing the costs of treatment

Most countries have taken steps to restrain expenditure on health care. In many the restraint has been simply the unavailability of investigations and treatments requiring high technology equipment, whereas in most developed countries positive steps have been taken to contain costs.

Unnecessary operations

Barnes (1977) perused the Transactions of the American Surgical Association from 1880 to 1942 and found testimonials to the value of operations for *visceroptosis*, which was widely practised from 1890 to 1928, the indications being 'neurasthenia' and non-specific abdominal pain; for *constipation*, which caused 'autointoxication' by subtotal colectomy; for *duodenal stasis* by duodenojejunostomy; for *prostatic obstruction* by orchidectomy; for *respiratory obstruction* by thymectomy; for *epilepsy, hypertension* and other conditions by thyroidectomy; for *angina* by cervicodorsal sympathectomy; for *Raynaud's disease* by periarterial sympathectomy; for *megacolon* by lumbar sympathectomy; for *cirrhotic ascites* by the Talma operation; and for *ischaemia* by ligation of veins.

None of these reports were controlled, and their acceptance was attributable to the authority of the authors, primitive comprehension of standards of objectivity in the judgement of outcome, incorrect diagnoses, incorrect comprehension of pathology, lack of ethical constraints, and poor and biased follow up. He need not have stopped in 1942.

There are still operations being done that are unnecessary, but more attention is being paid to guidelines and consensus statements, which are guided by the results of clinical trials. In the management of the 'acute abdomen' investigations such as ultrasonography, computer tomography, diagnostic peritoneal dialysis, and laparoscopy now offer valid alternatives to the policies of either 'wait and see' or 'look and see' (Paterson-Brown, 1991).

One of the most difficult decisions that a surgeon has to make is when not to operate. This applies particularly to patients with cancer, and there is little doubt that a laparotomy in a patient with advanced malignant disease does shorten the patient's life. It is, however, not only operations that can be done unwisely. Many patients are subjected to radiotherapy or chemotherapy with little or no prospect of palliation. There must come a time when doctors say 'enough's enough' and treat the patient's symptoms.

Unnecessary investigations

Good medicine is based on taking enough time to obtain a complete history and carry out a competent physical examination. If a doctor cannot make at least a tentative diagnosis without the need for elaborate and costly tests there is something wrong with his training.

Departments of pathology and imaging find it difficult to stem the steadily increasing flow of requests, and even the prominent display of guidelines for junior staff, the holding of seminars, joint review of casenotes, and redesigning of request forms has had little effect. In one unit there was a rule that if a junior member of staff asked for an investigation that would not change the management of the patient he was fined a small sum, which was placed in the unit 'amenity fund' – in other words, to pay for leaving parties. As Brewin (1981) wrote: 'The best reason – some would say the only reason – for ordering a test is to modify management if the findings so indicate.'

About one dollar in every three of the total health care bill in the United States goes on investigations. Competition for patients is so intense that some imaging centres encourage people to come in off the streets for magnetic resonance imaging, claiming that it gives useful information 'on a wide variety of common ailments' (Relman, 1991). The extensive and some would say excessive use of special tests is to be attributed partly to the fact that every investigation generates income, partly to the attitudes fostered by undergraduate and postgraduate education, partly to mere curiosity, without reflection whether the result of a particular investigation is going to benefit the patient, and partly to the sort of defensive medical practice that has been engendered by the large number of malpractice claims. A lot of money could be saved if every surgical unit drew up a strategy to guide junior staff about preoperative investigations (Anonymous, 1983).

The more advanced the diagnostic tools that are introduced, the greater the expense. Moore *et al.* (1987) examined the cost of computed tomography in 150 patients and concluded that the cost : benefit ratio was 1.3 : 1 because of reduction of time in hospital and of other investigations (including staging laparotomy for Hodgkin's disease).

The cost effectiveness of magnetic resonance imaging, on the other hand, has not been established, yet many American hospitals have installed the equipment, more in order to attract patients than because they believed it would produce clinical benefit (Hillman *et al.*, 1986). A study of 100 consecutive patients with intracranial symptoms and 100 with symptoms related to the spine who were referred for magnetic resonance imaging found that clinicians considered that the investigation made an important contribution to management in nearly three quarters of the patients, but that the quality of life of the patients was unchanged when they were assessed four months later (Dixon *et al.*, 1991)

Many investigations are ordered, both for the worried well and the seriously ill, not because the result will affect the management of the patient, but for other reasons. These include the availability of the equipment; the more it is used the less each investigation costs. There is also sometimes a fear on the part of the junior staff that a test not ordered will be the one that the consultant particularly wants. Special investigations may be ordered out of mere curiosity, or in order to avoid the risk of being sued (Reuben, 1984).

One of the least desirable ways in which money can be wasted and patients subjected to unnecessary irradiation is when X-ray examinations have to be repeated because films are not available for patients who attend clinics. One solution is to entrust the keeping of films to patients: this has the added advantage of solving the chronic problem of storage space in the radiology department (Burwood, 1989).

Defensive medicine is responsible for a large number of unnecessary X-rays. A working party of the Royal College of Radiologists (1979) audited the records of 10 619 patients undergoing elective non-cardiopulmonary operations to discover the extent of the use of preoperative chest X-rays. They found that the rate varied from 12% to 54% and concluded that:

'It is advisable, on financial and ethical grounds, that the preoperative chest radiology service should in future be used (i) selectively only in circumstances where the clinical history or signs place the patient at very high risk of postoperative pulmonary complications and where it is considered that the investigation will provide important additional information and (ii) routinely, perhaps only in population groups where the prevalance of undiagnosed chest disease is likely to be high (e.g. immigrants).'

In the developing world the diagnostic yield of chest X-rays is higher. Rajani *et al.* (1991) studied 1899 consecutive chest X-rays at the All India Institute of Medical Sciences in New Delhi that had been requested for 'routine diagnostic workup'. They found only 28 (3.1%) clinically important abnormalities among 899 X-rays of patients who had no symptoms or signs of chest disease. On the other hand, of 1000 X-rays of patients with symptoms or signs the yield of clinically important abnormalities was enormous – 413 (41.3%). Pulmonary tuberculosis was diagnosed in 186, and inflammatory consolidation in a further 106.

Guidelines for radiography of the skull in patients with head injuries are loss of consciousness or amnesia, neurological symptoms and signs, cerebrospinal fluid or blood issuing from the nose or ear, bruising or swelling of the scalp, and seizures. These patients should be admitted for observation, and in all cases computed tomography is more sensitive and can detect treatable intracranial fluid collections before clinical signs are apparent.

Substitution of paramedical workers for doctors

There is no doubt that this is cost effective. A trained secretary can, with the help of a questionnaire, elicit a history from a patient, and paramedical staff can do most of the examination and ordering of special tests. The problem remains that patients may not like this style of medicine, preferring closer contact with the doctor whom they have chosen. Spitzer *et al.* (1974) reported a randomised trial of the use of a nurse practitioner in a large suburban practice in Ontario. Families were randomly allocated in a ratio of 2 : 1 to be cared for by two doctors or two nurse practitioners. The health status was compared before and after the trial by mortality, physical functional capacity, social function, and emotional function. Satisfaction was high in both groups by both patients and professionals, but the authors concluded: 'Although cost effective from society's point of view, the new method of primary care was not financially profitable to doctors because of current restrictions on reimbursement for the nurse practitioner services.'

There are now over 15 000 nurse practitioners in the United States. The cost of training one is estimated to be about one sixth of the cost of training a doctor, and further savings on salaries are substantial. In Britain there has been little attempt to introduce nurse practitioners, but a pilot study was set up in Derbyshire in 1991.

Cost containment in the USA

In 1990 spending on health care took up over 12% of the gross national product of the United States, compared with 6% in 1960. The cost escalates year by year at twice the rate of inflation and is projected to absorb 16.4% of the gross national product by the year 2000 (Greenberg, 1991). Most of this money (19–24% of which is for administration – more than in any other country) is spent without government assistance, 60% of the population being insured. Health insurance is one of the perquisites of being employed in a big concern, the employer paying all or most of the premium (which is nearly $3000 a year). The problem is that nearly 40 million people lack sufficient, or even any, insurance; the system is in crisis (Friedman, 1991).

Utilisation Review

Utilisation Review was introduced in 1983 by CNA Insurance Companies of Chicago to try to limit costs by requiring pre-admission authorisation (which examines the appropriateness of the admission) by physicians, and concurrent review of treatment plans and projected length of stay by a nurse (Wickizer *et al.*, 1990). Employers often pay the premiums for private health insurance for their employees, and if an employee does not agree to pre-admission authorisation he is required to pay a percentage (usually 10%) of the hospital charges. Two thirds of private group insurers now require utilisation review before admission for a number of specified conditions, and this has reduced admissions by 12%, and inpatient expenditure by 8%.

Medicare and Medicaid

The twin programmes of Medicare (for the elderly) and Medicaid (for people whose income is below the official poverty level – about $12 000 a year for a family of four) are paid out of federal and state funds. Medicaid covers only 42% of the 31 million poor people in the USA, but the cost has risen from $23 billion in 1980 to a projected $65 billion in 1992 (Greenberg, 1991).

Most of the audit programmes that have been introduced have been concerned with limiting costs rather than with ensuring quality. Many have foundered because they have not been seen by doctors to lead to better health care.

California Relative Value program

A committee of the California Medical Association in the early 1950s recommended relative values of fees for medical, surgical, laboratory, and radiological work (Parks, 1983). Within each discipline (but not between disciplines) the committee published the relative value of services, using units and not dollars. Thus local excision of a skin lesion had a relative value of 1, replacement of the abdominal aorta 40. In medicine there were 150 procedures, in surgery 170, in radiology and pathology nearly 200 each. In 1979 the Federal Trade Commission charged that relative value studies restricted competition and were against the law. They were, however, a valuable index of surgical work load and allowed Nickerson *et al.* (1976) to conclude that 'far too many physicians perform surgical operations and ... work loads of surgical specialists are modest ... the total volume of operations in this study could have been handled by a substantially smaller cadre of busier surgical specialists'.

Hospital experimental payment program

This was instituted in New York in 1980 and followed the Canadian plan of giving each hospital a fixed prospective budget (Drucker *et al.*, 1983). An analysis of 2021 general surgical patients showed that 85 (4.2%) generated a disproportionate percentage of general surgical charges (26.8%) and number of days in hospital (27.6%). Nineteen of these patients (22%) died in hospital and 42 (49%) were dead within two years. Half had complex conditions and cure of one merely revealed another. Drucker *et al.* wrote that physicians, patients, and society should be aware that 'less expensive modes of diagnosis and therapy are an appropriate response to rationed health resources'.

In 1988 the United States Congress commissioned a study of doctors' pay by a team of public health professors at Harvard led by Dr W.C. Hsiao. Payment for services to Medicare patients has been based on 'customary, prevailing, and reasonable' charges (Hsiao *et al.*, 1988). The team looked at more than 4000 procedures and developed the Resource Based Relative Value Scale that included a doctor's workload, overheads, malpractice costs, and loss of earnings during long years of training. In 1991 Medicare managers made public the first schedule of national fees for doctors, which narrowed the pay difference between specialties, giving more to primary care physicians and less to surgeons, anaesthetists, and ophthalmologists (Roberts, 1991). The schedule is due to come into effect in 1992 and will no doubt be used as a guideline for payments by health insurance agencies.

Professional Standards Review Organisations

In October 1972 President Nixon signed Public Law 92-603, which established mandatory cost and quality controls for Medicaid and Medicare patients by Professional Standards Review Organisations (Welch, 1973). The purpose of these organisations was to contain costs by discouraging 'overutilisation' of hospital care. Local PSROs were to comprise all the doctors and osteopaths in a district and they were to establish norms of diagnostic pathways and treatment of diseases. Secondly they were to establish acceptable lengths of stay for all diseases and interventions. Thirdly, 'profiles' were to be established for each institution, doctor, and patient, and these were to be made public. Fourthly, ambulatory care surveillance was to be optional. The idea was that group decisions would replace individual vagaries.

In the event PSROs were set up in most places by 1975 and were soon found to be unworkable. They could assess whether a process was carried out, but not how well, and their impact on cost containment was negligible or even negative. As Komaroff (1978) wrote: 'If we expand research efforts designed to develop sound standards and effective quality assessment and assurance mechanisms, perhaps the insidious nihilism that undermines many of our efforts will be replaced by a spirit of cautious enthusiasm.' A few gains were made. As a result of an educational programme conducted by a PSRO in half of 120 hospitals, the use of X-ray pelvimetry, which is useless and potentially dangerous to the fetus, was reduced to one third of the control rate (Chassin and McCue, 1986).

On the whole, though, most medical audit by PSROs merely accumulated vast amounts of unusable data. The main difficulty was to define standards and to get doctors to agree with them. The immediate response of doctors criticised for deviating from standards of care was to reject the criteria. Data on outcome in particular were often greeted with nonchalance by doctors because they argued that their personal contribution to the poor outcome was negligible compared with social, public health, or constitutional factors (Nelson, 1976). PSROs were finally phased out in 1984 and were replaced by Peer Review Organisations.

Peer review organisations

The introduction of payment by diagnosis-related groups was linked to 'utilisation and quality control peer review organisations', the name being shortened to PRO (Dans, Weiner and Otter, 1985). The regulations are slightly different in Maryland, New York, New Jersey and Massachusetts, all of which have their own programmes of cost containment (Silver, 1983). PROs are contracted to the Health Care Financing Administration to ensure that services that are paid in part or in whole by Medicare will be:

- provided economically, and only when, and to the extent that, they are medically necessary;
- of a quality that meets professionally recognised standards of care;
- supported by evidence of medical necessity and quality in such form and at such time as may reasonably be required by a reviewing PRO.

A PRO contract can mean millions of dollars, and private organisations now compete for these lucrative contracts to oversee a certain region. The job of a PRO is to produce results, show that money is being saved, and that the public is being protected from incompetent doctors (Dunea,

1988). The review is done by nurses who descend on a hospital and demand to see the notes of patients who may have died or been discharged many months before. They use a book of written criteria for each disease, including what investigations should be done, what treatment should be given, whether the patient should be admitted to hospital, how long the patient should stay in hospital, and what follow up is necessary. If a visiting nurse finds deviations from the criteria she refers the case to medical reviewers for further evaluation. It is estimated that some deviation from ideal treatment is found in 2–3% of cases.

A PRO may apply sanctions against a doctor whose quality of care falls below an accepted level. These include withholding of payment, banning the doctor from further participation in the care of federally funded patients, and publishing these sanctions in the local newspaper. The American Medical Association has recommended legislation that would not allow sanctions by a PRO to be effected until the doctor had exhausted the right to judicial review, and would allow appeals to be heard before panels of doctors in active practice. The medical members of PROs are usually either retired doctors or inexperienced young people and there is considerable disquiet among American doctors about the operation of PROs.

There is little doubt that PROs promote efficiency, particularly by reducing the duration of inpatient stay, although whether this is balanced by the inordinate amount of money that is poured into PROs, and whether this reduction leads to a better outcome may be disputed. Fitzgerald *et al.* (1987) found that there had been a reduction in the mean stay in hospital after hip fractures from 16.6 to 10.3 days but that the number of patients discharged to nursing homes had more than doubled, and that patients were nearly four times more likely to be in a nursing home one year after discharge from hospital. They wondered if less time for rehabilitation might mean lower quality of life. It is crucial to know whether the reduction in postoperative stay that has been stimulated by payment by DRGs for Medicare patients has resulted in greater efficiency at the cost of lower effectiveness. There is a feeling that patients are being discharged quicker and sicker than before.

Health maintenance organisations

These organisations date back at least 50 years, and the past decade has seen a spectacular growth in their number (Richards 1986). One of the aims of HMOs is to keep people healthy and out of hospital and at first they encountered strong opposition from local doctors. The Group Health Association in Washington DC was founded in 1937, but the movement lost impetus during the Second World War. One of the biggest of the HMOs is the Kaiser Permanente Medical Care Program. This was started by Dr Sidney Garfield to serve the men constructing a pipe line to take water from the Colorado River to Los Angeles. It is now a national company. The Harvard Community Health Plan in Boston, Massachusetts has 207 000 members, 360 doctors, and nine health centres. The monthly fees for a family were $230 in 1986 and these are paid in whole or in large part by employers, the Federal Government paying 95% of the cost of Medicare patients.

Taylor (1989) investigated the conflicts that arise when patients and primary care physicians disagree about the need for referral to a consultant within a health maintenance organisation. Physicians concluded that the need to contain costs had:

- compromised their role as patient advocate;
- led to loss of trust because of perceived financial conflict of interests;
- led to withholding of information from patients;
- led to conflict between medical benefit and financial risk;
- led to loss of credibility of the doctor.

Cost containment in the UK

'If I were ill ... I should like good medical attention, by which I mean clinical service which combines technical competence with human care .... Inability to control the outcome of disease does not reduce the importance of the pastoral or samaritan role of the doctor. In some ways it increases it' (McKeown, 1979).

There can be no doubt that surgeons must find the most cost effective way of treating patients that is consistent with the greatest efficacy. As a correspondent in *The Times* (1983) commented after the first heart lung transplant in Britain, 'The NHS can afford a limited indulgence in experimental pyrotechnics, but its planners must never lose sight of the fact that what kills most of us, and darkens many lives before death, is humdrum everyday disease requiring humdrum everyday treatment.' Agmete Lausten, the Danish health minister, caused controversy by stating that Denmark would have to make choices and set priorities. One heart transplant meant 50 fewer hip replacements (Timmins, 1988).

The problem is that, unlike in industry, new technology inflates costs, not reduces them. Doctors, who make most of the management decisions like the admission and discharge of patients and the need for new diagnostic and therapeutic equipment, have no incentive to control costs. Trade unions resist redundancies and administrators have little control over decisions that have far reaching revenue consequences. Is it possible to devise incentives for low cost care, or sanctions against surgeons who use too many resources? The first and most obvious method is by auditing the performance of individual surgeons and individual hospitals, but the difficulty is to provide valid yardsticks of their performance. We consider two possible methods in Chapter 10.

The main drain on health care resources arises from keeping patients in hospital too long, from postoperative complications, and from terminal care (Eiseman and Stahlgren, 1987). In the USA it has been estimated that 80% of the health care costs of a lifetime are incurred during the last 6 months of life. As a fictional hospital administrator is reported to have said: 'Your last two weeks on earth may not be your most comfortable, but sure as Hell they'll be your most expensive.'

There are few data about the cost effectiveness of intensive care. A study from Los Angeles showed that 8% of the patients in an intensive care unit used half the resources, and that 70% of these high cost patients died (Oye and Bellamy, 1991). There is increasing pressure on doctors to use scoring systems to predict outcome and to ration care. Data about the quality of life of patients who survive a period of intensive care and are discharged home are even more scarce. How much does it cost to reintegrate them into the community, what is their quality of life, and what is their late mortality? There has been too little research on these subjects.

Domiciliary consultations

One of the curious anomalies of the British National Health Service is the payment to hospital consultants, over and above their normal salary, of fees for visiting patients in their homes at the request of primary care physicians. This wasteful use of consultants' time is a hangover from the more leisurely days before the introduction of the National Health Service. The service is supposed to be for patients who cannot, on medical grounds, attend hospital, and each visit has to be requested by, and should be attended by, a general practitioner. It is, however, rare for general practitioners to accompany consultants. The service is most widely used by specialists in geriatric medicine, psychiatry, general medicine, dermatology, and rheumatology. General and orthopaedic surgeons are asked to visit patients at home only rarely.

Domiciliary consultations can add considerably to a consultant's income and their abolition will not be welcomed by some doctors. Others realise that the hour or so that such a visit entails can be used far more profitably in the hospital, and that a patient who is too ill to travel to the hospital for a consultation should be admitted. The number has declined by between a quarter and a half in the past decade (Donaldson and Hill, 1991).

Cost containment in Canada

In 1971, faced with an escalation of costs that was paralleling that in the USA, the federal government of Canada took the step of substituting state funded provincial insurance for private insurance for most aspects of health care. Hospitals have cash limits and doctors, although they still receive a fee for each item of service, are paid from a budget for all medical services fixed by the federal government. The distribution of this money among doctors is determined by the doctors' own organisations. Canada, however, although spending 8.6% of gross national product on health care (compared with 12% in the USA), is facing the same kind of economic squeeze as the rest of the world (Dunlop, 1991). The federal government, faced with an annual bill for $28 billion, announced that it would cut the allocation by a fifth. The result is the closure of beds and the start of a system of rationing by the waiting list.

Cost containment in Europe

In France health insurance is compulsory. Basic insurance is organised by the state but often topped up by private non-profit making insurance funds, the *mutuelles*. Employers pay 12.6% of their employees' wages and employees 5.9% into the state scheme, which pays 70% of a person's health care expenditure, but all the expenses of the poor and of those incurred in the treatment of certain diseases such as cancer. The system is inefficient and top heavy and the costs of administration are high (5.2% of total expenditure, compared with 3.7% in Germany, 3.2% in Italy, and 0.9% in Spain). It is the most expensive system in Europe, costing 9.4% of gross domestic product. Rising costs of hospitals, laboratory tests, and drugs have added to the problems of unemployment and ageing of the population to put an increasingly severe strain on the Sécurité Sociale, which expects a deficit of up to 20 billion francs in 1991 (£2 bn) (Anonymous, 1991b). Higher taxes on individuals and the pharmaceutical industry are inevitable.

Both Germany and The Netherlands have similar systems of compulsory health insurance, together with private insurance. Doctors charge fees for items of service, and there are too many beds and too much highly sophisticated equipment. Lithotripters were a German invention and there are said to be enough lithotripters in Germany to treat all the patients with renal stones in Europe. Daschner (1988) wrote: 'In West Germany...hospital epidemiology will never become cost effective, because insurance companies pay the same amount of money for each day of hospital stay. Therefore hospital administrators try to keep patients in hospital for as long as possible so as to increase profits.' The unification of Germany has brought even greater problems. The East German system was possibly not particularly efficient; it may not even have been very effective; but at least it did provide health care for all its citizens. Their demands will drive the costs of care in the new Germany even higher.

Denmark has an efficient national health service funded by taxation and costing only 6.3% of gross domestic product (compared with Britain's 5.9%). There are no private hospitals, and the public hospitals are provided with budgets that encourage shorter stays in hospital, daycase and 5-day surgery. There are waiting lists, but as the health minister, Mrs Lausten, said: 'If you don't have any waiting time at all it would show that you weren't efficient, that you were just sitting down waiting for patients to come' (Timmins, 1988).

Cost containment in New Zealand

The health service in New Zealand was internationally admired as a model of universal health coverage combined with a simple system of funding and low administrative costs. Beset by the same problems of rising costs and expectations as everywhere else in the world, however, the government introduced several new measures in 1991, the effect of which may be to cause inequalities in the delivery of health care (Coney, 1991). Visits to primary care doctors will cost up to £25 even for elderly people, provided that their income exceeds £105 a week. Hospital outpatient visits will cost £6–10, and inpatient care £11–16 a night. Only the very poor will be exempt from these charges.

Conclusions

When a hospital is planning for greater efficiency, it must be prepared to change its practices in many ways, some of which we summarise here:

- Avoid admissions for tests
- Avoid unnecessary and expensive tests
- Shorten hospital stay
- Use convalescent homes or hotels
- Encourage day case and overnight stay surgery
- Establish five day wards
- Use operating rooms seven days a week
- Reuse disposable equipment
- Control prescribable drugs
- Keep drug stocks low
- Establish an antibiotic policy
- Keep records and make regular audit
- Arrange cross cover by junior staff
- Use taxis rather than ambulances
- Close underused hospitals

References

Anonymous (1983) Routine preoperative investigations are expensive and unnecessary. *Lancet*, **ii**, 1466–167

Anonymous (1991a) Operating to prevent stroke. *Lancet*, **337**, 1255–1256

Anonymous (1991b) *British Medical Journal*, **302**, 490–491

Baker, E.L. (1991) Surveillance of disorders caused by occupational hazards – principles and practice: a review. *Journal of the Royal Society of Medicine*, **84**, 418–422

Barnes, B.A. (1977) Discarded operations: surgical innovation by trial and error. In Bunker, J.P. Barnes, B.A. and Mosteller F., eds, *Costs, Risks and Benefits of Surgery*, Oxford University Press, New York, pp. 109–123

Benatar, S.R. (1991) Medicine and health care in South Africa – five years later. *New England Journal of Medicine*, **325**, 30–36

Brenner, M. (1979) Mortality and the national economy. *Lancet*, **ii**, 568–573

Brewin, T.B. (1981) The cancer patient – too many scans and X rays? *Lancet*, **ii**, 1098–1099

Burwood, R. (1989) Unnecessary x-ray examinations. *British Medical Journal*, **298**, 1517

Butler, J. and Vaile, M. (1984) *Health and Health Services.* Routledge and Kegan Paul, London

Chassin, M.R. and McCue, S.M. (1986) A randomized trial of medical quality assurance. Improving physicians' use of pelvimetry. *Journal of the American Medical Association*, **256**, 1012–1016

Coleman, J.S. (1970) Quoted in *The International Thesaurus of Quotations*, edited by R.T. Tripp. Penguin Books, New York, p. 958

Coney, S. (1991) New Zealand: health system reforms. *Lancet*, **338**, 374–375

Dans, P.E., Weiner, J.P. and Otter, S.E. (1985) Peer review organizations: promises and potential pitfalls. *New England Journal of Medicine*, **313**, 1131–1137.

Daschner, F.D. (1988) How cost-effective is the present use of antiseptics? *Journal of Hospital Infection*, **11** (suppl.A), 227–235

Dixon, A.K., Southern, J.P., Teale, A., Freer, C.E.L, Hall, L.D., Williams, A. and Sims, C. (1991) Magnetic resonance imaging of the head and spine: effective for the clinican or the patient? *British Medical Journal*, **302**, 79–82

Donaldson, L.J. and Hill, P.M. (1991) The domiciliary consultation service: time to take stock. *British Medical Journal*, **302**, 449–451

Drucker, W.R., Gavett, J.W., Kirshner, R., Messick, W.J. and Ingersol, G. (1983) Towards strategies for cost containment in surgical patients. *Annals of Surgery*, **198**, 284-298.

Dunea, G. (1988) Distrust. *British Medical Journal*, **296**, 1251–1252

Dunlop, M. (1991) Canada's health care has problems too. *British Medical Journal*, **303**, 8–9

Eiseman, B. and Stahlgren, L. (1987) *Cost-effective Surgical Management*. Saunders, Philadelphia

Fallowfield, L. (1990) *The Quality of Life*. Souvenir Press, London

Fitzgerald, J.F., Fagan, L.F., Tierney, W.M. and Dittus, R.S. (1987) Changing patterns of hip fracture care before and after implementation of the prospective payment system. *Journal of the American Medical Association*, **258**, 218–221

Fitzpatrick, R.M. (1986) Social and changing patterns of disease. In *Sociology as Applied to Medicine*, edited by D.L. Patrick and G. Scrambler. Baillière Tindall, London., pp. 16–29

Friedman, E. (1991) The uninsured: from dilemma to crisis. *Journal of the American Medical Association*, **265**, 2491–2495

Gopal, R. and Lipschitz, R. (1988) Head injury. In *Modern Surgery in Africa. The Baragwanath Experience*, edited by D. Pantanowitz. Southern Book Publishers, Johannesburg, p.8

Greenberg, D.S. (1991) Bush plays safe on health-care reforms. *Lancet*, **338**, 561–562

Health Education Authority (1989) *Strategic plan 1990–1995*. HEA, London

Hillman, B.J., Neu, C.R., Winkler, J.D. *et al.* (1986) *Diffusion of Magnetic Resonance Imaging into Clinical Practice*. Rand Health Insurance Experiment Series, New York

Hsiao, W.C., Braun, P., Dunn, D. and Becker, E.R. (1988) Resource-based relative values. An overview. *Journal of the American Medical Association*, **260**, 2347–2353

Kaiser, A.B. (1986) Antimicrobial prophylaxis in surgery. *New England Journal of Medicine*, **315**, 1129–1138

Kind, P., Rosser, R. and Williams, A. (1982) Valuations of quality of life: some psychometric evidence. In *The Value of Life and Safety*, edited by M.W. Jones-Lee. North Holland, Amsterdam, pp. 159–170

Klein, R. (1991) Society, health, and the NHS. *British Medical Journal*, **303**, 867–868.

Komaroff, A.L. (1978) The PRSO, quality assurance blues. *New England Journal of Medicine*, **298**, 1194–1196

Loudon, I. (1987) Pueperal fever, the streptococcus, and the sulphonamides, 1911–1945. *British Medical Journal*, **295,** 485–490

McKeown, T. (1979) *The Role of Medicine. Dream, Mirage, or Nemesis?* Basil Blackwell, Oxford

Medical Commission on Accident Prevention (1988) *Strategies for Accident Prevention*. HMSO, London

Mercy, J.A. and Houk, V.N. (1988) Firearm injuries: a call for science. *New England Journal of Medicine*, **319**, 1283–1285

Moore, A.T., Dixon, A.K., Rubinstein, D. and Wheeler, T. (1987) Cost-benefit evaluation of body computed tomography. *Health Trends*, **19,** 8–12

Navarro, V. (1990) Race or class versus race and class: mortality differentials in the United States. *Lancet,* **336,** 1238–1240

Oye, R.K. and Bellamy, P.E. (1991) Patterns of resource consumption in medical intensive care. *Chest*, **99**, 685–689

Nelson, A.R. (1976) Orphan data and the unclosed loop: a dilemma in PRSO and medical audit. *New England Journal of Medicine*, **295**, 617–619

Nickerson, R.J., Colton, T., Peterson, O.L., Bloom, B.S. and Hauck, W.W. (1976) Doctors who perform operations. A study on in-hospital surgery in four diverse geographic areas. *New England Journal of Medicine*, **295**, 921–926 and 982–989

Parks, P. (1983) Relative value studies: a historical perspective. *American College of Surgeons Bulletin*, **68**, 2–8

Paterson-Brown, S. (1991) Strategies for reducing inappropriate laparotomy rate in the acute abdomen. *British Medical Journal*, **303**, 1115–1118

Raffle, P.A.B. (1991) The cost of traffic casualties to the community. *Journal of the Royal Society of Medicine*, **84**, 390–392

Rajani, M., Sharma, S. and Sonekar, P. (1991) Is the routine chest X-ray necessary? *National Medical Journal of India*, **4**, 24–25

Relman, A.S. (1991) Shattuck lecture – the health industry: where is it taking us? *New England Journal of Medicine*, **325**, 854–859

Reuben, D.B. (1984) Learning diagnostic restraint. *New England Journal of Medicine*, **310**, 591–593

Richards, T. (1986) Medicine American style and the growth of HMOs. *British Medical Journal*, **292**, 330–332

Roberts, C.J. Farrow, S.C. and Charny, M.C. (1985) How much can the NHS afford to spend to save a life or avoid a severe disability? *Lancet*, **i**, 89–91

Roberts, J. (1991) Pay cuts for American doctors. *British Medical Journal*, **302**, 1420

Royal College of Radiologists' Working Party on the Effective Use of Diagnostic Radiology (1979) Preoperative chest radiology. *Lancet*, **ii**, 83–86

Sade, R.M. (1983) Cost versus efficacy of treatment. *Surgery*, **93**, 355

Schletky, D.H. (1985) Children and handguns. A public health concern. *American Journal of Diseases of Children*, **39**, 229–231

Silver, G.A. (1983) Solution by acronym. *Lancet,* **ii**, 1433–1434

Spitzer, W.O., Sackett, D.L., Sibley, J.C. *et al.* (1974) The Burlington randomized trial of the nurse practitioner. *New England Journal of Medicine*, **290**, 251–256

Taylor, T.R. (1989) Pity the poor gatekeeper: a transatlantic perspective on cost containment in clinical practice. *British Medical Journal*, **299**, 1323–1325

The Times (1983) *Surgery at the frontier*, 7 December, 17,3

Timmins, N. (1988) Efficient Danes under pressure to trim budgets. *The Independent*, 8 March, 12

Williams, A. (1985) Economics of coronary artery bypass grafting. *British Medical Journal*, **291**, 326–329

Welch, C.E. (1973) Professional Standards Review Organizations – problems and prospects. *New England Journal of Medicine*, **289**, 291–295.

Wickizer, T.M., Feldstein, P.J., Wheeler, J.R.C. and McDonald, M.C. (1990) Reducing hospital use and expenditure through utilization review. *Quality Assurance and Utilization Review*, **5**, 80–85

Audit of outcome

Chapter 12

Introduction

It would be a tragic irony if the current epidemic of malpractice lawsuits brought quiet concealment of unfavorable results, so that medical progress is impeded rather than promoted.

Couch, Tilney and Moore (1978)

It is easy for surgeons to view outcome in terms of the mortality and complication rate within 30 days of operation. This narrow view is being eroded by physicians and sociologists, and we now recognise that we must enquire into and audit all the following aspects of our work: quality adjusted life years; patient satisfaction; measurements of impairment, disability, and handicap; and assessment of pain and pain relief.

Sir Raymond Hoffenberg (1987), wrote: 'More than ever it is now necessary for us to introduce a system for assessing professional competence. If we do not we shall fail to satisfy the public and invite regulation from outside the profession.' He commented that meetings to audit the *process* of care have been held by the medical units at the Queen Elizabeth Hospital in Birmingham, UK, since 1978, but that these meetings are seldom attended by doctors whose work may need looking into because they feel threatened by them. The meetings do not take the form of the usual 'grand rounds' or 'morbidity and mortality conferences'. Instead, a firm of staff (consultant) physicians is given the notes of a random selection of one quarter of the inpatients managed by a different firm and is required to comment on the quality of the note keeping, the appropriateness of the tests performed and the drugs prescribed, the appropriateness of the length of stay in hospital, and the quality and timeliness of the discharge letters. This peer review of the process of care is valuable, and has resulted in better documentation and more appropriate investigations and treatment.

The assessment of outcome is much more difficult, and the rules are only now in the process of being worked out. There are enormous problems in assessing the professional competence of doctors in terms of the outcome of their care. Standards have to be set, and there are only a few interventions the outcome of which is widely known and are therefore suitable for the purpose. There are large variations in the rates of mortality and morbidity between hospitals and between doctors, and most of these variations are not publicised. Harman and Galbraith (1991), two British Members of Parliament, suggested that 'league tables' of hospitals should be published so that patients would know what risks they were running when they were admitted to a particular hospital. Clearly the outcome measures would have to be the avoidable mortality and the avoidable morbidity both in the short term and the long term.

One of the interventions particularly suitable for audit is the repair of uncomplicated inguinal hernias: if the rate of postoperative complications, including chest and wound infections, is greater than 2%, the matter needs looking into. The recurrence rate after hernia repairs is another aspect that could be monitored. The audit of both postoperative complications and recurrence rates poses another difficulty. For example, if a surgeon has a 4% complication rate after herniorrhaphy (compared with the expected maximum of 2%) that rate would have to be sustained for 240 operations before it could be shown that his poor results were other than chance occurrences. Michaels (1988) discussed the same problem in relation to carotid endarterectomy. If the 'acceptable standard' rate of complications is 10%, a surgeon would have to do 150 operations before it could be shown that his complication rate of 15% reflected poor performance rather than chance.

Quality is to be measured by appropriateness, accessibility, equity, effectiveness, relevance, and acceptability (Bowden and Gumpert, 1988). The effectiveness of medical care 'must be differentiated from efficiency ... quality is concerned with outcome and efficiency is related to the process of care' (Rutstein et al., 1976). These authors published three tables that can be used to audit health care in nations, communities, and individual hospitals. A condition is listed in Table A as a 'sentinel event' if the occurrence of a single case of disease or disability, or a single untimely death, would justify an immediate inquiry – 'why did it happen?' This table includes cases of tuberculosis, tetanus, major complications of syphilis, and carcinoma of the skin, mouth, larynx, bronchi, and cervix. It includes deaths in patients under the age of 65 as a result of hernias and cholecystitis, and man-made disease – for example, illnesses caused by toxic agents, physical or biological hazards, and accidents.

Table B is a list of 'limited use of quality-of-care indexes'. These include death under the age of 55 from peptic ulcers, surgical and medical complications and misadventures, nosocomial infections and other iatrogenic diseases. This table is to be used when more than a single case is required to initiate an inquiry. Table C is 'categories demanding better definition and special study' and includes alcoholism, suicide, and homicide.

Critical incident reporting

The reporting of critical incidents goes back to the 1940s (Flanagan, 1954). It is widely used in the aviation industry and has been adopted particularly in departments of anaesthesia (Cooper et al., 1978), and of intensive care (Wright et al., 1991). It is a cheap and valuable method of audit of outcome.

Readmission rates as proxy measures of outcome

There is a growing tendency to regard rates of unplanned and unexpected readmissions (which are easy to record and retrieve) as evidence of unfavourable outcomes. Planned readmissions, and unplanned readmissions that are necessitated by the progress of the patient's disease (and are usually late) are not causes for concern, but unexpected readmissions within a few days usually indicate inappropriate or incomplete treatment during the first admission.

Correlation of process and outcome

Several studies have shown that process and outcome correlate poorly. Brook and Appel (1973) abstracted the initial case notes and the final outcome notes of 196 patients and invited three physicians to judge first the efficiency of care (process) by implicit and explicit criteria, and subsequently the outcome by the same criteria. They concluded that what matters to patients is how the eventual outcome will affect their daily lives, and not how that outcome was achieved. They found no correlation between process as defined by their criteria, and outcome. As Schroeder (1987) wrote: 'Faced with a choice between good process with a poor outcome and poor process with a good outcome, most patients and physicians would opt for the latter.'

Brook (1990) equated 'good process' with 'appropriate treatment', and concluded that four combinations were equally likely to exist: appropriate treatment and good outcome; appropriate treatment and bad outcome; inappropriate treatment and good outcome; and inappropriate treatment and bad outcome. Gray *et al.* (1990) examined the appropriateness of coronary angiography and coronary artery bypass operations in the Trent region of Britain, having established criteria of appropriateness by consensus. They reported that 49% of 320 randomly selected patients had had appropriate angiography, in 30% the indications were equivocal, and in 21% the investigation was inappropriate. Of 319 randomly selected patients who had had coronary artery bypass operations, 58% were considered to have been operated on appropriately, in 26% the indication was equivocal, and in 16% inappropriate.

One must not be unduly influenced by reports that process and outcome are not correlated: they usually are, but it is the minutiae of the process of care that determine a good outcome. For example, patients who have had a myocardial infarct do better if they are given thrombolytic treatment (either by streptokinase or by recombinant human tissue plasminogen activator) within six hours after the onset of pain than if they are treated conventionally. Rapid and expert management of injured patients reduces the number of preventable deaths. In both cases good process is followed by good outcome. Most analyses of process do not, however, go deeply enough into the matter, contenting themselves with the overall picture shown by statistics on work load.

There are disadvantages in considering outcome alone as an index of quality. Treatment may fail despite excellent care because of the constitution of the patients and the stage of advancement of their disease. For accurate assessment large samples and long follow up are needed; the final outcome may be years away; patient compliance with treatment cannot always be relied on; risk factors may not be accurately recorded; and finally the wrong measures of outcome may be used. Prospective surveys, controlled clinical trials, and consumer research can all contribute to improvement in the quality of care.

Joint Commission on Accreditation of Healthcare Organizations

The Joint Commission in the USA was set up as a non-governmental organisation in 1951. The title was changed from Joint Commission on Accreditation of Hospitals in 1989 because of the addition of accreditation programmes for long term care, ambulatory care, mental health and disability care, hospice care, home care, and managed care.

The Joint Commission in the United States and the Higher Surgical Training Committee of the Royal College of Surgeons of England have until recently relied solely on the examination of structure and process to determine whether a hospital shall be accredited for the training of surgeons. They have been concerned with the adequacy of equipment in the operating theatres, in the diagnostic departments, and in the library. They have assured themselves that the processes of selection of medical and surgical staff were properly carried out and that staff were properly trained. They have enquired into hospital activities such as postgraduate lectures, grand rounds, and deaths and complications conferences. They have verified the processes of communication with other doctors and of proper recording of data in patients' casenotes.

The Joint Commission announced an 'agenda for change' for the 1990s. It will require health care organisations to demonstrate not only their *potential* for change (by evaluation of the process of care), but their actual *provision* of care within acceptable clinical outcome ranges (Couch, 1989). The Commission will 'monitor and evaluate' health care by reference to agreed standards, of which the Commission has published six manuals.

The Agency for Health Care Policy and Research of the US Department of Health and Human Services has established a research programme called the Medical Treatment Effectiveness Program. The Agency will support research into effectiveness of treatments, development of databases, and methods of dissemination of the results of the research to health care workers.

Australian Council on Healthcare Standards Care Evaluation Program – clinical indicators

In 1990 the Australian Council followed the lead of the American Joint Commission and, with the cooperation of the national Royal Colleges, published specific indicators of the outcome of clinical care which will establish national standards. To deal with the problem of case mix and to compare like with like, the Council will identify patient and disease groups that are as homogeneous as possible. For example, one of the indicators will be the wound infection rate after elective cholecystectomy in women aged 30–60, excluding those who also had exploration of the common bile duct, and those with other diseases.

There are far fewer Australian indicators than those of the American Commission. This is partly because the large number of indicators in the USA require that enormous numbers of records will have to be reviewed at enormous cost. It is also because the Australians believe that it is possible to get bogged down in 'audit for audit's sake', resulting in disenchantment among healthcare providers. Furthermore, many of the American indicators are not accepted by the Australians – from the list of 21 American clinical indicators in obstetric care, for example, only two were accepted by a group of Australian obstetricians.

The following is an example of the clinical indicators that apply to one branch of surgery – gynaecology:

- Hysterectomy in women under 35 years of age
- Diagnostic laparoscopy for indications other than investigation of infertility
- Blood transfusion apart from radical hysterectomy and similar operations
- Injury, unplanned repair, or unplanned removal of an organ during an operation
- Unplanned return to operating room
- Wound infection
- Unplanned hospital readmission.

Consensus statements, guidelines, and standards

Clinical freedom is everywhere being challenged, and nowhere is this more apparent than in the USA, where the federal Agency for Health Care Policy and Research has been charged with developing and maintaining:

'... clinically relevant guidelines that may be used by physicians ... to assist in determining how diseases, disorders, and other health conditions can most effectively and appropriately be prevented, diagnosed, treated, and managed clinically ... and standards of quality, performance measures, and medical review criteria'.

Eddy (1990) suggested that:

'The solution is not to remove decision-making power from physicians, but to improve the capacity of physicians to make better decisions. To achieve this solution we must give physicians the information they need; we must institutionalise the skills to use that information; and we must build processes that support, not dictate, decisions.'

It might be assumed that somewhere there must be, for each departure from normal health, a consensus view from experienced clinicians about how to measure and record outcome, and how to distinguish poor outcomes from good ones. In reality this is seldom the case, not only because experts do not agree, but also because measurements of outcome are often subjective and observers can vary considerably in their judgement of the outcome for any patient. Most guidelines are decided in a pragmatic way by groups of experts supported by the results of published work, including random controlled trials and meta-analyses (Jenkins, 1991). The problem is that for the treatment of many diseases there are no adequate random control clinical trials; indeed many treatments are given for no better reason than that clinical intuition tells the doctor that the treatment seems sensible.

Guidelines introduced by national organisations such as the Joint Commission in the USA, or the Royal Colleges and specialist societies in Britain, carry a lot of weight, but even they have to be upgraded regularly in the light of further advances in knowledge and techniques. Guidelines must be seen as temporary snapshots rather than tablets of stone.

It is worrying that consensus statements might gain medicolegal validity and the slightest deviation from protocol could be used in litigation. They are, however, valuable as yardsticks against which to judge the effectiveness of one's own work. Holdsworth (1991) reported the results of 466 vascular operations over a period of five years. The incidence of complications (30%), of further operations (14%), and of death (9%) was high, and the author regretted the absence of national consensus statements on the outcome of unselected patients undergoing vascular operations.

Guidelines and consensus must not be allowed to take over from clinical judgement. Once a rigid protocol starts to be applied there is a danger that common sense will depart and thinking will stop. They must not be followed rigidly in recipe book fashion, but they are better than '... the alternative, practising in complacent uncertainty...' (Bracken, 1987).

Finally, you may introduce guidelines and standards, but the difficulty is to get the doctors to use them. We consider this aspect again in the context of malpractice. Some doctors will complain about the abrogation of their clinical freedom and claim that every patient is unique and deserves unique consideration and treatment.

Meta-analyses

The detection of small improvements in outcome when the failure rate is below 10% would require controlled trials in thousands of patients. The value of meta-analysis is that it allows the results that have been reported in numerous publications to be pooled, and a consensus arrived at (Sacks *et al.*, 1987). There are, however, several obstacles in the path of meta-analysts. They must first make a thorough search of the literature, and not rely simply on a MEDLINE search. Secondly, they have to face the fact that there is a publication bias in favour of positive results; a good meta-analysis will also include trials that have not been published. Thirdly, they must judge the scientific validity of the trials that they are analysing; this requires that potential biases in each paper must be sought and recognised, and that at least two observers must give their judgement about the validity of each trial; a high rate of exclusions or withdrawals in any trial should put the analysts on their guard. Given these provisos, valid consensus statements have been made about, for example, antibiotic prophylaxis in biliary tract surgery (Meijer, Schmitz and Jeekel, 1990), and endoscopic treatment of haemorrhage from peptic ulcers (Henry and Cook, 1991).

Mortality

The yardstick most commonly used to judge the outcome of care is postoperative mortality. This, however, although it is easy to monitor, is fallible because a surgeon may refuse to operate on patients who have a high risk of dying, preferring either to pass them on to another surgeon or another hospital, or to deny the patients the chance that operation might offer. As Moore (1971) wrote:

'As to mortality rates, every surgeon understands the potential false-hood of low mortality rates in large series of operations undertaken for serious disease. It is possible to maintain a low mortality rate in cancer of the colon or advanced disease of the heart valves if the surgeon simply avoids operating on difficult patients. The strength of character of an institution as well as a man can be judged by willingness to take on difficult cases, realizing that some will be salvaged while others will be lost. That salvage will be obtained at the expense of a mortality rate higher than that of an institution which seeks only to perfect its statistics by confining its attention to the easy cases, leaving the other ones go.'

Avoidable and unavoidable deaths

Deans *et al.* (1987) attempted to give a truer account of postoperative mortality by dividing deaths into 'expected' and 'unexpected'. They defined unexpected deaths as 'those in which, after careful consideration of the prevailing clinical circumstances at the time of operation, the probability of death following operation was felt to be low'. They published an audit of 9165 major or intermediate operations in 11 years. There were 125 deaths (1.4%), of which 96 were expected and 29 unexpected.

Carr-Hill, Hardman, and Russell (1987) concluded that 'the proposition that avoidable mortality is a useful outcome indicator has not been established and is unlikely to be established for some time'. They analysed regional data for the years 1976 to 1983 for four major causes of avoidable mortality (hypertension, carcinoma of cervix, pneumonia, and perinatal deaths) and concluded that mortality correlated fairly well with three social indicators (unemployment, rateable value of houses, and number of motor cars owned) but not with the amount of money spent on health care.

There are great problems in describing postoperative deaths as 'avoidable' or 'unexpected'. Both adjectives suggest an element of negligence in management. Perhaps the adjective should be qualified by an adverb - 'possibly' or 'probably' – and the reason given. Could the death have been avoided by better structure or process, was the management less than ideal or, finally, did negligence play a part? Surgeons are apt to feel threatened when a patient dies and the death is recorded as avoidable.

Pollack, Ruttiman, and Getson (1987) observed a sixfold difference in mortality in paediatric intensive care units among nine teaching hospitals in the United States. When, however, these rates were adjusted for differences in the initial severity of illness, the differences disappeared. Dubois *et al.* (1987) examined the case records of 205 000 patients discharged from 93 hospitals and developed a model that accounted for 64% of the variance in hospital death rates. The four independent variables were the index of case mix, the proportion of patients over the age of 70 years, of emergency admissions, and of admissions from nursing homes. They identified 11 hospitals in which the observed death rate was more than two standard deviations greater, and nine in which it was more than two standard deviations less, than the expected. They examined six in each group for the quality of care of pneumonia, myocardial infarction, and stroke. The 'high outliers' had more high risk patients – they cared for sicker patients – but they could not exclude the possibility that these hospitals might also have provided poorer care.

Shortell and Hughes (1988) approached the problem from another angle. They analysed the records of 214 839 Medicare patients discharged from 981 hospitals in 45 states in 1983–84. They examined the mortality rates for 16 conditions, including five operations (cholecystectomy, transurethral resection of the prostate, repair of inguinal hernia, mastectomy, and excision or destruction of a local lesion in the bladder). They found positive correlations between mortality and two clinical and three sociopolitical variables. The clinical ones were indexes of disease severity and case mix; case mix was measured by the proportion of hospital days in intensive care units, by the index of the Health Care Financing Administration, 1984, and by the presence of comorbid conditions. The sociopolitical variables were the stringency of state programmes to review rates of admission to hospital, the stringency of 'certificate of need' legislation, and the intensity of competition. This last was measured not by the number of hospitals available, but by the proportion of the population enrolled in Health Maintenance Organisations (which are assumed to shop around for the cheapest deal). Hospitals in states with the most stringent review procedures for hospital admission rates and for certificates of need had mortality rates that were 5–10% higher than expected. There was no correlation between mortality and ownership (for profit or not for profit) of the hospitals.

The grading of severity of illness

Crude death rates are meaningless unless adjusted for the severity of the illness. 'The success of an operation depends on a number of factors, prominent among which are the nature of the disease for which the operation is undertaken, the quality of care, and the ability of the patient to withstand the insults of both the disease and the operation' (Playforth *et al.*, 1987). If we are to undertake audits of outcome to compare the competence of surgeons, we must include an objective evaluation of the preoperative fitness of each patient (Carter and Campbell, 1988, Goldman *et al.*, 1977), and an enumeration and declaration of outcome of the patients who were denied operation for whatever reason, a compilation of postoperative complications as well as of deaths, and an account of the improvement in the length and quality of life resulting from each intervention.

Daley *et al.* (1988) from the Health Care Financing Administration in Baltimore produced the Medicare Mortality Predictor System as a computer program to help in assessing whether variations in mortality from myocardial infarction, stroke, pneumonia, and congestive cardiac failure could be explained by variations in the severity of these illnesses. The system incorporates the APACHE II score, gender, age, ability to walk, presence of metastatic cancer, blood urea concentration, fever, blood pressure, Glasgow coma scale, and 'do not resuscitate' instructions on admission. The system was calibrated from the casenotes of a stratified random sample of 5888 discharges and deaths. They concluded that:

'Medicare Mortality Predictor System accounts for 13–25% of the variation in mortality for individual patients ... but the source of the majority of variations in outcome remains unmeasured. They include risk factors for which we do not have data, disease processes that we call random because we do not fully understand them, and variations in the effectiveness of care.'

Numerous other efforts have been made to score the severity of illnesses, and we consider scores and scales for physical, mental, and social ill health in Chapter 15.

Technical factors as determinants of outcome

When audit is used as a tool of quality assurance, one of its main purposes is to identify deficiencies in surgical craftsmanship. Its purpose is not to conduct a witch hunt of substandard surgeons but to allow them to achieve better skills by education and example.

Accurate and complete audit has allowed the discovery of wide variations in mortality and morbidity among surgeons for the same disease. McArdle and Hole (1991) studied the immediate and late outcome of the treatment of 645 consecutive patients with colorectal cancer by 13 surgeons at the Royal Infirmary in Glasgow. The overall postoperative mortality varied among surgeons from 8% to 30%. After 'curative' resection the local recurrence rate varied from 0% to 21% and the 10 year survival from 20% to 63%. After taking into account identified risk factors the hazard rate ratio varied from 0.56 to 2.03 for curative resections.

One of the problems about setting standards of excellence is that a common reaction of surgeons who do not attain these standards is one of nonchalance because they argue that their personal contribution to the outcome was negligible compared with social, public health, or constitutional factors (Nelson, 1976). Nevertheless, many surgeons agree with Russell (1987) who suggested that improvements in operative skills were more important in determining postoperative outcome than attention to preoperative nutritional state.

Pettigrew, Burns, and Carter (1987) studied the outcome of 113 alimentary resections. Nine patients died and major complications (including deaths) comprised 12 leaking anastomoses, 2 reoperations for haemorrhage, 2 myocardial infarctions, 2 cerebrovascular accidents, 1 respiratory failure, 1 septicaemia, 1 pseudomembranous enterocolitis, 1 colonic infarction, 1 pancreatitis, and 1 burst abdomen. They found that preoperative assessment of risk by an independent physician was just as accurate a predictor of complications as a preoperative concentration of albumin in the serum of < 30 g/l. Even more valuable, however, was the assessment immediately after operation by the operating surgeon; if this indicated a high risk, judged by the technical difficulty of the operation, it was an even more sensitive indicator of the likelihood of complications.

Matheson (1987) wrote:

> 'It is a welcome trend that differences in craftsmanship are now being ... recognized as crucial to surgical outcome. That recognition is the foundation for reassertion of the importance of technical skill as a necessary attribute for a surgical career .... Technical ability ... should be a major consideration in the regular local review of trainees ... and those that are inadequate technically should be counselled at an early stage and led in other directions.'

The difficulty is that there is as yet no working definition of superior surgical ability, nor validated methods of selecting young doctors who will make good surgeons (Graham and Deary, 1991).

Under the patients' charter in Britain patients have the right 'to be given detailed information on local health services, including quality standards and maximum waiting times'. Are hospitals to publish in the newspapers the rates of mortality and morbidity of individual surgeons? Toynbee (1991) reported that Birmingham Central district has the highest postoperative death rate in the country at 41.2/1000 operations, compared with 0.3 in Cambridge district. If such figures are to be published they must be accompanied by an analysis of case mix: it is natural that the death rate at a tertiary referral hospital should be higher than at a district general hospital.

The fallibility of death certificates

'If we stop questing, we stop finding. It's as simple as that' (Prutting, 1978). It is not unknown for a patient to collapse a few days after an intestinal anastomosis and die soon after. The patient was elderly, ill, and had an advanced cancer. No necropsy is requested and the death certificate reads 'congestive cardiac failure due to coronary atheroma'. From the standpoint of the audit of outcome this is misleading: how can we be sure that the fatal outcome was not the result of breakdown of the anastomosis?

Scottolini and Weinstein (1983) reported the results of an attempt to correlate the causes of death identified at necropsy with those that were listed clinically. In 30 of 100 necropsies the cause of death was not mentioned in the clinical notes, and in 6 of the 30 the clinical cause of death was not confirmed. They have established weekly clinicopathological conferences in the mortuary, the proceedings of which are stamped 'confidential and not for the chart'.

In Britain a Report of the Joint Working Party of the Royal College of Pathologists, the Royal College of Physicians of London, and the Royal College of Surgeons of England (1991) concluded that the rate of clinical (as opposed to coroners') necropsies is too low, and that the cause of death recorded on the death certificate is fully confirmed in only about half of all cases. The report recommended that death certificates should be completed by senior doctors, who should also be responsible for asking permission from relatives for necropsy; that the necropsy rate should be increased; and that the consultant, the relatives and the general practitioner should be informed of the results of the necropsy as soon as possible.

Hospital and medicolegal necropsy findings should be part of audit, and a member of the clinical team should be present at the necropsy of every patient who dies in that unit. This is a valuable teaching method and has the additional advantage of making the pathologist's job more interesting. The addition of still photographs and video recordings can add considerably to the educational value of the necropsy.

Minimum necropsy rates are no longer part of the requirements for accreditation of hospitals in the United States. The decline of the necropsy is the result of several factors: it is not a reimbursable expense; there is a fear of malpractice litigation if a mistake is exposed; pathologists are not keen; and there is a belief that advances in clinical diagnostic procedures have rendered it unnecessary (Goldman *et al.*, 1983). Dorsey (1978) quoted McManus as saying that 'We should realize that the necropsy is the understaffed, underfinanced, and generally neglected final step of the continuum of medical care, which otherwise is so prodigiously financed in our affluent society.' Dorsey claimed that the total cost of a necropsy can be as much as $1000.

In Scotland, Cameron and McGoogan (1981) divided clinical diagnoses into 'agreed' (the necropsy confirmed the clinical diagnosis), 'underdiagnosed' (first discovered at necropsy), and 'overdiagnosed' (clinical diagnosis disproved at necropsy). They gave the figures shown in Table 12.1.

Table 12.1

Disease	Agreed	Underdiagnosed	Overdiagnosed
Peritonitis	31	34	3
Acute abdomen	30	24	7
Peptic ulcer	18	58	2
Cholecystitis	12	11	1
Cardiac infarct	198	51	58
Pulmonary embolus	44	110	35
Carcinoma of colon	19	12	13

The necropsy rate in Stockholm has been reported to be as high as 96% (Britton, 1974). In Sweden it is apparently normal practice for permission for necropsy to be requested and it is seldom refused. The underlying cause of death (defined by the World Health Organisation as 'the disease or injury which initiated the train of morbid events leading directly to death') was confirmed as correct in 57% and erroneous in 30%. Errors were more frequent if the patient was over the age of 70.

Audit of postoperative complications

If the audit of postoperative deaths is beset with difficulties, that of postoperative complications is even more so. Unless a surgeon insists that all complications are looked for and listed as they arise, they can be missed from the discharge summary and the audit proforma. For this reason the statistics collected by hospitals for administrative purposes are likely to be misleading.

There are three statistics that are valuable in implying the presence or absence of complications without revealing their nature. They are:

- The actual length of postoperative stay in hospital with reference to the expected length of stay
- The pyrexial score – the sum of the degrees by which the patient's temperature rises above 37°C recorded on a twice daily chart, multiplied by the number of days that this occurs. Postoperative pyrexia confined to a total of 3 degrees on no more than 3 days can be regarded as normal; a pyrexial score of 10 or more indicates an infective complication
- The rates of unscheduled returns to the operating theatre, and of unscheduled readmissions to hospital

Audit of long term results of interventions

Doctors cannot follow all the patients who have come under their care for ever – the outpatient clinics would soon become unmanageable. Macintyre (1989) suggested that it is so important to know what happens to patients years after an intervention that follow up should be done by mail and that it should be prospective, that it should embrace every patient with the condition that is under investigation, and that it should be computer based. Some of the most valuable research publications in the fields of oncology and gastroenterology have resulted from just this sort of enquiry.

Conclusions

Audit of outcome is more useful, but also more difficult, than audit of structure or process. Postoperative mortality, even standardised for age, is of little value unless account is taken of the severity of the diseases being audited, of the fitness of patients for operation, and of the proportion of patients not operated on and the outcome in these patients. Death certificates are unreliable, and the proportion of necropsies in patients who die after operations should be increased. Postoperative complications should be carefully looked for and recorded.

References

Bowden, D. and Gumpert, R. (1988) Quality versus quantity in medicine. *Royal Society of Art Journal*, **136**, 333–346

Bracken, M.B. (1987) Clinical trials and the acceptance of uncertainty. *British Medical Journal*, **294**, 1111–1112

Britton, M. (1974) Diagnostic errors discovered at autopsy. *Acta Medica Scandinavica*, **196**, 203–210

Brook, R.H. and Appel, F.A. (1973) Quality of care assessment: choosing a method for peer review. *New England Journal of Medicine*, **288**, 1323–1329

Brook, R.H. (1990) Relationship between appropriateness and outcome. In *Measuring the Outcomes of Medical Care*, edited by A. Hopkins and D. Costain. Royal College of Physicians, London, pp. 59–67

Cameron, H.M. and McGoogan, E. (1981) A prospective study of 1152 hospital autopsies. II Analysis of inaccuracies in clinical diagnoses and their significance. *Journal of Pathology*, **133**, 285–300

Carr-Hill, R.A., Hardman, G.F. and Russell, I.T. (1987) Variations in avoidable mortality and variations in health care resources. *Lancet*, **i**, 789–792

Carter, D.C. and Campbell, D. (1988) Evaluation of the risks of surgery. *British Medical Bulletin*, **44**, 322–340

Cooper, J.B., Newbower, R.S., Long, C.D. and McPeek, B. (1978) Preventable anesthesia mishaps: a study in human factors. *Anesthesiology*, **49**, 399–406

Couch, J.B. (1989) In *Providing Quality Care*, edited by N. Greenfield and D.B. Nash DB. American College of Physicians, Philadelphia, pp. 201–224

Couch, N.P., Tilney, N.L. and Moore, F.D. (1978) The cost of misadventures in colonic surgery. A model for the analysis of adverse outcomes in standard procedures. *American Journal of Surgery*, **135**, 641–646

Daley, J., Jencks, S., Draper, D., Lenhart, G., Thoas, N. and Walker, J. (1988) Predicting hospital-associated mortality for Medicare patients. *Journal of the American Medical Association*, **260**, 3617–3624

Deans, G.T., Odling-Smee, W., McKelvey, S.T.D., Parks, G.T. and Roy, D.A. (1987) Auditing perioperative mortality. *Annals of the Royal College of Surgeons of England*, **69**, 185–187

Dorsey, D.B. (1978) A perspective on the autopsy. *American Journal of Clinical Pathology*, **69 (suppl)**, 217–219.

Dubois, R.W., Rogers, W.H., Moxley, J.H. III, Draper, D. and Brook, R.H. (1987) Hospital inpatient mortality: is it a predictor of quality? *New England Journal of Medicine*, **317**, 1674–1680

Eddy, D. (1990) Practice policies – what are they? *Journal of the American Medical Association*, **263**, 877–880

Flanagan, J.C. (1954) The critical incident technique. *Psychological Bulletin*, **51**, 327–358

Goldman, L., Calderea, D.L., Nussbaum, S.B. *et al.* (1977) Multifactorial index of cardiac risk in noncardiac surgical procedures. *New England Journal of Medicine*, **297**, 845–850

Goldman, L., Sayson, R., Robbins, S., Cohn, L.H., Bettmann, M. and Weisberg, M. (1983) The value of the necropsy in three medical eras. *New England Journal of Medicine*, **308**, 1000–1005

Graham, K.S. and Deary, I.J. (1991) A role for aptitude testing in surgery? *Journal of the Royal College of Surgeons of Edinburgh*, **36**, 70–74

Gray, D., Hampton, J.R., Bernstein, S.J., Kosecoff, J. and Brook, R.H. (1990) Audit of coronary angiography and bypass surgery. *Lancet*, **335**, 1317–1320

Harman, H. and Galbraith, S. (1991) Operating in a free market. *The Times*, December 17, 14, 2–7

Henry, D. and Cook, D. (1991) Meta-analysis workshop in upper gastrointestinal haemorrhage. *Gastroenterology*, **100**, 1481–1482

Hoffenberg, R. (1987) The Rock Carling Fellowship 1986. *Clinical Freedom*. Nuffield Provincial Hospitals Trust, London

Holdsworth, J.D. (1991) Five-year vascular audit from a district hospital. *British Journal of Surgery*, **78**, 601–606

Jenkins, D. (1991) Investigations: how to get from guidelines to protocols. *British Medical Journal*, **303**, 323–324

McArdle, C.S. and Hole, D. (1991) Impact of variability among surgeons on postoperative morbidity and mortality and ultimate survival. *British Medical Journal*, **302**, 1501–1505.

Macintyre, I.M.C. (1989) Extending surgical audit: the assessment of postoperative outcome. *British Journal of Surgery*, **76**, 531–532

Matheson, N.A. (1987) Surgical technique. *British Journal of Surgery*, **74**, 1190

Meijer, W.S., Schmitz, P.I.M. and Jeekel, J. (1990) Meta-analysis of randomized clinical trials of antibiotic prophylaxis in biliary tract surgery. *British Journal of Surgery*, **77**, 283–290

Michaels, J.A. (1988) Surgical audit and carotid endarterectomy. *Lancet*, **ii**, 110–111

Moore, F.D. (1971) The quality of care. Gallie memorial lecture delivered before the Royal College of Physicians and Surgeons of Canada, Ottawa, p. 130

Nelson, A.R. (1976) Orphan data and the unclosed loop: a dilemma in PSRO and medical audit. *New England Journal of Medicine*, **295**, 617–619

Pettigrew, R.A., Burns, H.J.G. and Carter, D.C. (1987) Evaluating surgical risk: the importance of technical factors in determining outcome. *British Journal of Surgery*, **74**, 791–794

Playforth, M.J., Smith, G.M.R., Evans, M. and Pollock, A.V. (1987) Preoperative assessment of fitness score. *British Journal of Surgery*, **74**, 890–892

Pollack, M.M., Ruttiman, U.E. and Getson, P.R. (1987) Accurate prediction of the outcome of pediatric intensive care: a new quantitative method. *New England Journal of Medicine*, **316**, 134–139

Prutting, J. (1978) Autopsies – benefits for clinicians. *American Journal of Clinical Pathology*, **69 (suppl)**, 223–225

Report of the Joint Working Party of the Royal College of Pathologists, the Royal College of Physicians of London, and the Royal College of Surgeons of England (1991) *The Autopsy and Audit*. Royal College of Pathologists, London

Russell, R.C.G. (1987) Surgical technique. *British Journal of Surgery*, **74**, 763–764

Rutstein, D.D., Berenberg, W., Chalmers, T.C., Child, C.G., Fishman, A.P. and Perrin, E.B. (1976) Measuring the quality of medical care. A clinical method. *New England Journal of Medicine*, **294**, 582–588

Sacks, H.S., Berrier, J., Reitman, D., Ancona-Berk, V.A. and Chalmers, T.C. (1987) Meta-analysis of randomized controlled trials. *New England Journal of Medicine*, **316**, 450–455

Schroeder, S.A. (1987) Outcome assessment 70 years later: are we ready? *New England Journal of Medicine*, **316**, 160–162

Scottolini, A.G. and Weinstein, S.R. (1983) The autopsy in clinical quality control. *Journal of the American Medical Association*, **250**, 1192–1194

Shortell, S.M. and Hughes, E.F.X. (1988) The effects of regulation, competition, and ownership on mortality rates among hospital inpatients. *New England Journal of Medicine*, **318**, 1100–1107

Toynbee, P. (1991) A question of life or death. *The Times*, November 8, 16, 1–2

Wright, D., MacKenzie, S.J., Buchan, I., Cairns, C.S. and Price, L.E. (1991) Critical incidents in the intensive therapy unit. *Lancet*, **338**, 676–678

Chapter 13

Surveillance of hospital-acquired infections

There must be some Rules; therefore certain Rules are here set forth; which, as they are few in number, so they are plain and easy to be understood.

Thomas Cranmer (1549)

About one in 20 patients in acute care hospitals will develop an infection. The commonest are those of the urinary tract, followed by surgical wounds, pneumonia, and bacteraemia. In 1976, 19% of hospitals in the United States were providing information on infection rates to their staff. In 1983 this figure had declined to 13%, presumably because of difficulty in collecting accurate data (Berg, 1986) but, largely as a result of the initiative of the Centers for Disease Control, the figure is now much higher.

There are two ways of finding out about infection rates in a hospital. The first is to study the incidence. This is expensive and often inaccurate. The second, which is much cheaper, is to find out the prevalence of all infections at a certain time of a certain day; it has the additional merit of being accurate.

The collection, retrieval, analysis, and display of data relating to surgical infections in comprehensible form require a computer with appropriate software. The software must be dedicated to the task it has to do; it must provide confidentiality by requiring passwords to gain access to data; it must allow daily entry of all operations and classification of operations according to the extent of bacterial contamination – any operation wound that becomes infected can then be recalled and the extent of contamination recorded; it must allow microbiological data about all nosocomial infections to be recorded in the appropriate place; it must allow regular and speedy production of figures, bar charts, and graphs which relate wound infections to particular operations, particular surgeons, and particular wards, and other infections to particular risk factors.

There are many such software programs, one of the most versatile of which is the Automated Infection Control Expert (AICE) from Infection Control and Prevention Analysts Inc of Austin, Texas. The Hospital Infections Program of the Centers for Disease Control in Atlanta developed their own software, which incorporates patient risk factors (Hughes, 1991). A program for the surveillance of surgical wound infections in which surgeons are themselves responsible for entering data about every operation is in use in Denmark (Cordtz *et al.*, 1989).

The SENIC program

The Study on the Efficacy of Nosocomial Infection Control (SENIC) was carried out over 10 years in the 1970s. It was coordinated by the Hospital Infection Program of the Centers for Disease Control in Atlanta, Georgia (Haley *et al.*, 1985). A random sample of 1000 patients from each of 338 hospitals in the United States was studied – a total of 338 000 patients. Details about each patient were recorded and analysed. The commonest site of infection was the urinary tract, but the category that cost most in terms of delayed discharge from hospital and increased money costs was wound infection. The average increased cost was estimated to be $2700 for each case, of which the hospital is reimbursed only $51 from the Diagnosis Related Groups formula.

The SENIC data allowed measurement of the intensity of surveillance, of control efforts, of policy development and teaching, and whether hospitals regularly reported rates of surgical wound infection to surgeons. If these criteria were met, the wound infection rates after operations with comparable potential bacterial contamination were 20% lower than in hospitals with less stringent programmes. If in addition there was a physician on the staff who was interested in infection control, the wound infection rate was 38% lower than in control hospitals.

The key factor in bringing about a reduction in the rate of infection appears to be feedback to individual surgeons, based on accurate and complete recording. Nobody can discern differences in event rates when the rate is below about 20% unless the data are collected prospectively. Surgeons (who must be identified by number, not by name, to maintain complete confidentiality) must be told regularly what their infection rates are, in comparison with average rates for the types of operation. Experience in many centres has shown reduction in infection rates, particularly after clean operations, if there is regular feedback (Cruse and Foord, 1980, Condon *et al.*, 1983). This is known as the Hawthorne effect.

The lesson of the SENIC programme can be summarised: if the best processes of care are followed, and if the outcome is carefully and speedily monitored and the results communicated to surgeons, then the quality of care will improve.

Surveillance in Minneapolis

The surgical wound surveillance programme at the Veterans Administration Center in Minneapolis has been run by a single nurse-epidemiologist for 10 years (Condon *et al.*, 1988). She makes daily rounds on all surgical wards, often helped by experienced ward nurses. Any wound that discharges pus is recorded as infected and microbiological cultures of wound discharges are routinely done. Prospective surveillance has four elements: stratification of surgical operations, detection of wound infections, regular reporting of infection rates, and education of the operating team. The stratification used in Minneapolis is confined to three categories – clean, clean-contaminated, and contaminated. The fourth category, dirty, is not used. About 75% of all wound infections occur in hospital, and many of the 25% that occur at home require the patients' readmission. Wound infection rates are reported to surgeons every month and discussed at regular surgical conferences, in which such factors as the use of antibiotics, bowel preparation, preoperative disinfection of the skin, and lapses in asepsis, are discussed.

The aetiology of surgical wound infection should take account of four determinants – the standard of the surgeon and of the hospital, the bacteria, the local host defences, and the systemic host defences. It may be impossible to record any of these with any accuracy but no good can come of a comparison of wound infection rates in two equally bacterially 'clean' operations – for example, thyroidectomy and femoropopliteal bypass operations. Both local and systemic host defences are likely to be compromised in the lower limb operation.

Surveillance in Florida

The South Florida Hospital Consortium for Infection Control was formed in 1972 to monitor and improve the incidence of outbreaks (as opposed to endemic occurrences) of nosocomial infections (Ehrenkranz, 1986). In general and orthopaedic surgical units the incidence was decimated in the eight years 1975–1982, largely as a result of feedback to the hospitals and acceptance by the surgeons. The incidence of outbreaks in intensive care units (mainly in oncology) remained static.

Surveillance in Hong Kong

French *et al.* (1989) studied the prevalence of hospital acquired infections at 12 noon on a single day, and repeated the study every six months. Guidelines were agreed with clinicians and nurses and the monitoring was done by infection control nurses. After adjusting for risk factors the prevalence fell from 9.9% to 6.0% after three years.

Surveillance in Britain

There have been numerous studies of both incidence and prevalence of nosocomial infections, but few of them have shown the effect of the surveillance and feedback to clinicians. An exception was published by Raine (1991), who reported that the incidence in a district general hospital fell from 1203/15 790 (7.6%) in 1978 to 805/20 259 (3.9%) in 1988. One of the remarkable aspects of this study was that it was done without the help of a computer.

References

Berg, R. (1986). Software for infection control. *American Journal of Infection Control*, **14**, 139–145

Condon, R.E., Schulte, W.J., Malangoni, M.A. and Anderson-Teschendorf, M.J. (1983). Effectiveness of a surgical wound surveillance program. *Archives of Surgery*, **118**, 303–307

Condon, R.E., Haley, R.W., Lee, J.T. and Meakins, J.L. (1988). Does infection control control infection? *Archives of Surgery*, **123**, 250–256

Cordtz, T., Kjaeldgaard, P., Sejberg, D., Kjaelgaard, E., Silleman, M.P., Andersen, J.C. and Jepson, O.B. (1989). The DANOP-DATA system: a low cost personal computer based program for monitoring wound infections in surgical wards. *Journal of Hospital Infection*, **13**, 273–280

Cranmer, T. (1549). Preface to the First Prayer Book

Cruse, P. and Foord, R. (1980). The epidemiology of wound infection: a ten-year prospective study of 62 939 wounds. *Surgical Clinics of North America*, **60**, 27–40

Ehrenkranz, N.J. (1986). The efficacy of a Florida hospital consortium for infection control: 1975-1982. *Infection Control*, **7**, 321–326

French, G.L., Cheng, A.F.B., Wong, S.L. and Donnan, S. (1989). Repeated prevalence surveys for monitoring effectiveness of hospital infection control. *Lancet*, **ii**, 1021–1023

Haley, R.W., Culver, D.H., White, J.W., Morgan, W.M., Emori, T.G., Munn, V.P. and Hooton, J.M. (1985). The efficacy of infection surveillance and control programs in preventing nosocomial infections in US hospitals. *American Journal of Epidemiology*, **121**, 182–205

Hughes, J.M. (1991). Role of surveillance in the prevention of surgical wound infections: data collection, analysis, and use. In *Sterilization of Medical Products*, edited by R.F. Morrissey and Y.I. Prokopenko, Polyscience Publications, Morin Heights, pp. 258–266

Chapter 14

Confidential enquiry into perioperative deaths

A man's dying is more the survivors' affair than his own.
Thomas Mann (1924)

Deaths after surgical operations are an obvious subject for peer review, and many hospitals conduct confidential mortality and morbidity conferences. On a national scale, however, no concerted attempts have been made to audit these deaths until recently, and the idea of avoidable and unavoidable deaths remains to be refined.

Maternal and neonatal deaths

Maternal deaths during or after childbirth in Britain were recorded by the Royal College of Obstetricians and Gynaecologists from 1932 to 1952, when the audit was taken over by the Department of Health and Social Security. This is the longest running clinical audit in the world, and the latest report (1991) deals with the years 1985–1987. The maternal death rate for those years was 6.7/100 000 (compared with 640 in Africa, a mean of 30 in all developed countries, and 10 in northern and middle Europe). The report recommended five measures:

- Consultants should deal with emergencies in labour wards
- Women with complications should be transferred to consultant units early
- General practitioners should keep abreast of changes in practice
- Maternity units should be part of general hospitals
- Blood for transfusion should always be available.

The New York Academy of Medicine studied all maternal deaths in New York City in the early 1930s. The mortality then was 643 per 100 000, but declined to 290 in 1940, 160 in 1945, 80 in 1950, and 33 in 1973 (Rutstein *et al.*, 1976).

A confidential inquiry into neonatal deaths in the Wessex Health Authority region in England disclosed that there were 66 256 births in 1981 and 1982 and 386 (5.8 per 1000) neonatal deaths (Wood, Catford and

Cogswell, 1984). Lethal malformations accounted for 37% of the deaths and 'possible adverse factors in medical care' were found in 38 deaths. The authors concluded that 'the greatest scope for improving the outcome of childbirth in Wessex would be offered if there were further advances in obstetric rather than neonatal care. It is expected that systematic regional perinatal mortality surveys will be in place by 1991' (Kirkup, 1990).

Deaths associated with anaesthesia

Statistics about deaths associated with anaesthesia were first collected in the United States in 1948 (Beecher and Todd, 1954), and other countries followed. In Britain Edwards *et al.* (1956) collected information on anaesthetic deaths by means of postal questionnaires. They concluded that 'in the great majority of the reports there were departures from ideal practice'. The Association of Anaesthetists of Great Britain and Ireland conducted a national enquiry in 1980 (Lunn and Mushin, 1982) and concluded that the demise of many poor risk patients was related to surgical factors as well as anaesthesia. That enquiry was conducted without any input from surgeons. Lunn and Mushin (1982) estimated that 280 patients may have died each year solely from anaesthetic causes (1 in 10 000 anaesthetics), but 1800 deaths may have been due partly to anaesthetics (1 in 1700). They commented that trainee anaesthetists were too often left alone, that monitoring equipment was often inadequate, that anaesthetic records were sometimes not kept, that some recovery units were inadequate, and that there was insufficient consultation between surgeons and anaesthetists, particularly concerning comorbidities.

Cooper, Newbower, and Long (1982) introduced the reporting of 'critical incidents' at Massachusetts General Hospital. These were defined as any occurrence that could have led or did lead to an undesirable outcome of anaesthesia. In addition it must involve an error or a failure of equipment, and it must have been preventable. No adverse effects followed 95% of the incidents reported. Eichhorn *et al.* (1986) at Harvard Medical School in Boston, Massachusetts, drew up standards for the practice of anaesthesia. They included the presence of the anaesthetist in the operating room at all times, taking the blood pressure every five minutes, continuous electrocardiography, monitoring ventilation preferably by measuring end-tidal carbon dioxide concentration, monitoring circulation by pulse palpation, an alarm system to warn of disconnection of any part of the breathing system, continuous monitoring of the inspired oxygen concentration, and (in special cases) recording of the body temperature. They encountered no resistance to the acceptance of these standards.

The reporting of anaesthetic 'incidents' has been adopted widely throughout the world. In Adelaide, South Australia, anaesthetists are required to report any adverse incident to a coordinator. These reports are confidential in the sense that the identity of the anaesthetist and the patient are not disclosed, but the form stresses that 'If you are still concerned about possible medicolegal consequences, DO NOT complete this report.' The report comprises eight items:

1. Description of incident
2. Keywords
3. What happened?
      Circuitry incident
      Circuitry involved
      Equipment involved
      Pharmacological incident
      Airway incident
4. Why did it happen?
      Factors contributing to incident
      Factors minimising incident
      Suggested corrective strategies
5. Anaesthesia and procedure
      Emergency Yes/No
      Procedure category
      Type of anaesthesia
      Monitors in use
6. When and where did it happen?
      When alerted to incident
      Phase when alerted
      Location
7. Patient outcome
      Outcome
      Duration of outcome
8. Who it happened to
      Rank of person immediately responsible for anaesthesia
      Years in this rank
      Rank of person who discovered incident
      Years in this rank
      Patient age group
      Patient risk (ASA)

Medicare mortality rates

In 1986 the Office of Research of the Health Care Financing Administration
bowed to pressure from consumer groups who cited the *Freedom of
Information Act* and subsequently published the mortality rates of Medicare
patients over the age of 64 years in 5888 hospitals in the United States
(Jencks *et al.*, 1988). The data comprised 10 million admissions and 735 000
deaths either in hospital or at home within 30 days of admission to hospital. The publication was intended 'to inform, not infuriate', but it succeeded
in infuriating doctors in hospitals with higher than average death rates, and
allowed others to advertise that, for example, 'we have the lowest mortality for heart surgery in the country'. Protesting doctors claimed that the data
were primitive and inadequate, and that they took no account of case mix,
severity of illness, or socio-economic circumstances (Dunea, 1988).

   Risk adjustment methods do not show whether higher than expected
death rates resulted from chance, or because of unmeasured differences
in patients' risk at the time of admission, or because of ineffective care.

Surgical deaths in Britain

Until 1986 there were no national audits of surgical deaths in Britain apart from that conducted by the European Dialysis and Transplant Organisation, which audits the results of the treatment of end stage renal failure, and the United Kingdom Cardiac Surgical Register (established in 1977), which audits the deaths following cardiac operations (English *et al.*, 1984). Reports are issued periodically, one of which examined the results of percutaneous coronary angioplasty (Hubner, 1990). Of a total of over 5000 angioplasties the mortality was 0.77%, myocardial infarction complicated 2.4% of interventions, and emergency bypass grafting was required in 2.7%.

Confidential Enquiry into Perioperative Deaths (CEPOD)

In 1986 the surgeons and anaesthetists in three regions in England (Northern, South Western, and North East Thames) took part in a pilot study of perioperative deaths. They were approached by a surgeon (H.B. Devlin) and an anaesthetist (J.N. Lunn) on behalf of the Association of Surgeons and the Association of Anaesthetists of Great Britain and Ireland and asked to fill in detailed pro formas concerning the deaths of all patients that occurred during, or within 30 days after, operations (Buck, Devlin and Lunn, 1987). This Confidential Enquiry into Perioperative Deaths (CEPOD) was extended to the whole of the United Kingdom in 1989.

One of the first problems that had to be overcome was that of confidentiality. This was achieved, first of all by removing from all forms and other documents anything that could identify the hospital, the surgeon, the anaesthetist, or the patient. Second, by ensuring that all the assessors were based outside the three regions being audited. Third, only the clinicians in charge of a case could receive the assessors' reports, and then only by telephone to the coordinating centre. Finally, all documents and computer tapes were destroyed and the data could not be produced in court in the event of an action for negligence.

Each form was sent to at least two assessors, one of whom was a surgeon and the other an anaesthetist, who were asked to score from 0 (total failure of care) to 10 (unavoidable death) the following aspects, some of which applied only to the anaesthetist assessor:

- Appropriateness of the operation
- Appropriateness of the preoperative preparation
- Appropriateness of the grade and special interests of the surgeon
- Soundness of the organisation
- Equipment failure
- Adverse drug reaction
- Human failure:
    Lack of knowledge
    Failure to apply knowledge
    Lack of experience
    Lack of care
    Inadequate supervision

Fatigue
Physical or mental impairment
Other.

The authors of this report analysed 2391 (59%) of the 4034 deaths after 485 850 operations (0.8%); data on the remaining 41% were incomplete. No less than 70% of the deaths were of patients over the age of 70 years, and over half were admitted as emergencies. Some disquieting facts emerged, notably that 30% of the deaths in the Northern and South Western regions, and 50% of those in the North East Thames region were of patients who had had no consultant (staff surgeon) contribution to their care. The trainee surgeons and anaesthetists who performed these operations were not being properly supervised, but were being used to lighten consultants' work load.

The report disclosed that 195 deaths (8% of the deaths analysed) were due solely to deficiencies in surgical care, and that between 8% and 25% of all deaths (depending on age) were avoidable. Among the deficiencies revealed were inappropriateness of the operation (assessors would have declined to operate on 5.6% of the patients who died), inappropriateness of the preoperative management, particularly operating on patients who had not been adequately resuscitated, operations by surgeons who were not qualified to perform that operation, and operations in inadequately equipped and staffed hospitals.

Conclusions of CEPOD

'1. The overall death rate after anaesthesia and surgery, analysed in this Enquiry, was low. The mortality of over half a million operations was 0.7% and most of these were in the elderly (over 75 years old) and were unavoidable due to the progression of the presenting condition, such as advanced cancer, or coexisting diseases such as heart and (or) respiratory failure. Death was solely attributable to avoidable surgical or anaesthetic factors in a very small proportion of operations.
2. The majority of clinicians in the relevant disciplines cooperated in this system of clinical audit.
3. There were important differences in clinical practice between the three Regions studied.
4. There were deficiencies in the Hospital Activity Analysis data. There were also problems with the storage, movement, and retrieval of patients' notes, particularly those of deceased patients.
5. Many surgeons and anaesthetists did not hold regular audits of their operation results (mortality and morbidity meetings). The proportion varied with the sub-specialty but joint meetings between the two disciplines were very rare.
6. There were important differences in the consultants' supervision of trainees.
7. There were a number of deaths in which junior surgeons or anaesthetists did not seek the advice of their consultants or senior registrars at any time before, during or after the operations.

8. The preoperative assessment and resuscitation of patients by doctors of both disciplines were sometimes compromised by undue haste to operate. This was a greater problem than delayed operations and it is possible that pressure to fit an operation into a very tight theatre schedule was one of the responsible factors.
9. There were instances of patients who were moribund or terminally ill having operations that would not have improved their condition.
10. There were examples of surgeons operating for conditions for which they were not trained or performing operations outside their field of primary expertise.
11. There were examples of difficulties in transferring patients for specialised treatment to other hospitals in the area.'

Recommendations of CEPOD

'1. There is a need for an assessment of clinical practice on a national basis. Our experience suggests that our colleagues would welcome this.
2. Consultants in every District should ensure that their own coding and input to information systems (including the Körner systems) is accurate and up to date; without :this, any audit is flawed. Every District should urgently review the storage, movement, and retrieval of patients' notes, particularly those of deceased patients.
3. Clinicians need to assess themselves regularly. Effective self assessment needs time; time to attend autopsies, mortality/morbidity meetings and clinical review with other disciplines.
4. All departments of anaesthetics and surgery should review their arrangements for consultants' supervision of trainees. Locally agreed guidelines are important to ensure appropriate care of all patients, but particularly when responsibility is transferred from one clinical team or shift to another. No senior house officer or registrar should undertake any anaesthetic or surgical operation as an emergency or urgent matter without consultation with their consultant or senior registrar.
5. Resuscitation, assessment, and management of medical disease take time and may determine the outcome; their importance needs to be restated. Arrangements which permit this in every case are important.
6. The decision to operate on the elderly and the very sick is important and should be taken at consultant or senior registrar level. For the most seriously ill patients, consultant anaesthetists and surgeons should consult together before the operation.
7. The decision not to operate is difficult. Humanity suggests that patients who are terminally ill or moribund should not have operations but should be allowed to die in peace with dignity.
8. Districts should review their facilities for out-of-hours work and concentrate anaesthetic, surgical, and nursing resources at a single location. A fully staffed and fully equipped anaesthetic room, resuscitation room, operating room, recovery area, and high dependency or intensive therapy unit should be available at all times.

9. The implementation of the CEPOD classification of operations (emergency, urgent, scheduled, and elective) would concentrate the attention of all staff on the fact that very few operations need to be performed at night.

10. Operations should only be performed by consultants or junior surgeons accountable to consultants who have had adequate training in the specialty relevant to the operation. Health Authorities should therefore balance surgical specialties so that appropriate urological and vascular trained surgeons are provided in each District. In the case of small Districts this may necessitate sub-Regional units to ensure adequate sub-specialty care. Neurological and neonatal surgery should be carried out at special Regional units.'

The obvious defect in recording perioperative death rates is the fact that faint-hearted surgeons will refuse to operate on patients who may die, preferring either to pass them on to another surgeon or to treat them medically. The perioperative mortality of such surgeons will be lower than that of their more courageous colleagues who are prepared to offer even desperate cases the chance of survival that only surgery can offer.

Among the discouraging facts disclosed by this report was that the necropsy rate when death occurred within 48 hours of operation was 44%, but it was only about 30% when death occurred later. Most of the early deaths were .reported to coroners, and some coroners were unhelpful about releasing reports of necropsies they had requested. We have referred to the discrepancies between information on death certificates and the findings at necropsy, so the necropsy rate in this study was disappointing. For example, the diagnosis of massive pulmonary embolism (reported to have caused 189 deaths) cannot be substantiated without the evidence of a necropsy. Another disturbing revelation was that only about half the participating hospitals held regular mortality and morbidity conferences, and that these were ill attended. Finally, a ludicrously low percentage of surgeons (6%) and anaesthetists (4%) sought to be told the opinion of assessors concerning deaths that they had reported.

National Confidential Enquiry into Perioperative Deaths

This study investigated deaths within 30 days of any surgical or gynaecological operation in all hospitals in the United Kingdom except Scotland. In the first report (Campling, Devlin and Lunn, 1990), which recorded 20 247 deaths, a special study was made of the 417 deaths in children aged 10 years or less, for 295 of whom completed surgical questionnaires were received. The main conclusions of this report were that the data produced for NHS purposes are inadequate for effective clinical audit; that the needs of children referred to single surgical specialty units are unmet; and that greater care should be taken in the appointment of locum senior surgeons to posts with reponsibilities for children. Further publications are expected.

References

Beecher, H.K. and Todd, D.P. (1954) A study of the deaths associated with anesthesia and surgery based on a study of 599 428 anesthesias in 10 institutions 1948–52 inclusive. *Annals of Surgery*, **140**, 2–35

Buck, N., Devlin, H.B. and Lunn, J.N. (1987) *The Report of a Confidential Enquiry into Perioperative Deaths*. Nuffield Provincial Hospitals Trust, London

Campling, E.A., Devlin, H.B. and Lunn, J.N. (1990) *The Report of the National Confidential Enquiry into Perioperative Deaths 1989*. NCEPOD, London

Cooper, J.B., Newbower, R.S. and Long, C.D. (1982) Human errors in anesthesia management. In *The Quality of Care in Anesthesia*, edited by B.L. Grundy and J.S. Gravenstein. Thomas, Springfield, pp. 114–130

Dunea, G. (1988) Distrust. *British Medical Journal*, **296**, 1251–1252

Edwards, G., Morton, H.J.V., Pask, E.A. and Wylie, W.D. (1956) Deaths associated with anaesthesia. *Anaesthesia*, **11**, 194–220

Eichhorn, J.H., Cooper, J.B., Cullen, D.J., Maier, W.R., Philip, J.H. and Seeman, R.G. (1986) Standards for patient monitoring during anesthesia at Harvard Medical School. *Journal of the American Medical Association*, **256**, 1017–1020

English, T.A.H., Bailey, A.R., Dark, J.F. and Williams, W.G. (1984) The UK cardiac surgical register 1977-82. *British Medical Journal*, **289**, 1205–1208

Hubner, P.J.B. (1990) Cardiac interventional procedures in the United Kingdom during 1988. *British Heart Journal*, **64**, 36–37

Jencks, S.F., Daley, J., Draper, D., Thomas, N., Lenhart, G. and Walker, J. (1988) Interpreting hospital mortality data. The role of clinical risk adjustment. *Journal of the American Medical Association*, **260**, 3611–3616

Kirkup, W. (1990) Perinatal audit: does confidential enquiry have a place? *British Journal of Obstetrics and Gynaecology*, **97**, 371–373

Lunn, J.N. and Mushin, W.W. (1982) *Mortality Associated with Anaesthesia*. Nuffield Provincial Hospitals Trust, London

Mann, T. (1924) *The Magic Mountain*. Translated by H.T. Lowe-Porter. Secker and Warburg, London, 1927, p. 532

Report on Confidential Enquiries Into Maternal Deaths in the United Kingdom 1985–7 (1991). HMSO, London

Rutstein, D.D., Berenberg, W., Chalmers, T.C., Child, C.G., Fishman, A.P. and Perrin, E.B. (1976) Measuring the quality of medical care. A clinical method. *New England Journal of Medicine*, **294**, 582–588

Wood, B., Catford, J.C. and Cogswell, J.J. (1984) Confidential inquiry into neonatal deaths in Wessex, 1981 and 1982. *British Medical Journal*, **288**, 1206–1208

Chapter 15

Scores for assessment of fitness

No human investigation can be called true science without passing through mathematical tests. Leonardo da Vinci (1452–1519)

When something can be expressed in a numerical way, it is an aid to more precise and accurate thinking. Richard Asher (1983)

Concern about the quality of clinical care must not blind us to the fact that wars, poverty, unemployment, ignorance, unrestrained growth of populations, and poor education are potent causes of death and ill health. Nor should we forget that hand guns, motor vehicles, cigarette smoking, and alcohol cause more premature deaths and disablement than any diseases that we are called upon to treat. Methods designed to assure the quality of clinical care can have no impact on these.

It is only during the past 150 years that Western nations have collected 'vital statistics', which are designed to measure the health of populations. Careful interpretation of these statistics resulted in important social and medical reforms in the nineteenth century. Without the collection of such statistics William Farr, Edwin Chadwick, and Florence Nightingale, to name but three of the crusaders for better health in Britain, would not have been able to bring about their reforms.

The health of individuals is harder to measure than the health of nations. For one thing, there is no standard 'healthy person'. All we can hope to do is to measure *indicators* of good health or deviations from health, and give each indicator a score. We can then add these scores to produce a picture of that person's health.

Scales and scores serve three functions: they may be *predictive* (this includes all the staging systems, such as the TNM classification of cancer); they may be *descriptive* (distinguishing between those with and those without a disease); or they may be *evaluative* (assessing health and the quality of life before and after an intervention) (Charlson *et al.*, 1991).

No assessment of the outcome of clinical care can be valid unless we have ways of measuring the extent of the reduction in health before an intervention, and the change in health resulting from that intervention. Sometimes this is easy. For example, a woman who was previously well is brought into hospital with acute appendicitis. She is in pain and is nauseated and anorexic. Following appendicectomy there is no immediate improvement, but within a day or two her health has improved greatly, and within a month she has returned to normal.

More often, however, the judgement of the quality of care by referring to the outcome of that care is much more difficult. It is in these circumstances that scores and scales are valuable.

Some scores allow us to judge only the extent of deviation from physical health, and others include psychological health and the quality of life (McDowell and Newell, 1987, Bowling, 1991). We have chosen those that are of historical interest and those that have been shown to be reliable and valid. We have also considered the cost, and the ease with which a score or scale can be calculated. The following are examples.

Predicting outcome in injured patients

Injury severity score

The injury severity score was introduced by Baker *et al.* (1974) as a development of the abbreviated injury scale, in which the severity of injury was classified from 1 (minor), to 2 (moderate – for example, an undisplaced fracture of the tibia), 3 (serious – for example, a head injury with recovery of consciousness within an hour), 4 (severe – for example, a major laceration of the liver), 5 (critical – for example, an incomplete transection of thoracic aorta), to 6 (lethal). The injury severity score is the sum of the squares of the three most serious injuries in the six anatomical regions – head and neck, abdominal and pelvic contents, bony pelvis and limbs, face, chest, and body surface. Grade 6 is automatically given a score of 75, which is the maximum score. The American College of Surgeons Committee on Trauma estimated that death should be preventable if the injury severity score is less than 32, but the outlook is worse in older people.

Outcome predictive score

The injury severity score pays no attention to the profound suppression of immune competence associated with trauma. Cheadle *et al.* (1989) produced an outcome predictive score by combining the injury severity score with factors that took account of the age of the patient, the degree of bacterial contamination, and a measure of immune competence – the proportion of peripheral monocytes that expressed the human leucocyte antigen DR (HLA-DR).

Revised trauma score

The revised trauma score is calculated from measurements of the systolic blood pressure, the respiratory rate, and the Glasgow coma scale. It was derived from statistical analysis of a large database in the USA and each coded value is multiplied by a weighting factor, which reflects the relative value of the measurement in determining survival (Table 15.1). The score,

Table 15.1 Revised trauma score

	Coded value	X weight = score
Systolic blood pressure		
>89	4	.....
76–89	3	.....
50–75	2	0.7326 .....
1–49	1	.....
0	0	.....
Respiratory rate		
10-29	4	.....
>29	3	.....
6-9	2	0.2908 .....
1-5	1	.....
0	0	.....
Glasgow coma scale		
13-15	4	.....
9-12	3	.....
6-8	2	0.9368 .....
4-5	1	.....
3	0	.....
		Total score.........

by convention, is recorded when the patient first arrives in the accident and emergency department.

TRISS Score

The revised trauma score has been combined with the injury severity score to make the TRISS (*TR*auma score, *I*njury *S*everity *S*core) score (Boyd, Tolson and Copes, 1987) to indicate the probability of survival. It is weighted by a factor for age over 55 years, and for blunt injury (which is more deadly than penetrating injury). It ranges from 0 (unconscious, not breathing, no recordable blood pressure) to 7.84 (normal). It reflects not only the severity of injury but also the physiological disturbance to the patient of that injury. Data were obtained on the outcome of over 25 000 patients and the expected outcome can be matched against the observed outcome in any institution (Yates, 1990). The correlation is good, except for elderly people with fractured necks of femur, whose mortality is greater than would be predicted by application of the TRISS method.

Table 15.2 Glasgow coma scale

Verbal response		Motor response		Eye opening	
None	1	None	1	None	1
Incomprehensible	2	Extending	2	To pain	2
Inappropriate	3	Abnormal flexion	3	To speech	3
Confused	4	Flexion to pain	4	Spontaneous	4
Orientated	5	Localising pain	5		
		Obeying commands	6		

Glasgow coma scale

This scale, introduced by Teasdale and Jennett in 1974, is valuable not only in the triage of patients with head injuries and diseases of the brain, but also as an essential part of scores that assess derangements of acute physiology in many diseases. It is unusual in that low numbers are allocated to the more severe disturbances, the maximum (15) being allocated to a near normal condition. The scale is as shown in Table 15.2.

Leeds prognostic score for severe head injury

Gibson and Stephenson (1989) introduced a score to help to discriminate between patients with severe head injuries who were going to die (and for whom further interventions were pointless), and those who might live if they were given aggressive medical and surgical treatment. Scores from 1 to 4 were given for deviations from the optimum for age, pupillary reactions, intracranial pressure, systolic blood pressure, Glasgow coma scale, the presence of other injuries, and of high density lesions shown on computed tomography. They found that no patient with a score of 12 or more survived in a group of 187 studied retrospectively and only one of 52 who were studied prospectively. The certainty of these findings was challenged by Feldman *et al.* (1991). Of 131 consecutive patients who required monitoring of intracranial pressure they reported that 8 survivors had scores of 12 or more; 2 of these, however, were moderately disabled, 2 were severely disabled, and 4 were in a vegetative state three months later.

Innsbruck coma scale

Gerstenbrand *et al.* (1984) scored seven aspects of coma from 0 to 3 and an eighth from 0 to 2, making a total of 23. Observations were made daily and aggregate scores were calculated. They found that 100 patients died of 102 who scored under 6 at the time of admission, and all died whose mean aggregate score was under 11. The score differs slightly from the Glasgow coma scale, as shown in Table 15.3.

Benzer *et al.* (1991) used this modified Glasgow coma scale and found that all 79 (out of 421) patients who scored 0 or 1 on the Innsbruck coma scale died within 21 days.

Predicting outcome of operations

Feinstein (1970) wrote: 'The neglect of comorbidity has many detrimental effects on general statistics of disease, but some of the worst clinical consequences occur during efforts to evaluate treatment.... The omissions create misleading data in mortality rates for a general population, and in fatality rates for an individual disease.'

There have been many attempts to devise methods of assessing the ability of patients to withstand major operations, but most of them have concentrated on only a few aspects, or have been subjective.   The most widely used is the American Society of Anesthesiologists (ASA) classification.

Table 15.3 Innsbruck coma scale

Reaction to noise	Turning towards	3
	Purposeful movement	2
	Non-purposeful movement	1
	No movement	0
Reaction to pain	Appropriate reaction	3
	Withdrawal	2
	Extension	1
	No reaction	0
Body posture	Normal	3
	Partly extended	2
	Completely extended	1
	Limp	0
Eye opening	Spontaneous	3
	In response to noise	2
	In response to pain	1
	None	0
Pupil size	Normal	3
	Small	2
	Dilated	1
	Fixed dilated	0
Pupil reaction	Normal	3
	Sluggish	2
	Barely perceptible	1
	Absent	0
Eye movements	Normal	3
	Not following	2
	Sometimes divergent	1
	Fixed divergent	0
Vocal sounds	Spontaneous	2
	In response to stimuli	1
	None	0

ASA classification

This originated from deliberations as long ago as 1940, and the system
commonly used today divides patients into five categories.   Class 1
comprises patients who are healthy, class 2 those with mild systemic
disease, class 3 those with severe systemic disease, class 4 those with potentially lethal systemic disease, and class 5 those who are moribund. A full
description of the classes was given by Buck, Devlin and Lunn (1987):

'Class 1. The patient has no organic, physiological, biochemical, or
psychiatric disturbance. The pathological process for which operation is
to be performed is localized and does not entail a systemic disturbance.
Examples: a fit patient with inguinal hernia; fibroid uterus in an otherwise healthy woman.

Class 2. Mild to moderate systemic disturbance caused either by the
condition to be treated surgically or by other pathophysiological
processes. Example: non- or only slightly limiting organic heart disease,
mild diabetes, essential hypertension, or anaemia. Some might choose
to list the extremes of age here, both neonates and octogenarians, even
though no discernible systemic disease is present. Extreme obesity and
chronic bronchitis may be included in this category.

Class 3. Severe systemic disturbance or disease from whatever cause, even though it may not be possible to define the degree of disability with finality. Examples: severely limiting organic heart disease; severe diabetes with vascular complications; moderate to severe degrees of pulmonary insufficiency; angina pectoris or healed myocardial infarction.

Class 4. Severe systemic disorders that are already life threatening, not always correctable by operation. Examples: patients with organic heart disease showing marked signs of cardiac insufficiency, persistent angina, or active myocarditis; advanced degree of pulmonary, hepatic, renal, or endocrine insufficiency.

Class 5. The moribund patient who has little chance of survival but is submitted to operation in desperation. Examples: the burst abdominal aneurysm with profound shock; major cerebral trauma with rapidly increasing intracranial pressure; massive pulmonary embolus. Most of these patients require operation as a resuscitative measure with little if any anaesthesia.'

Owens, Felts and Spitznagel (1978) sent descriptions of 10 hypothetical patients to 304 board-certified anaesthesiologists, requesting them to assign an ASA class to each patient. They analysed the 235 replies and found that there was considerable inconsistency in the classification of four of the 10 patients. They concluded that 'The ASA Physical Status Classification is useful but suffers from a lack of scientific precision.'

Goldman's cardiac index

'Heart attacks and their complications are the main cause of death after anesthesia and surgery' (Mangano, 1990). Goldman constructed an index from a multivariate linear discriminant analysis of risk factors and outcome in 1001 patients over the age of 40 years having operations on organs other than the heart (Goldman *et al.*, 1977). They identified and allocated scores to nine risk factors predicting serious cardiac complications or cardiac death, as shown in Table 15.4.

Table 15.4 Goldman cardiac index

Third heart sound or jugular venous distension	11
Myocardial infarction within six months	10
More than 5 ventricular extrasystoles/minute	7
Not in sinus rhythm	7
Age more than 70 years	5
Intraperitoneal, thoracic, or aortic surgery	3
Emergency operation	4
Aortic stenosis	3
Poor general medical condition	3

'Poor general medical condition' included patients who were bedridden, or who had signs of chronic liver disease, abnormal hepatic enzyme activities, blood urea > 8 mmol/l, serum creatinine > 260 mmol/l, serum potassium < 3 mmol/l, serum bicarbonate < 20 mmol/l, PaO_2 < 8.0 kPa, or $PaCO_2$ > 6.7 kPa.

They graded their patients into one of four classes. Class I scored 0–5, class II 6–12, class III 13–25, and class IV over 25. Table 15.5 shows the results.

Table 15.5 Outcome in 1001 patients

	I	*II*	*III*	*IV*
Total	537	316	130	18
Cardiac deaths	1	5	3	10
Major cardiac complications	4	16	15	4

They recommended that 'only truly life saving procedures be performed on patients with risk index scores of 26 points or more, and that those with scores of 13 to 25 should have medical consultations and treatment'.

Detsky *et al.* (1986) added 'angina' to the list, scoring 10 for controlled, and 20 for unstable, angina.

Malnutrition as a determinant of outcome of operations

There has been a plethora of studies suggesting that clinical, anthropometric, or biochemical measurements of protein-calorie malnutrition can identify patients at risk of developing postoperative complications.

Baker *et al.* (1982) suggested that 'carefully performed history taking and physical examination are sufficient for nutritional assessment'. Two clinicians agreed in 48 of 59 patients on the clinical classification of patients before operations into normal, mildly malnourished, and severely malnourished. These patients were also investigated by anthropometric, biochemical, and immunological tests. There was a strong correlation between clinical and laboratory classifications, and between these assessments and the incidence of postoperative infective complications.

Pettigrew and Hill (1986) concluded that careful clinical assessment combined with measurements of serum protein concentrations (transferrin and pre-albumin being more sensitive than albumin) were more valuable than anthropometric measurements in predicting which patients were at high risk.

They allotted a score of 1 each for bronchitis, smoking, treated hypertension, mild angina, past history of rheumatic fever or tuberculosis, diabetes, high alcohol intake, and mild nutritional deficiency. A score of 2 was given to patients with moderate nutritional deficiency, and 3 to those with severe deficiency.

A score of 4 each was allotted to: severe obstructive airways disease; current chest infection; recent myocardial infarction; presence of a pacemaker; previous pneumonectomy; jaundice; failure of renal, cardiac or respiratory function; prolonged high doses of steroids; thrombocytopenia; metastatic cancer or myeloma; major sepsis; and past history of venous thrombosis or pulmonary embolism. In their system a score of 6 or more indicated a high risk of death or complications.

Neither clinical nor laboratory measurements can, however, separate the effects of malnutrition from those of other aspects of illness.

Preoperative assessment of immune competence

Immunological deficiencies are most easily recognised either by reduction in the number of circulating lymphocytes or by intradermal injection of four or five recall antigens (mumps, Candida, trichophyton, purified protein derivative of old tuberculin, and streptokinase/streptodornase); the diameter of the resulting weal is measured 24 and 48 hours later (MacLean *et al.*, 1975). The test has been simplified by the introduction of the Multitest ICM (Institut Merieux, Lyon). The dose of each antigen is lower than those used in the traditional intradermal injections of each antigen separately, and subjects may fail to react and so be falsely declared anergic.

People with normal cell-mediated immunity produce a palpable weal greater than 5 mm in diameter at the sites of two or more antigens, relatively anergic people to one, and anergic people to none. Anergy or relative anergy is certainly associated with trauma and sepsis, but its importance as a preoperative predictor of death or complications is controversial. Work in Scarborough (Ausobsky *et al.*, 1982) and in

Table 15.6 Preoperative assessment of fitness score

Score 1 for each:
   Cardiac symptoms controlled by treatment
   Short of breath on climbing stairs
   Morning cough
   Stroke or myocardial infarct > 6 months ago
   Haemoglobin < 100 g/l
   Serum albumin 30–35 g/l
   Plasma urea 10–19 mmol/l
   Steroid treatment
   Controlled diabetes
Score 2 for each:
   Age 70–79 years
   Cardiac symptoms poorly controlled
   Short of breath on walking
   Persistent cough with sputum
Score 3 for each:
   Clinical jaundice
   Serum albumin < 30 g/l
   Loss of 10% weight in one month
   Plasma urea > 20 mmol/l
   Short of breath at rest
   Myocardial infarction within 6 months
   Confusion
   Cytotoxic treatment
Score 4 for each:
   Age > 80 years
   Palliative operation for cancer
   Intestinal obstruction
   Perforations, pancreatitis, and intraperitoneal abscess (excluding perforated appendicitis)
   Haemorrhage or anaemia requiring transfusion

Manchester (Brown *et al.*, 1982) failed to confirm that patients who were anergic or relatively anergic before elective operations had significantly higher morbidity or mortality than patients who reacted normally.

Preoperative assessment of fitness score

Playforth *et al.* (1987) introduced this score to concentrate the attention of auditors on those patients with low scores (indicating relative fitness) who had major complications or died after operations. The score is predominantly clinical, relying on only three laboratory tests — estimation of the concentrations of haemoglobin, urea, and albumin in the blood (Table 15.6).

The scores are added together, a fit young person being given a score of 0 and the maximum score being 10. The score was used in a prospective study of 1517 patients who were operated on. Table 15.7 shows the results.

Table 15.7 Results in 1517 patients

Score	Number of patients	Number (%) who died
0–5	1095	7 (0.6)
6	105	16 (15.2)
7–8	191	74 (38.7)
9–10	126	70 (55.6)

POSSUM

Copeland, Jones, and Walters (1991) combined a 12 factor, four grade, physiological score with a six factor, four grade, operative severity score to produce their physiological and operative severity score for the enumeration of mortality and morbidity. The physiological factors – graded from 1 (no deviation from reference range) to 8 (profound disturbance) – were: age, cardiac signs, respiratory history, systolic blood pressure, pulse rate, Glasgow coma scale, haemoglobin, white cell count, urea, sodium, potassium, and electrocardiogram. The operative severity score similarly graded took into account the extent of the operation, performance of multiple procedures, total blood loss, peritoneal soiling, presence of malignancy, and whether the operation was done electively or as an emergency. In an audit of 1372 patients they found a close correlation between observed and predicted mortality and morbidity.

A simple score to predict surgical risk

Ramsay *et al.* (1988) examined a number of variables by stepwise discriminant analysis and found that, by multiplying the age in years by 3 and subtracting the percentage of lymphocytes in a peripheral blood count, they obtained a score which, if it was above 105, predicted a high risk of death and complications after elective and emergency major laparotomy.

Scores for assessment of specific conditions

Stratification of risk in perforated peptic ulcers

Boey, Wong and Ong (1982) studied the effect on mortality of three deviations from normal physiology in patients with perforated duodenal ulcers. They scaled from 0 (no deviation) to 3 (profound deviation) the blood pressure on admission, delay from onset of symptoms to operation of more than 24 hours, and coexistent serious illness. Irvin (1989) added age over 70 years, and validated the scale in a consecutive series of 265 patients operated on for perforation of peptic ulcers. Nineteen patients were not operated on, and 16 died (Table 15.8).

Table 15.8 Deaths after perforated peptic ulcers

	Age <70 years		Age >70 years	
	Total no.	No (%) of deaths	Total no.	No (%) of deaths
Scale 0	70	2 (3)	53	6 (11)
Scale 1	23	4 (17)	75	20 (27)
Scale 2	8	3 (38)	29	16 (55)
Scale 3	2	2 (100)	5	5 (100)

Stratification of risk of surgical wound infection

Haley *et al.* (1985) studied two groups, each of about 60 000 patients, operated on five years apart. They entered 10 risk factors into a multivariate program and identified only four as significant. These were: an operation within the abdomen, an operation lasting more than two hours, an operation classified as contaminated or dirty, and a patient with three or more underlying diseases. They identified risk groups from 0 (low risk) to 4 (high risk) and found wound infection rates of <1% when the score was 0 and >25% when it was 4.

Cirrhosis of the liver

Child (1964) was one of the first physicians to introduce a scale to classify a disease by its severity. His classification of cirrhotic patients in terms of their hepatic reserve has not been superseded. The scale, A, B, and C, is shown in Table 15.9.

Table 15.9 Child's classification of cirrhosis

Variable	A	B	C
Serum bilirubin (μmol/l)	<34	34–51	>51
Plasma albumin (g/l)	>35	30–35	<30
Ascites	None	Minimal	Massive
Encephalopathy	None	Minimal	Coma
Nutrition	Good	Moderate	Poor
Risk of operation	Low	Moderate	High

Pugh *et al.* (1973) modified Child's scale, retaining the A, B, and C grades, but giving them numerical values. Grade A was assigned if the total score was 5 or 6, grade B if 7–9, and grade C if 10–15. The modified scale is shown in Table 15.10.

Table 15.10 Pugh's modification of Child's scale

Variable	Points		
	1	*2*	*3*
Serum bilirubin (µmol/l)	<34	34–51	>51
Plasma albumin (g/l)	>35	28–35	<28
Ascites	None	Slight	Severe
Encephalopathy	None	Slight	Severe
Prothrombin index	<1.3	1.3–1.5	>1.5

Tumour–nodes–metastases (TNM) staging of cancers
The Union Internationale Contre le Cancer devised the TNM grading, which is applied to many cancers. T1, T2, T3, and T4 refer to increasing size and local spread of the tumour. N0, N1, N2, and N3 refer to the extent of lymph node involvement, and M0 and M1 to the absence or presence of metastases. No audit of the results of treatment of cancer can be reliable unless the stage of the cancer is known.

Dukes' classification of colorectal tumours
This was one of the earliest attempts to stage a cancer. First published in 1932, it was later slightly amended by subclassification of stage C into C1 and C2. Stage A means a tumour confined to the rectal wall (not, as later workers have assumed, to the submucosa). Stage B is applied to tumours that have penetrated through the rectal wall, and stage C to those in which lymph nodes contain cancer cells. Some workers have refined stage B into B1 and B2, according to the depth of spread, and others refer to stage C1 when up to four nodes are involved, and C2 when more than four. The inclusion of stage D when the cancer is incurable surgically seems logical.

Anatomy–function–pathology score for reflux oesophagitis
The results of medical or surgical treatment of reflux oesophagitis depend not only on the effectiveness of the treatment but also on the severity of the disease. The classification of severity has three components: anatomical, functional, and pathological, and these have been combined into the AFP score (Feussner *et al.*, 1991). Anatomically, hiatus hernias are graded from 0 (no hernia) to 3 (mixed sliding and paraoesophageal, or pure paraoesophageal, hernia). Function is graded by 24 hour pH monitoring from 0 (no reflux) to 3 (nocturnal reflux), and pathology from 0 (no mucosal abnormality) to 4 (penetrating ulcers, strictures, longitudinal fibrosis). By adding the scores for each element an overall score can be calculated and the results of treatment assessed. What matters to patients, however, is not the anatomy, function, or pathology, but the symptoms. These do not form part of the AFP score.

Iowa hip score

Larson (1963) introduced this score to assess the severity of arthritis of the hip before and after operation. Points from 0 (the worst) to 100 (the best) were allocated to social functioning, pain, gait, deformity, and range of movements.

Acute pancreatitis

It is important in assessing the effectiveness of treatment of acute pancreatitis to distinguish between mild attacks, which resolve spontaneously and cause no serious complications or deaths, and severe attacks, the mortality of which ranges from 16% to 100%. The first useful classification of the severity of the disease was by Ranson *et al.* (1974). Later classifications by Imrie *et al.* (1978), and by APACHE II (Wilson, Heath, and Imrie, 1990) yielded similar discrimination between mild and severe attacks. The scores of Ranson and Imrie are similar, the measurements shown in Table 15.11 being indicative of a severe attack; the more of these criteria that are satisfied, the higher the mortality. We have converted Ranson's measurement to SI units.

Table 15.11 Two measures of severity of acute pancreatitis

Measurement	Ranson	Imrie
Age	>55 years	Not included
White cell count (x 10^9/l)	>16	>15
Blood glucose (mmol/l)	>11.1	>10
Lactic dehydrogenase (IU/l)	>700	>600
AST/ALT (u/l)	>100	>100
Blood urea (mmol/l)	Rise >1.8	>16
PaO_2 (kPa)	<8.0	<8.0
Serum calcium (mmol/l)	<2.0	<2.0
Serum albumin (g/l)	Not included	<32
Haematocrit fall (%)	>10	Not included
Base deficit (mmol/l)	>4	Not included
Fluid sequestration (l)	>6	Not included

In a retrospective study of 519 patients with acute pancreatitis Jacobs *et al.* (1977) found a total mortality of 12.9%, and significantly higher mortality associated with old age, shock on admission, abnormal lung function, white cell count >20 x 10^9/l, albumin <30 g/l, prothrombin time >14 seconds, haematocrit <30%, serum creatinine >177 mmol/l, blood urea >10.7 mmol/l,bilirubin >68 µmol/l, and calcium <2.0 mmol/l. Later in the course of the disease death could be predicted by abnormalities on chest X-ray pictures, acute renal failure, respiratory failure requiring ventilation, bacteraemia, bleeding complications, and massive colloid requirements.

Stratification of severity of sepsis

Three scores that have been used to define the severity of sepsis are the sepsis severity score of Stevens (1983), the score of Elebute and Stoner (1983), and the APACHE score of Knaus *et al.* (1981).

Sepsis severity score

Stevens recognised that the outcome of patients with failure of two or more organ systems is worse than would be indicated from a mere addition of the deleterious effect of each one separately. He assigned values from 1 to 5 to varying grades of dysfunction of lungs, kidneys, coagulation system, cardiovascular system, liver, gastrointestinal tract, and neurological system. He squared these values and added them to produce a sepsis severity score. The mean score of survivors was 29, of those who died 49.

Elebute and Stoner score

Elebute and Stoner scored the local and secondary effects of sepsis and fever, and laboratory measurements, and added the resulting scores. If the total score exceeded 20, death was likely. The scores were as follows:

Score 1: fever <38.4°C, compensated acidosis, single positive blood culture, white cell count 12–30 × 10^9/l, haemoglobin 70–100 g/l, platelet count 100–150 × 10^9/l, serum albumin concentration 30–35 g/l, bilirubin >20 μmol/l.

Score 2: one wound dressing/day, local peritonitis, chest infection without sputum, fever 38.5–39°C, jaundice, uncompensated acidosis, white cell count >30 × 10^9/l, haemoglobin <70 g/l, platelets <100 × 10^9/l, serum albumin 25-30 g/l

Score 3: fever >39 or <36°C, renal failure, mental deterioration, diffuse intravascular coagulation, two or more positive blood cultures, or positive blood culture together with a cardiac murmur or history of an invasive procedure, white cell count <2.5 × 10^9/l, serum albumin <25 g/l.

Score 4: more than 1 dressing/day, purulent sputum.

Score 6: general peritonitis, pneumonia, intra-abdominal abscess.

APACHE

APACHE (Acute Physiology and Chronic Health Evaluation) was introduced by Knaus *et al.* in 1981 to assess the severity of illness in patients in intensive care units, but has been modified to apply to other sick patients. The number of variables was reduced from 34 to 12 (Knaus *et al.*, 1984), and this is the form of the widely used APACHE II. The score is closely correlated with mortality. Counts of 0 to 4 are awarded for each of 12 findings on the day of admission to the intensive care unit, depending on how far they deviate from normal; a count of 2 is added for age between 45 and 54, 3 between 55 and 64, 5 between 65 and 74, and 6 for age over 75 years. If the patient has serious coexistent disease, or his immune system is substantially impaired, a count of 2 is added after elective operations, and 5 after emergency operations. The 12 findings are core temperature, mean blood pressure, heart rate, respiratory rate, partial pressure of arterial oxygen as a proportion of percentage of inspired oxygen, arterial pH, creatinine, sodium, and potassium concentrations in serum, haemoglobin concentration and white cell count, and Glasgow coma scale subtracted from 15.

The mortality by score is on the whole higher in medical than in surgical patients, and varies from 1% for a score of 0–4 in surgical patients, to one of 40% for a score of 20–24 in medical patients, and of 86% for a score of over 35 in surgical patients.

The importance of the APACHE system is that it allows comparisons of the results of treatment within a unit and between one unit and another. Knaus *et al.* (1982a) surveyed 795 consecutive admissions to intensive care units in five hospitals in the United States and found that the APACHE score accurately predicted the death rates, ranging from 5% for a score less than 5, 6% for scores of 6 to 10, 10% for scores of 10 to 15, 20% for scores of 16 to 20, 30% for scores of 21 to 25, 50% for scores of 26 to 30, 60% for scores of 31 to 35, and 75% for scores of over 35. They further validated the score by an international comparison of the results in five United States hospitals with those in seven French hospitals (Knaus *et al.*, 1982b).

Meakins *et al.* (1984) used the APACHE score with weightings for increasing age to define a surgical infection stratification system for intra-abdominal infections, taking account of the varying prognoses of infections originating in the stomach and duodenum (group I), small intestine (group II), large intestine (group III), and as a result of postoperative anastomotic breakdown (group IV). They pointed out that the reported mortality rate from peritonitis in some therapeutic trials of antibiotics in 'serious intra-abdominal infections' has been as low as 3.5%, whereas audits of consecutive cases often show mortality rates in excess of 30%. It is clear that stratification for risk must be made in all therapeutic trials.

APACHE III

Concern about several aspects of APACHE II led Knaus *et al.* (1989) to introduce APACHE III, validation of which is awaited. Five blood tests will be added to the 12 that comprise APACHE II. They are the concentrations of urea, bilirubin, glucose, and albumin, and the $PaCO_2$. Urinary output will also be included.

Intensive care units in some hospitals take patients before they are stabilised. These patients have high APACHE II scores, and correlation of these scores with mortality could be interpreted as showing that they perform better than units in other hospitals, which take patients only after they have been stabilised. The intention is to give each patient a score not only on admission, but also during the first 24 hours in the unit. The delay between admission to the hospital and to the intensive care unit will be monitored.

Secondly, APACHE III will further refine not only the part of the score that is concerned with chronic health evaluation, but also enquire further into the role of the presenting disease in determining the mortality. For example, postoperative peritonitis is more lethal than primary peritonitis.

Thirdly, 26 hospitals will be randomly selected to provide data from other than tertiary referral centres, to give a better idea of what transpires in the average hospital.

Fourthly, the study will try and document preventable deaths by measuring individual risks before treatment in a large number of cases.

Finally, there is a prospect that a refined and accurate estimate of the probability of death may allow doctors to decide that aggressive treatment is not indicated for an individual patient and that such a patient should be offered comfort and communication. There is at present no justification for withholding treatment from patients whose APACHE II scores are above 35: the score is not designed to give a prognosis of individual patients.

Conclusion

Audit of outcome can have meaning only if we are comparing like with like. We still cannot be certain that doctors or hospitals whose patients have a high mortality or a low rate of cure are practising poor quality medicine, or whether they are dealing with sicker patients. One of the essential requirements is that the extent of patients' departure from normal health must be given numerical values, even if they are only on an ordinal scale. Scores and scales are constantly being improved, and we neglect them at our peril.

References

Asher, R. (1983) *A Sense of Asher*. British Medical Association, London, p. 46

Ausobsky, J.R., Bean, P., Proctor, J. and Pollock, A.V. (1982) Delayed hypersensitivity testing for the prediction of postoperative complications. *British Journal of Surgery*, **69**, 346–348

Baker, J.P., Detsky, A.S., Wesson, D.E. *et al.* (1982) Nutritional assessment. A comparison of clinical judgment and objective measurements. *New England Journal of Medicine*, **306**, 969–972

Baker, S.P., O'Neill, B., Haddon, W. and Long, W.B. (1974) The injury severity score: a method for describing patients with multiple injuries and evaluating emergency care. *Journal of Trauma*, **14**, 187–196

Benzer, A., Mitterschiffthaler, G., Marosi, M. *et al.* (1991) Prediction of non-survival after trauma: Innsbruck Coma Scale. *Lancet*, **338**, 977–978

Boey, J., Wong, J. and Ong, G.B. (1982) A prospective study of operative risk factors in perforated duodenal ulcers. *Annals of Surgery*, **195**, 265–269

Bowling, A. (1991) *Measuring health. A review of quality of life measurement scales*. Open University Press, Milton Keynes

Boyd, C.R., Tolson, M.A. and Copes, W.S. (1987) Evaluating trauma care: the TRISS method. *Journal of Trauma*, **27**, 370–378

Brown, R., Bancewicz, J., Hamid, J., Tillotson, G., Ward, C. and Irving, M. (1982) Delayed hypersensitivity skin testing does not influence the management of surgical patients. *Annals of Surgery*, **196**, 672–676

Buck, N., Devlin, H.B. and Lunn, J.N. (1987) *The Report of a Confidential Enquiry into Perioperative Deaths*. Nuffield Provincial Hospitals Trust, London

Charlson, M.E., Johanson, N.A. and Williams, P.G. (1991) In Troidl, H. *et al.. Principles and Practice of Research*, Ch. 20. Springer Verlag, New York

Cheadle, W.G., Wilson, M., Hershman, M.J., Bergamini, D., Richardson, J.D. and Polk, H.C. Jr (1989) Comparison of trauma assessment scores and their use in prediction of infection and death. *Annals of Surgery*, **209**, 541–546

Child, C.G. III (1964) *Liver and Portal Hypertension*. Saunders, Philadelphia

Copeland, G.P., Jones, D. and Walters, M. (1991) POSSUM: a scoring system for surgical audit. *British Journal of Surgery*, **78**, 356–360

Detsky, A.S., Abrams, H.B., Forbath, N. and Hillard, J.R. (1986) Cardiac assessment for patients undergoing non-cardiac surgery. *Archives of Internal Medicine*, **146**, 2131–2134

Elebute, E.A. and Stoner, H.B. (1983) The grading of sepsis. *British Journal of Surgery*, **70**, 29–31

Feinstein, A.R. (1970) The pre-therapeutic classification of co-morbidities in chronic disease. *Journal of Chronic Diseases*, **23**, 455–468

Feldman, Z., Contant, C.F., Robertson, C.S., Narayan, R.K. and Grossman, R.G. (1991) Evaluation of the Leeds prognostic score for severe head injury. *Lancet*, **337**, 1451–1453

Feussner, H., Petri, A., Walker, S., Bollschweiler, E. and Siewert, J.R. (1991) The modified AFP score: an attempt to make the results of anti-reflux surgery comparable. *British Journal of Surgery*, **78**, 942–946

Gerstenbrand, von F., Hackl, J.M., Mitterschiffthaler, G., Poewe, W., Prugger, M. and Rumpl, E. (1984) Die Innsbrucker Koma-Skala: Clinisches Koma-Monitoring. *Intensivbehandlung*, **9**, 133–144

Gibson, M.R. and Stephenson, G.C. (1989) Aggressive management of severe closed head trauma: time for reappraisal. *Lancet*, **ii**, 369–371

Goldman, L., Calderea, D.L., Nussbaum, S.B. *et al.* (1977) Multifactorial index of cardiac risk in noncardiac surgical procedures. *New England Journal of Medicine*, **297**, 845–850

Haley, R.W., Culver, D.H., Morgan, M., White, J.W., Emori, T.G. and Hooton, T.M. (1985) A simple multivariate index of patient susceptibility and wound contamination. *American Journal of Epidemiology*, **121**, 206–215

Imrie, C.W., Benjamin, I.S., Ferguson, J.C. *et al.* (1978) A single centre double blind trial of Trasylol therapy in primary acute pancreatitis. *British Journal of Surgery*, **65**, 337–341

Irvin, T.T. (1989) Mortality and perforated peptic ulcer: a case of risk stratification in elderly patients. *British Journal of Surgery*, **76**, 215–218

Jacobs, M.L., Daggett, W.M., Civetta, J.M. *et al.* (1977) Acute pancreatitis: analysis of factors influencing survival. *Annals of Surgery*, **185**, 43–51

Knaus, W.A., Zimmerman, J.E., Wagner, D.P., Draper, E.A. and Lawrence, D.E. (1981) APACHE – acute physiology and chronic health evaluation: a physiologically based classification system. *Critical Care Medicine*, **9**, 591–603

Knaus, W.A., Draper, E.A. and Wagner, D.P. (1984) APACHE II: final form and national validation results of a severity of disease classification system. *Critical Care Medicine*, **12**, 213

Knaus, W.A., Draper, E.A., Wagner, D.P. *et al.* (1982a) Evaluating outcome from intensive care: a preliminary multihospital comparison. *Critical Care Medicine*, **10**, 491–496

Knaus, W.A., Wagner, D.P., Loirat, P. *et al.* (1982b) A comparison of intensive care in the USA and France. *Lancet*, **ii:**, 42–46

Knaus, W.A., Draper, E. and Wagner, D. (1989) APACHE III study design: analytic plan for evaluation of severity and outcome. Chapter 1, Introduction. *Critical Care Medicine*, **17**, S176–S180

Larson, C.B. (1963) Rating scale for hip disabilities. *Clinical Orthopedics*, **31**, 85–93

Leonardo da Vinci (1452–1519) *Trattato della Pittura*. Published 1651, translated by J.P. Richter 1883, p. 4

Maclean, L.D., Meakins, J.L., Taguchi, K., Duignan, J.P., Dhillon, K.S. and Gordon, J. (1975) Heat resistance in sepsis and trauma. *Annals of Surgery,* **182**, 207–217

Mangano, D.T. (1990) Perioperative cardiac mortality. *Anesthesiology*, **72**, 153–184

Meakins, J.L., Solomkin, J.S., Allo, M.D., Dellinger, E.P., Howard, R.J. and Simmons, R.L. (1984) A proposed classification of intra-abdominal injections: stratification of etiology and risk for future therapeutic trials. *Archives of Surgery,* **119**, 1372–1378

Owens, W.D., Felts, J.A. and Spitznagel, E.L. (1978) ASA physical status classifications: a study of consistency of ratings. *Anesthesiology*, **49**, 239–43

Pettigrew, R.A. and Hill, G.L. (1986) Indicators of surgical risk and clinical judgement. *British Journal of Surgery*, **73**, 47–51.

Playforth, M.J., Smith, G.M.R, Evans, M. and Pollock, A.V. (1987) Preoperative assessment of fitness score. *British Journal of Surgery*, **74**, 890–892

Pugh, R.N.H., Murray-Lyon, I.M., Dawson, J.L. *et al.* (1973) Transsection of the oesophagus for bleeding oesophageal varices. *British Journal of Surgery*, **60**, 646–649

Ramsay, G., McGregor, J.R., Murray, G.D., Neithercut, D., Ledingham, I.Mc.A. and George, W.D. (1988) Prediction of surgical risk in adults. *Surgical Research Communications*, **3**, 95–103

Ranson, J.H.C., Rifkind, K.M., Roses, D.F. *et al.* (1974) Prognostic signs and the role of operative management in acute pancreatitis. *Surgery, Gynecology and Obstetrics*, **139**, 69–75

Stevens, L.E. (1983) Gauging the severity of surgical sepsis. *Archives of Surgery*, **118**, 1190–1192

Teasdale, G. and Jennett, B. (1974) Assessment of coma and impaired consciousness. *Lancet*, **ii,** 81–84

Wilson, C., Heath, D.I. and Imrie, C.W. (1990) Prediction of outcome in acute pancreatitis: a comparative study of APACHE II, clinical assessment, and multiple factor scoring systems. *British Journal of Surgery*, **77**, 1260–1264

Yates, D.W. (1990) Scoring systems for trauma. *British Medical Journal*, **301**, 1090–1094.

Chapter 16

Quality of life after surgery

Health is not only the absence of infirmity and disease but also a state of physical, mental, and social well-being

World Health Organisation (1947)

Williams (1991) proposed that seven Ds should be used to audit the outcome of interventions. They are: death, disability, disease, discomfort, dissatisfaction, disruption, and destitution.

It is natural for a surgeon to ask a patient on whom he has operated, 'How are you?' and 'Is there anything specially troubling you?' Yet, in reports on the outcome of operations, it is unusual to find any mention of the patients' quality of life, most authors being concerned only with rates of morbidity and mortality.

It is, however, not enough to consider the correction of an abnormality or the cure of a disease. We should now be equally concerned with a person's ability to perform his daily activities, and with the concepts of happiness and the quality of life. If patients have not been restored to their previous level of activity and contentment with their lot – or an improved level – then your operation has failed. The evaluation of the quality of life both before and after an intervention should be part of the routine assessment of any patient.

It is important to realise that the correlation betweeen objective measurements (for example, of lung function after pneumonectomy) and patients' assessment of their quality of life may not be correlated. The objective measurement may indicate an excellent result, whereas the patient may regard himself as totally disabled. Conversely, semi-objective scores such as return to work or Karnofsky index may indicate a poor quality of life, whereas subjective impressions of happiness, well-being, and satisfaction with life may give a totally different result (Evans, 1991). It appears that most people can adapt to adverse circumstances. As Bowling (1991) wrote: 'What matters is how patients feel, rather than how doctors think they ought to feel.'

Whatever score or scale is used to measure the quality of life, it should take into account not only physical symptoms and functions, but also social and psychological aspects, including the patient's own perception of well-being. Spitzer (1987) discussed the validation of measures of the quality of life and concluded that no gold standard exists and that the proliferation of scores during the last 10 years has not served to make the assessment of the quality of life any easier. It is no easier to define health than it is to define illness, but if we are going to compare treatment with no treatment (for advanced cancer, for example), or to compare surgical with medical treatment for the same disease, the patient's quality of life and his perception of that quality are just as important end points as the rates of complications and death. From the patient's point of view, the fear of recurrence of cancer can overwhelm other considerations. This is probably present in every patient after an operation for cancer. It tends to lessen as time goes by without recurrence, and is probably exacerbated by adjuvant radiotherapy and chemotherapy.

Measurements of the quality of life after operations

Surgeons are apt to think that they have done their job properly when they have cured the disease with which the patient presented. More and more, however, it is being realised that the judgement of success by the surgeon and by the patient may be at odds, and that clinical decisions have got to be made in cooperation with the patient.

The purpose of surgical treatment is to cure a disease, but it is often done at the expense of introducing new symptoms. Honest audit of the results of surgical interventions must take account not only of mortality and immediate morbidity, but also of long term disturbance of the *quality* of life. As Streiner and Norman (1989) wrote: 'There is increased awareness of the impact on health and health care on the quality of human life ... methods must be devised to measure what was previously thought to be unmeasurable, and assess in a reproducible and valid fashion those subjective states which cannot be converted into the position of a needle on a dial.'

In surgical publications the three conditions that have received most attention from the point of view of the quality of life are diseases of the breast, of the gastrointestinal tract, and of the kidney.

Lasry *et al.* (1987) examined 123 women who had received treatment for breast cancer in accordance with the National Surgical Adjuvant Breast Project (protocol B-06) a mean of 3.5 years previously. The three arms of this trial were total mastectomy, partial mastectomy, and partial mastectomy followed by local irradiation. They found that women who had had a total mastectomy were significantly less satisfied with their body image, that there were no significant differences among the groups concerning fear of recurrence, and that those patients who had had postoperative radiotherapy were significantly more depressed than those in the other two groups. They commented that 'radiation therapy could well be more frightening to breast surgery patients than had been anticipated by doctors'.

In recent years there has been a striking movement away from abdominoperineal excision towards sphincter saving operations for cancer of the rectum. Williams and Johnston (1983) reported a better quality of life in terms of return to work, lack of impairment of sexual function, and reduction in the use of drugs in patients who had had a sphincter saving operation.

The advent of laparoscopic cholecystectomy may encourage surgeons to operate on patients with gall stones that are causing few symptoms. An audit by self-administered questionnaire in 274 patients one year and two years after cholecystectomy showed that one third of them still had abdominal pain, flatulence, or indigestion (Bates *et al.*, 1991). On a linear analogue scale just over half the patients rated the operation a 'complete success'. The authors advised that patients who accept operation for gall stones should be told about the relatively high incidence of continued symptoms.

Troidl *et al.* (1987) compared the quality of life, both disease specific and sociopersonal, in 45 patients before and after total gastrectomy for cancer. The questions that were related to the disease concerned appetite, swallowing, size of meals, vomiting, and loss of weight. The general questions concerned tiredness, pain, and ability to sleep, to work or practice a hobby, and to go for a walk. They concluded that the pouch operation was better than the straight oesophagojejunostomy but, of even greater importance, that patients whose operation was palliative (those who died of the cancer in less than a year) never regained their preoperative quality of life. It is possible that these patients should not have been submitted to such a radical operation as total gastrectomy.

The treatment of end stage renal failure by chronic dialysis or renal transplantation depends more on the supply of kidneys than on anything else, renal transplantation being much more cost effective than dialysis. A multicentre study (Evans *et al.*, 1985) of 859 patients undergoing dialysis or transplantation reported significantly better quality of life after transplantation than with dialysis, in spite of the necessity for immunosuppression and frequent monitoring.

Long term backache is common after childbirth, and 1132 (10%) of 11 701 women who had been delivered in a maternity hospital in Birmingham had had it for over a year (MacArthur *et al.*, 1990). There was a significant association with epidural anaesthesia: nearly twice as many women who had had epidural anaesthesia during labour had long term backache as women who had had other forms of anaesthesia.

Measurement of pain

Pain cannot be assessed accurately and analysed statistically until it is given numerical values. The simplest measure of pain is the linear analogue scale, marked at one end 'no pain' and at the other 'the worst pain imaginable'. This system, however, does not distinguish the presence of pain from the psychological reactions to that pain (fear, anxiety, and so on). Melzack (1975) separated the sensory qualities of pain from the affective and evaluative qualities. He introduced the McGill Pain Questionnaire, comprising 20 descriptions of pain and five degrees of pain in each description. The system has been widely used, but it does require an interviewer to interpret the categories to patients.

Scores that measure physical, psychological, and social health

These scores are by their very nature subjective, but many of them have been validated by seeking intraobserver and interobserver variations. They are related to impairment and disability, and they all test the quality of life (McDowell and Newell, 1987). Most of them are questionnaires, which can either be self-administered, or they may require that subjects be interviewed. A few require the direct observation of people.

Karnofsky scale

This was one of the earliest attempts to evaluate the quality of life after an intervention. Karnofsky and Burchenal (1948) recognised that the outcome of the treatment of cancer with chemotherapeutic drugs should be judged not only by objective measurements such as the dimensions of the tumour, but also by the well-being of the patient. They put forward a 10-point scale, graded from worst (score 1) to best (score 10):

1. Moribund.
2. Very ill; admission to hospital for treatment needed.
3. Severely disabled; spends a lot of time in hospital.
4. Disabled; needs special care most of the time.
5. Needs a lot of assistance and frequent medical care.
6. Needs occasional help, but can usually cope.
7. Can care for self but cannot carry on normal activities.
8. Has some symptoms and normal activity is an effort.
9. Has some symptoms but can carry on normal activities.
10. Has no complaints.

Visick score

This was also published in 1948 (Visick, 1948).It measures the quality of life after gastric operations. It is graded from I to IV. Grade I is given patients who have no gastric symptoms apart from 'fullness after extra large meals'. Grade II is applied when the patient has 'no pain, and mild occasional symptoms only, easily controlled by care; care includes rest, limitations of size of meal, and rejection of certain articles of diet'. Grade III implies 'mild symptoms not controlled by care. This grade is subdivided into IIIs (satisfactory) and IIIu (unsatisfactory)'. Grade IV comprises patients who are 'not improved'. Visick wrote:

'it is almost impossible to convey in statistical tables a true picture of our own conception of a "satisfactory" or an "unsatisfactory" result. This can only be gained by visiting the follow-up clinic. Figures alone are never so convincing as the practical demonstration, and no written word can compare with the dramatic sincerity and entertaining expressions with which the patients describe their feelings'.

Katz's index of independence in activities of daily living

Katz first introduced the index in 1959 (Katz *et al.*, 1963). It is generally abbreviated to ADL, and depends on a simple questionnaire. It is still valid over a wide range of diseases and disabilities. It examines the independence of patients in feeding, continence, transferring (getting out of bed), going to toilet, dressing, and bathing, and grades them from A (independent in all functions) to G (dependent in all functions). The index has been widely used and has formed the background for numerous other scales that have examined the activities of daily living, the most widely used of which is the Barthel index.

Barthel index

This was developed by Mahoney and Barthel (1965) and is limited to measuring physical activities in patients in institutions; it does not take psychological or social factors into account. The score can be compiled rapidly by a non-medical observer and covers nine aspects of daily activity:

- Feeding
- Ability to get from bed to chair
- Ability to wash or shave or put on make-up
- Ability to get on and off the toilet
- Ability to take a bath
- Ability to walk on a level surface
- Ability to walk up and down stairs
- Ability to dress
- Continence.

Each activity is scored and a total is calculated from 0 (totally dependent) to 100 (fully independent).

Sickness impact profile (SIP)

This emphasises dysfunction related to illness (Bergner *et al.*, 1976). The questionnaire can be filled in by the patient or by an observer; it is rather long and repetitive, but it is sensitive to change and is therefore valuable in the assessment of chronic illness. There are 136 questions concerning dysfunction in 12 areas: work, recreation, emotion, affect, home life, sleep, rest, eating, walking, mobility, and social interaction (Bowling, 1991). A score from 0 (healthy) to 100 (severely handicapped) is calculated, but the scores tend to be skewed toward the lower end, and few patients – however severely handicapped – score more than 30.

Nottingham health profile

This differs from the sickness impact profile in that it was developed with the help of lay people, and is couched in lay terms (Hunt, McEwen and McKenna, 1986). It is particularly useful in assessing patients' estimation of their improvement (or lack of it) after operations. It is self-administered and comprises statements about physical mobility, pain, sleep, energy, social isolation, and emotional reactions. For example, under physical mobility there are eight statements ranging from 'I find it hard to reach for things' to 'I'm unable to walk at all.' There are eight statements about pain, ranging from 'I'm in pain when going up or down stairs or steps' to 'I'm in constant pain'. The five statements about sleep range from 'I'm waking up in the early hours of the morning' to 'I lie awake for most of the night'. The three statements about energy are 'I soon run out of energy', 'Everything is an effort', and 'I'm tired all the time'. The five statements about social isolation range from 'I find it difficult to get on with people' to 'I feel I am a burden to people', and the nine statements about emotional reactions range from 'The days seem to drag' to 'I feel that life is not worth living'. Each statement is given a numerical weight and the total score reflects the subject's perceived quality of life.

Quality of life (QL) index

This index was devised by Spitzer *et al.* (1981). It is derived from a questionnaire that is divided into five sections – the ability of the patient to work, to take care of himself, to interact with friends and the family, and to perceive his own health as good or bad; finally a section is devoted to rating the patient's mood. The index varies from 0 to 10, and is accompanied by a visual analogue scale that summarises the overall quality of life. It is a simple and quick test that was originally applied to patients with cancer but has subsequently been validated for other diseases and disabilities and in many countries and languages.

Quality adjusted life years

The Rosser (Kind, Rosser and Williams, 1982) scale depends on allocating a letter from A to D for degree of distress and a Roman number from I to VIII for degree of disability. It has been applied on both sides of the Atlantic mainly in the field of health care economics and the cost of quality adjusted life years (QALYs) has been calculated for various diseases and interventions. One of the problems associated with this work is that the long term outlook after many interventions is unknown, and the figures attached to QALYs are at best conjectural.

Reintegration to normal living index

Wood-Dauphinee and Williams (1987) introduced this index. It can best be summed up by the single phrase 'return to autonomy'; the questionnaire seeks information about patients' mobility with or without external aids like wheelchairs, ability to look after themselves with or without special equipment or assistance, ability to perform useful and recreational activities, ability to take part in social and family activities, and general perception by the patients that they are autonomous.

   A patient's reintegration after a devastating injury or disease depends on the patient's own determination and personality as much as on any intervention. Quality of life as an end point in surgical audit and research can, therefore, be used only as a guide, and not to to give an accurate assessment of individual patients.

Scales to assess psychological wellbeing

These scales, usually administered by questionnaire, derive from the health opinion survey, which was first used in 1951 and published in 1957 (McDowell and Newell, 1987). One of the most popular derivatives is the general health questionnaire in either its original 60-question format, or in abbreviated versions that enquire into somatic symptoms, anxiety and insomnia, social dysfunction, and severe depression.

Scales to measure social health

These are of two types: social adjustment scales and measurements of social support. One of the best validated is Weissman's social adjustment scale. This is derived from a questionnaire containing 42 questions covering work, leisure activities, and relationships with the extended family, with the spouse, parents, and members of the family unit.

Conclusions

Audit of the quality of life after surgical treatment tends to be neglected by surgeons; it is, however, just as important as audit of morbidity and mortality. Unless our treatments improve the quality of life we are probably doing our patients more good by not operating on them.

References

Bates, T., Ebbs, S.R., Harrison, M. and A'Hern, R.P. (1991) Influence of cholecystectomy on symptoms. *British Journal of Surgery*, **78**, 964–967

Bergner, M., Bobbitt, R.A., Pollard, W.E. *et al.* (1976) The sickness impact profile: validation of a health status measure. *Medical Care*, **14**, 57–67

Bowling, A. (1991) *Measuring Health. A review of quality of life measurement scales.* Open University Press, Milton Keynes, p. 60

Evans, R.W., Manninen, D.L., Garrison, L.P. *et al.* (1985) The quality of life of patients with end-stage renal disease. *New England Journal of Medicine*, **312**, 553–559

Evans, R.W. (1991) Quality of life. *Lancet*, **338**, 636

Hunt, S.M., McEwen, J. and McKenna, S.P. (1986) *Measuring Health Status.* Croom Helm, London

Karnofsky, D.A., Abelman, W.H., Craver, L.F. and Burchenal, J.H. (1948) The use of nitrogen mustards in the palliative treatment of carcinoma. *Cancer*, **1**, 634–656

Katz, S., Ford, A.B., Moskowitz, R.W. *et al.* (1963) Studies of illness in the aged. *Journal of the American Medical Association*, **185**, 914–919

Kind, P., Rosser, R. and Williams, A. (1982) Valuation of quality of life: some psychometric evidence. In *The Value of Life and Safety*, edited by M.W. Jones-Lee. North Holland, Amsterdam

Lasry, J-C.L., Margolese, R.G., Poisson, R. *et al.* (1987) Depression and body image following mastectomy and lumpectomy. *Journal of Chronic Diseases*, **40**, 529–534

MacArthur, C., Lewis, M., Knox, E.G. and Crawford, J.S. (1990. Epidural anaesthesia and long term backache after childbirth. *British Medical Journal*, **301**, 9–12

McDowell, I. and Newell, C. (1987) *Measuring Health: a guide to rating scales and question-naires*. Oxford University Press, Oxford

Mahoney, F.I. and Barthel, D.W. (1965) Functional evaluation: the Barthel index. *Maryland State Medical Journal*, **14**, 61–65

Melzack, R. (1975) The McGill Pain Questionnaire: major properties and scoring methods. *Pain*, **1**, 277–299

Spitzer, W.O., Dobson, A.J., Hall, J. *et al.* (1981) Measuring the quality of life in cancer patients. A concise QL-Index for use by physicians. *Journal of Chronic Diseases*, **34**, 585–597

Spitzer, W.O. (1987) State of science 1986: quality of life and functional status as target variables for research. *Journal of Chronic Diseases*, **40**, 465–471

Streiner, D.L. and Norman, G.R. (1989) *Health Measurement Scales. A practical guide to their development and use*. Oxford University Press, Oxford

Troidl, H., Kusche, J., Vestweber, K-H., Eypasch, E. and Maul, U. (1987) Pouch versus esophagojejunostomy after total gastrectomy: a randomized clinical trial. *World Journal of Surgery*, **11**, 699–712

Visick, A.H. (1948) Measured radical gastrectomy. Review of 505 operations for peptic ulcer. *Lancet*, **i**, 505–508

Williams, J.I. (1991) Strategies for quality of life assessment – a methodologist's view. *Theoretical Surgery*, **6**, 152–157

Williams, N.S. and Johnston, D. (1983) The quality of life after rectal excision for low rectal cancer. *British Journal of Surgery*, **70**, 460–462

Wood-Dauphinee, S. and Williams, J.I. (1987) Reintegration to normal living as a proxy to quality of life. *Journal of Chronic Diseases*, **40**, 491–499

Chapter 17

Mishap and malpractice

They have not the courage to correct, because they have not the courage to stand correction.   Montaigne (1580)

It is all my fault, gentlemen, it is all my fault.   Robert E. Lee (1863)

McQuade (1991), who is a lawyer in North Carolina, laid down six principles concerning compensation for medical injuries:

- Injured people should be compensated
- Money should be available to compensate as many injured people as necessary
- Compensation costs should not unreasonably affect the cost and availability of medical treatment
- Competent and capable people should not be discouraged from entering the practice of medicine
- Competent and conscientious doctors should be allowed quiet enjoyment of their profession
- Incompetent or impaired doctors should be identified and removed from practice, or retrained and rehabilitated.

In 1991 the Medical Protection Society in Britain recommended that the government should consider a pilot scheme for the compensation of brain-impaired infants, irrespective of the aetiology of their condition. This arose out of the uncertainty about whether damage to the brain of an infant has arisen because of obstetric errors or from natural causes. Equity demands that such a child should be supported financially without having to prove negligence on the part of an obstetrician or paediatrician. This is rather a grey area. Some would argue that it is no more right to support a child with cerebral palsy than one with, say, spina bifida.

Battery and negligence

In nearly all countries there are two allegations that, if substantiated, result in injured patients being compensated. They are battery and negligence. In addition, if a patient has entered into a contract with a doctor for treatment that the doctor has promised will have a certain outcome, and that outcome does not eventuate, the patient may have a right to sue for breach of contract. This is rare.

Battery (sometimes erroneously confused with assault) is the touching of a person without his or her consent. It is a criminal offence, the civil law equivalent being 'trespass to the person'. It is rarely invoked as the cause of a claim, because only if consent was obtained by fraud or misrepresentation can it be said that it was not true consent. Negligence, on the other hand, can be claimed not only in the performance of an operation (or indeed in the preoperative or postoperative care or the prescription of a drug), but also in the failure of the doctor to warn the patient sufficiently about the risks associated with the treatment that has been recommended, accepted, and carried out.

In the United States some monstrously unjust claims have succeeded. Bernard Levin (1988) quoted several such cases, including that of a Mr Febesh, who was sitting outdoors at his country club in New York State when he was stung by a wasp and suffered a severe anaphylactic reaction. He sued the club and was awarded $1.5 million in damages.

Medical negligence no defence against charge of murder

In the case of *R v Smith (1959 2 All ER 193)* a man's appeal against a conviction for murder was dismissed (Brahams, 1991a). The facts were that a soldier received a bayonet wound to his arm and back in a barrack room brawl, the wound in the back piercing a lung. He was taken to the reception room where he was inadequately treated and died two hours later. Lord Parker CJ stated that 'If at the time of death the original wound is still an operating cause and a substantial cause, then the death can properly be said to be the result of the wound .... Only if it can be said that the original wound is merely the setting in which another cause operates can it be said that death does not result from the wound'.

In 1991 the Court of Appeal in *R v Cheshire* dismissed an appeal from a verdict of guilty of an assailant who had shot a man in the leg and stomach. His victim died two months later of respiratory arrest caused by tracheal stenosis at the site of a tracheostomy. The appeal judge concluded that even though negligent treatment was the immediate cause of the victim's death, that death was caused by the assailant.

Error of judgement or negligence?

When does an error of judgement achieve the status of negligence? Lord Denning concluded that errors of judgement do not necessarily equal negligence, and that 'if doctors were to be found liable whenever they did not effect a cure or whenever something happened to go wrong, it would be a great disservice not only to the profession itself but to society at large' (Lister, 1980).

In England the distinction between errors and negligence was laid down by the highest court in the land. This was in the case of *Whitehouse v*

Jordan in the House of Lords (reported in [1981] 1 All ER at page 267). The relevant judgment is summarised in the following terms:

'To say that a surgeon has committed an error of clinical judgement is wholly ambiguous and does not indicate whether he has been negligent, for while some areas of clinical judgement may be completely consistent with the due exercise of professional skill, other acts or omissions in the course of exercising clinical judgement may be so glaringly below proper standards as to make a finding of negligence inevitable. The test whether a surgeon has been negligent is whether he has failed to measure up in any respect, whether in clinical judgement or otherwise, to the standard of the ordinary skilled surgeon exercising and professing to have the special skill of a surgeon [the Bolam test].'

Three Law Lords added to this statement.
Lord Edmund Davies said:

'...doctors and surgeons fall into no special category and, to avoid any future disputation of a similar kind, I would have it accepted that the true doctrine was enunciated, and by no means for the first time, by McNair J in *Bolam v Friern Barnet Hospital Management Committee* [1957] 2 All ER page 118 in the following words: "...Where you get a situation which involves the use of some special skill or competence, then the test as to whether there has been negligence or not is not the test of the man on the top of a Clapham omnibus because he has not got this special skill. The test is the standard of the ordinary skilled man exercising and professing to have that special skill." If a surgeon fails to measure up to that standard in any respect (clinical judgement or otherwise), he has been negligent and should be so adjudged.'

Lord Fraser of Tullybelton said:

'Merely to describe something as an error of judgement tells us nothing about whether it is negligent or not. The true position is that an error of judgement may, or may not, be negligent; it depends on the nature of the error. If it is one that would not have been made by a reasonably competent professional man professing to have the standard and type of skill that the defendant holds himself out as having, and acting with ordinary care, then it is negligent. If, on the other hand, it is an error that a man, acting with ordinary care, might have made, then it is not negligence.'

Finally, Lord Russell of Killowen said:

'My Lords, I wish at the outset to emphasise one matter. Some passages in the Court of Appeal might suggest that if a doctor makes an error of judgement he cannot be found guilty of negligence. This must be wrong. An error of judgement is not per se incompatible with negligence, as Donaldson LJ pointed out. I would accept the phrase "a mere error of judgement" if the impact of the word "mere" is to indicate that not all errors of judgement show a lapse from the standard of skill and care required to be exercised to avoid a charge of negligence.'

What it all means is that you can get it wrong without being negligent if it is an error that a responsible body of the specialty might have made.

Negligence or recklessness?

In 1991 the medical establishment in Britain was shocked to read of the conviction on a charge of manslaughter of two young doctors (Dyer, 1991). The story is that Malcolm Savage was 16 years old when he died as a result of an injection of vincristine given intrathecally instead of intravenously. He had had leukaemia since the age of four, and Drs Barry Sullman aged 27 and Michael Prentice aged 25, both junior medical officers at Peterborough General Hospital, mistakenly injected vincristine instead of methotrexate intrathecally. The judge directed the jury that if they found that the doctors had acted recklessly rather than negligently they were entitled to find them guilty of manslaughter. A person was guilty of recklessness if he took a risk when he knew of the harm that could arise, and also if he gave no thought to the possibility of such a risk. The case is to go to appeal, but the real lesson is that these young doctors were not sufficiently trained or supervised.

Incidence of medical accidents

There is almost universal ignorance (or concealment) of the incidence of medical accidents. A study in California in 1974 reported that 140 000 (4.7%) iatrogenic injuries arose in association with 3 million operations and that 24 000 (0.08%) of these could be attributed to negligence (Vincent, 1989). The Harvard Medical Practice Study (1990) looked at 30 121 records of admissions in 51 hospitals in New York State in 1984 and found 1133 (3.8%) adverse events arising from medical mismanagement, of which a quarter were judged to be caused by negligence, but only about one in 10 of these resulted in litigation.

There are remarkably few other reports of mishaps, notable exceptions being the inquiries into maternal deaths and the Confidential Enquiry into Perioperative Deaths (see Chapter 14). No system of audit is going to fulfil its proper function if medical mishaps are not fully documented and an attempt made to find out why they happened.

An analysis of 5612 surgical patients admitted to the Peter Bent Brigham Hospital in Boston, Massachusetts, showed that 1% suffered iatrogenic injuries, nearly all because of 'unnecessary, contraindicated, or technically defective surgical activity' (Couch et al., 1981). In a previous publication (Couch, Tilney and Moore, 1978) these authors reported 16 surgical disasters arising from one of three errors: failure to recognise and treat peritonitis of colonic origin; failure to provide proximal colonic diversion in the presence of a precarious anastomosis or at the time of leakage from a colonic anastomosis; and doing a colostomy so badly that it retracted and caused sepsis. 'It seems,' they wrote, 'that among the most common errors in colonic surgery, as typified by the above cases, are those that arise from unwarranted confidence in colonic anastomoses and misplaced optimism when postoperative sepsis occurs.' They commented that the reporting of 'critical incidents' for the National Surgical Study in the United States was 'crippled in several hospitals because of a reluctance to disclose adverse results' and concluded: 'it would be a tragic irony if the current epidemic of malpractice lawsuits brought quiet concealment of unfavorable results, so that medical progress is impeded rather than promoted'.

The growth of malpractice claims can lead to refusal by doctors to take part in audit, refusal to ask for necropsies, overinvestigation of patients, refusal by surgeons to operate on high risk patients or patients whom they perceive might be litigious, slowing down of throughput resulting in increasing waiting lists, and impoverishment of health authorities (Black, 1990).

The problems associated with litigation for alleged negligence are not confined to the medical profession. Solicitors, barristers, accountants, architects, engineers, and surveyors all face similar dilemmas, and the professional indemnity insurance market is in chaos. Many professionals are refusing to take on work that may entail claims for negligence, and some solicitors, particularly in Scotland, have formed themselves into limited liability companies so that a successful claim cannot force an individual, or all the partners in a practice, into bankruptcy.

Insurance by doctors against malpractice claims

In the United States and many other countries this is a purely commercial affair and premiums are adjusted to take account of risks. In Britain all doctors working in the National Health Service are obliged to belong to one of the organisations that are not insurance companies, but do arrange reinsurance through commercial channels. The first to be established was the Medical Defence Union, founded in 1885 by Charles Rideal and six other men, none of whom was a doctor (Hawkins, 1987). It would have foundered but for the appointment two years later of the surgeon Lawson Tait as president, a post he held until his death at the age of 54 of a kidney disease. The main functions of the Union, of the Medical Protection Society founded in 1892, and of the Medical and Dental Defence Union of Scotland were at first not the protection of doctors against claims for damages but the prosecution of unqualified practitioners and the defence of doctors against criminal charges.

Annual reports are published by both the Medical Defence Union and the Medical Protection Society and are useful reminders to all doctors of the pitfalls that they may so easily encounter themselves. The Medical Defence Union reports have been produced since 1888. In 1894 there were only five cases of alleged negligence among the 100 cases reported, but since 1927 they have made up the bulk of the cases.

Why has litigation against doctors increased?

There has been an exponential increase in the number of law suits alleging medical and surgical malpractice in the last 50 years, both in Britain and the United States. Obstetricians, neonatologists, and neurosurgeons are most at risk of being sued in the United States, whereas plastic and cosmetic surgeons are probably the biggest risk category in Britain. The annual insurance premium for a neurosurgeon in New York exceeds $100 000. The position is not as critical in Britain, and this is reflected in the annual subscription to the defence societies, which was just over £1000 ($1700) in 1988, and has since been reduced as a result of the National Health Service taking over responsibility for settling claims for malpractice (negligence) against doctors in its employ.

The chances of successful litigation in cases in which there was indeed medical negligence has been estimated to be between 10% and 25%. The fact is that most doctors do something wrong every day. Patients seldom suffer permanent injury from these deviations from ideal practice, but even if they do their chances of compensation are less than 50%. Many people who have suffered a mishap have no desire for financial compensation. What they want is to know precisely what happened and why, and that every effort will be made to see that no one else suffers in a similar way. In Britain a charity called Action for Victims of Medical Accidents was formed by Arnold Simanowitz, who said:

> 'The complaints machinery with its five separate channels is needlessly complex. The delay in processing claims is a disgrace. Doctors need to appreciate that it is not money that most patients are after but an explanation, an apology, reassurance that those concerned will be called to account, and steps taken to ensure that the same "mistake" does not happen again' (Richards, 1989).

The escalation in claims alleging medical malpractice has occurred for several reasons (McQuade, 1991). Firstly, the public has come more and more to the conclusion that if something goes wrong, somebody must be to blame; people's expectations of a perfect outcome from every intervention have been fuelled by the media (particularly by television soap operas that show perfect facial reconstructions), and by the technological advances of the last half century.

Secondly, more and more lawyers are making a good living out of medical malpractice litigation. It is sometimes thought that the contingency fee system in the United States – a lawyer will take on a case without payment, but takes half the award if the case is won – has been partly responsible for the fact that 2 million suits are filed there every year. On the other hand, an American lawyer is not going to waste his time on a claim that has no foundation, or one that he anticipates will attract damages of less than $100 000. It has been estimated that no more than 15% of all potential claimants are taken on.

The third reason for the escalation of claims in the United States is the emergence of the professional medical expert witness. There are now estimated to be 3000 doctors practising as legal consultants for plaintiffs at fees of $3000 to $5000 per day plus expenses (Quam, Fenn and Dingwall, 1987).

The fourth cause of the rapid growth in malpractice claims in both the USA and in Britain is the only one that doctors can control directly – it is that there are some careless or incompetent doctors, doctors who fail to keep good records, and doctors who are impaired by illness or drug abuse and they are no longer getting away with it. A study from Florida reported that 85% of payments to settle claims for malpractice were made on behalf of 3% of doctors (Sloan, 1989). The public is nothing like as gullible in medical matters as it was 50 years ago. People in the USA are fed publications by organisations such as the Health Research Group, headed by Dr Sidney Wolfe, which reports questionable activities by doctors and drug companies and produces a monthly Health Letter containing the Outrage of the Month.

There are some actions that betray such carelessness that a claim for negligence is bound to succeed. The law of *res ipsa loquitur* was laid down in the seventeenth century and covers such actions as operating on the wrong person or the wrong digit. It also applies to leaving a swab or an instrument in the abdomen inadvertently. These actions cannot be defended and claims are normally settled out of court.

Financial disincentives to litigation in Britain

In Britain there is no contingency fee system, and there are only two ways of pursuing a claim for malpractice. The first is to take the risk that the claim will be successful and be prepared to pay the lawyers whether it is successful or not, and the second is to apply for legal aid. Equity demands that litigation should be made affordable both to the litigant and to the taxpayer. Between 1985 and 1990 the gross spending by the legal aid fund rose from £70 million a year to £153 million, and the office of the Lord Chancellor issued a consultation paper in 1991, suggesting that there should be a 'safety net', so that people could start legal claims privately, but if the costs exceeded a certain sum (depending on the claimant's means) they would be entitled to claim legal aid.

Legal aid is available without charge to people whose disposable income (in 1991) is less than £2860 a year (increased to between £5000 and £7000 for a person with a spouse and dependent children), and whose disposable capital – not including the house they live in – is less than £3000. If the disposable income is between £2860 and £7000, or the disposable capital is between £3000 and £8000 the claimant will have to pay a contribution up to one quarter of the difference between the income and £2860. If the disposable income is more than £7000 (or £11 000 if the person has a family), or the disposable capital is more than £8000 there is no entitlement to legal aid. If the claim is successful, the claimant will have to repay money paid to the lawyers by the legal aid fund. If, on the other hand, it is unsuccessful, the defendant doctor will not be able to recover his exper.

Not   ryers are willing to take on legal aid cases because the hourly rate is   2, which many lawyers regard as paltry.

What is to be done about malpractice litigation?

Hawkins and Paterson (1987) studied 100 files taken at random from those of 324 medicolegal cases against hospitals in the West Midlands. At the end of three years, 73 actions had been withdrawn, 12 were settled out of court, one was lost by the plaintiff, and 14 were pending. They made a plea for the presence of a medical expert on legal aid panels and commented that this would save public money as legal aid is so often provided for fruitless cases.

In June 1988 the Civil Justice Review was published in England (Dyer, 1988). The purpose of this review is to reduce costs, delays, and complexities attending actions for damages. The key proposal is that documents, opinions, and reports by expert witnesses should be exchanged between plaintiff and defendant as soon as possible after the issue of a writ and that opposing experts should consult and issue a joint statement of points of agreement and disagreement.

A Citizen Action Compensation Campaign has been set up under the presidency of Lord Scarman (Gibb, 1988). Lord Scarman said: 'There must be law reform so that people who suffer personal injury as a result of personal accidents in our high-risk society should be able to get fair and prompt compensation at reasonable cost.' The campaign wants judicial inquiries after cases such as that involving the drug Opren, it wants to introduce class actions so that groups of victims can seek compensation jointly, and finally it wants a reappraisal of the contingency fee system of payment of lawyers in compensation cases.

Risk management

Nearly all major claims for damages arising out of alleged malpractice concern hospital treatment, and many hospitals in the USA have established departments that have two aims: to reduce the number of incidents that might lead to litigation, and to reduce the number and cost of claims by improving communications between health care workers and patients (Morlock, Lindgren and Mills, 1989). The process of risk management starts with the obligatory reporting of 'adverse incidents' by doctors and other workers, continues with the sympathetic handling of dissatisfied patients, and ends with diffusion of details of the incident (omitting names of doctors and patients) to the entire staff of the hospital. If a doctor is responsible for several incidents, particularly if they are all connected with the same activity, the risk managers can require that that doctor should attend courses; if the incidents are repeated, the doctor's credentials for working at that hospital can be withdrawn.

In Britain the Medical Defence Union laid down four components of risk management (Dingwall, 1991):

- Systematic identification of risks, whether by internal initiatives (reporting of incidents or perusal of casenotes), or by external means (examination of patients' complaints and claims for negligence)
- Prevention of adverse incidents by imposition of clinical protocols, changes in structure, and continuing education

- Minimisation of claims by rapid and sympathetic reactions to adverse outcomes of treatment
- Prompt collection of evidence and decisions about the validity of claims, so that they can be settled or refuted without delay.

Tort reform in the USA

Tort reform Bills have been passed in some states in the past 15 years. The principal provisions of these Bills are that counter suits would be allowed, that contingency fees were to be limited, that damages for pain and suffering be abolished or limited, that punitive damages be abolished, that untrue allegations be withdrawn, and that expert witnesses practise at least 75% of their time in the speciality that is the subject of litigation. Many have required that there shall be no notification of the quantum of damages sought, so as to reduce the newsworthiness of the claim. Some states require a sworn statement from a qualified medical practitioner that a plaintiff's injuries were caused by negligence before an action can be started. The period between the discovery of an injury and the start of an action has been shortened in some states. A clause requiring pretrial screening panels was declared unconstitutional in some states and was dropped.

Alternative dispute resolution in the USA

ADR proposals are attracting a good deal of attention. In their pure form they comprise a panel of three lawyers – one from the plaintiff's side, one from the defendant's, and one who is neutral. They weigh up all the evidence and decide both the existence of negligence and the amount of the damages. Either party is entitled to refuse the award and elect for trial by jury, but this happens in only about 5% of cases.

Consent

Judge Robins in Ontario (*Malette v Shulman. Supreme Court of Ontario, Court of Appeal: Robins, Catzman, and Carthy JJA, March 30 1990*) confirmed that:

> 'Patients have the decisive role in the medical decision-making process. Their right of self-determination is recognised and protected by law...it is the patient who has the final say on whether to undergo the treatment...regardless of how unwise or foolish those choices may appear to others.'

The court awarded $Can 20 000 damages to a Jehovah's Witness who carried a card forbidding blood transfusion and was given a life-saving blood transfusion while unconscious.

The law governing consent to treatment differs somewhat between the United States and Britain. In America some of the States have adopted the 'prudent patient' test, while others have been content to continue with the 'reasonable doctor' approach to the disclosure of risks. The 'prudent patient' test was laid down by the United States Court of Appeals in 1972 in the decision in the *Canterbury v Spence* case. Four propositions were enunciated.

1. The root premise is the concept that every human being of adult years and of sound mind has a right to determine what shall be done with his own body.
2. The consent is the informed exercise of a choice, and that entails an opportunity to evaluate knowledgeably the options available and the risks attendant on each.
3. The doctor must, therefore, disclose all 'material risks'; what risks are 'material' is determined by the 'prudent patient' test, which was formulated by the court (464 F 2d 772 at 787): 'A risk...is material when a reasonable person, in what the physician knows or should know to be the patient's position, would be likely to attach significance to the risk or cluster of risks in deciding whether or not to forgo the proposed therapy.'
4. The doctor, however, has what the court called a 'therapeutic privilege'. This exception enables a doctor to withhold from his patient information as to risk if it can be shown that a reasonable medical assessment of the patient would have indicated to the doctor that disclosure would have posed a serious threat of psychological detriment to the patient.

In Massachusetts a jury awarded damages of $1 million to a plaintiff for whom prednisone had been prescribed after an operation to remove a piece of metal from his eye, and who suffered aseptic necrosis of both hips three years later (Curran, 1986). On appeal to the Massachusetts Supreme Judicial Court the verdict was overturned, because of the extreme rarity of such a complication of prednisone treatment. Justice O'Connor concluded that the likelihood of the complication was 'negligible' and that there was no onus on the eye surgeon to inform the patient of the possibility.

The 'reasonable doctor' approach is accepted on both sides of the Atlantic as applied to errors of diagnosis and treatment. Negligence may, however, be alleged for not disclosing the risks of an operation or other intervention. In England the matter was put to the legal test in 1957 in the case of *Bolam v Friern Barnet Hospital Management Committee*. This case was heard by Mr Justice McNair and a jury. The plaintiff, a voluntary patient in the defendants' mental hospital, sustained fractures in the course of electroconvulsive treatment and claimed damages, alleging negligence in (1) failing to administer a relaxant drug before treatment, (2) failing to provide manual restraint during treatment, and (3) failing to warn him of the risks involved in the treatment. The judge directed the jury that a doctor is not guilty of negligence if he acts 'in accordance with a practice accepted as proper by a responsible body of medical men skilled in that particular art'. This means that the law imposes a duty of care, but the standard of care is a matter of medical judgement. The claim was dismissed.

The Bolam test has been used in other cases involving the disclosure or non-disclosure of risks. One case (*Sidaway v Bethlem Royal Hospital Governors and others*) eventually reached the House of Lords (1985 1 All ER 643–666). The plaintiff, Mrs Amy Sidaway, accepted an operation on her neck (a laminectomy of C4 and a facetectomy or foraminectomy of the C4–5 disc space) for the relief of pain in both arms. Spinal cord damage, presumably caused by interference with the blood supply, resulted in permanent disability. No claim was made that the operation was negligently performed, but Mrs Sidaway claimed that she would not have undergone the operation if she had been informed about the risk, estimated by expert witnesses at between 1 and 2%. Her claim was dismissed and Mrs Sidaway appealed. In the Court of Appeal the claim was again dismissed, but Sir John Donaldson, the Master of the Rolls, elaborated on the Bolam criterion by adding the word 'rightly'. 'The duty is fulfilled' he said 'if the doctor acts in accordance with a practice *rightly* accepted as proper by a body of skilled and experienced medical men' (Legal correspondent, 1984). The Law Lords (Lord Scarman, Lord Diplock, Lord Keith of Kinkel, Lord Bridge of Harwich, and Lord Templeman) also dismissed the claim, adding a proviso that the disclosure of a particular risk of serious adverse consequences might be so obviously necessary for the patient to make an informed choice that no reasonably prudent doctor would fail to disclose that risk.

The alternative approach to the question of when it is not legally incumbent on the surgeon to warn a patient of all the risks of an operation (the 'prudent patient' test) was applied in the case in England of *Sharon Smith v Barking, Havering, and Brentwood Health Authority* (Cowley, 1989). At the age of 9 years Sharon had an operation to drain a cyst of the cervical cord. Symptoms returned nine years later and all her limbs became weak. A further operation was suggested, to which she agreed, but unfortunately the operation was followed by immediate and permanent quadriplegia. She sued the surgeon, claiming that if she had been properly informed about the risks she would not have consented to the operation. The trial judge, however, applied the 'prudent patient' test, saying: 'Reflection on what she was told would have let a reasonable patient to say to herself: "Well, it seems I'm going to be paralysed anyway in a very short time. This operation gives me a reasonable chance of avoiding that condition perhaps for a few years. True, there is a real risk that the operation will not be successful and I'll then be paralysed even sooner, but the possible benefits clearly outweigh the possible detriment and the chance is one well worth taking."'

Consent by proxy

It is customary for the parents or guardian of a child under the age of 16 years or of a mentally incapable adult to give or withhold consent to investigation and treatment on behalf of the patient, although that consent or refusal of consent is not valid if the intervention (or failure of intervention) is not for the good of the patient. What constitutes the good of the patient must often be decided not by doctors but by the courts. In the

Supreme Court of British Columbia in the case of *Re Superintendent of Family & Child Service and Dawson, 1983:145 DLR (3d) 610* Judge McKenzie said:

> 'I do not think that it lies within the prerogative of any parent or of this court to lay down upon a disadvantaged person and judge the quality of that person's life to be so low as not to be deserving of continuance'.

In the Court of Appeal in London in October 1990 Lord Donaldson of Lymington, Master of the Rolls, and Lords Justices Balcombe and Taylor, *In re J (a Minor) (wardship: Medical Treatment)   The Times* Law Report October 23 1990 – approved:

> 'the continuance of treatment in respect of J within the parameters of a medical report advising that in the event of his requiring further resuscitation it would not be in his best interests to do so by a ventilation machine unless that course seemed appropriate to the doctors caring for him in the prevailing clinical situation.'

The history of J was that he was born very prematurely at 27 weeks, weighing only 1.1 kg; he was placed on a ventilator for four months and suffered convulsions. When he was weaned off the ventilator it was apparent that he was blind and deaf and quadriplegic, but could still feel pain. The doctors asked the court to endorse their opinion that further artificial ventilation should not be undertaken.

In the case of *Gillick v West Norfolk and Wisbech Area Health Authority* it was held that:

> 'Children under the age of 16 may legally consent to medical treatment provided they have the intelligence and maturity to make up their own minds and have achieved a sufficient understanding and intelligence to understand fully what is proposed'(Brahams, 1991b).

This concept of 'Gillick competence' was applied in the 1991 case of *In re R (A Minor, Medical Treatment)*. A 15-year-old girl who had been made a ward of court and who had a serious psychiatric disorder refused treatment, but the Court of Appeal ordered that she should have the treatment because she was not at all times sufficiently intelligent and mature to be able to make up her own mind.

Three Appeal Court judges in England ruled that the common law will not penalise doctors who carry out treatment that is in the best interests of the patient when the patient is either unconscious or too mentally impaired to give valid consent. Their judgement arose out of the perceived necessity to sterilise a sexually active woman aged 36 years whose mental age was 5 (Dyer, 1989).

In England, as opposed to a number of other developed countries, there is no statutory power that allows anyone, be they doctors, relatives, or even courts of law to take decisions on treatment for mentally incompetent patients, whether they be mentally handicapped, mentally ill, or brain damaged. Indeed it has never been decided how impaired a mentally impaired person has to be before he or she is deemed incapable of making decisions about treatment. The Law Commission (1991) has issued a consultation paper, which calls for suggestions for amending the law to allow guardians of mentally impaired people to take decisions about treatment; the most feasible method might be for the guardian together with two doctors to make the decision and, if there were disagreement, to call in the services of an ethics committee.

In Scotland, on the other hand, there is a useful device which has recently been used more frequently for making decisions about mentally incapacitated patients. The Court of Sessions can answer a petition by appointing a *tutor dative*, who is empowered to make decisions relating to a person's welfare, and this could include medical treatment (Jennett and Dyer, 1991).

There have been occasions both in the United States and in Britain when a patient's or parent's refusal of consent has been overruled by a court of law. This happened in Britain some years ago when a child of parents who were Jehovah's Witnesses was made a ward of court and given a blood transfusion with the consent of the court.

A tragic case was reported from the Hastings Center in New York (Annas, 1988). A court in the United States decided to order a caesarean section on a woman of 28 who was 26 weeks' pregnant and terminally ill with cancer. The woman refused the operation on the grounds that the baby would probably be severely handicapped after such an early delivery. The court overruled her wishes, the operation was done, and both mother and baby died.

No fault insurance for injured patients

Justice demands that patients who are seriously injured by medical or surgical mishaps should be compensated, in the same way as those injured in other ways. Overt medical negligence should result in the disciplining of the doctor. Hodges (1992) stressed the desirable features of any system of compensation:

- Every aggrieved party should have free and speedy access to an independent tribunal
- Remedies should be adequate without unduly penalising doctors who make mistakes, but the fact that the injury arose from a mistake must be established
- The system should operate in such a way as to minimise recurrence of the error that caused the mishap
- Reparation should be made by the person responsible for the mishap.

In most countries there are ways in which people who have suffered misfortunes are supported both financially and by the provision of services. There remains, however, the ancient moral conviction that wrongdoers should be made to compensate their victims. Clothier (1989) (who was the Parliamentary Commissioner for Administration and Health Service Commissioner for England, Wales, and Scotland, 1979 to 1984) suggested that an inquisitorial system should be set up to take the place of the present adversarial system. A Clinical Judgement Review Board of doctors and lawyers would examine all the evidence, call witnesses, and deliver a verdict about the cause of a medical mishap. If the Board concluded that a doctor was negligent, the High Court would be asked to assess damages. A bill to provide no-fault compensation was heavily defeated in the House of Commons in 1991.

The Health Secretary in England has now sent out a consultation paper, the purpose of which is to speed up claims for medical negligence by allowing them to be examined – by scrutiny of documents, including casenotes and depositions by both plaintiff and defendant – by a tribunal of two senior doctors and a lawyer. It would be their judgement whether negligence had or had not been responsible for the patient's injury.

In Sweden, Finland, and New Zealand a patient who has suffered an unexpected and avoidable injury as a result of medical or surgical treatment does not have to prove negligence on the part of the doctor (Rosenthal, 1987). Sweden set up a Medical Responsibility Board, financed by a community charge or 'poll tax'. As a result, Swedish doctors pay annual premiums of only 65 Kronor (£7 or $11) for malpractice insurance. The chairman of the Medical Responsibility Board is a judge and the other members are two senior doctors, four members of parliament, three union representatives related to health care, and one representative of the county councils. The claims of aggrieved patients are presented by independent doctors and judged by the Board. The difficulty of proving that the injury was caused by an action on the part of the doctor has resulted in only about 42% of claims succeeding (Hodges, 1992). If a claim succeeds the patient is compensated by a yearly sum of money, not a lump sum as in Britain or America, and negligence by the doctor may or may not be shown. There are two main reservations about such a system. The first is that it could prove enormously expensive. The second is that it can blur the distinction between mishap and malpractice, although in Sweden an injured patient is quite entitled to sue his doctor in the courts for damages for negligence, and in New Zealand to bring a complaint about his doctor to the Medical Practitioners' Disciplinary Committee.

References

Annas, G.A. (1988) She is going to die: the case of Angela C. *Hastings Center Report*, **18**, 23–25

Black, N. (1990) Medical litigation and the quality of care. *Lancet*, **335**, 35–37

Brahams, D. (1991a) Responsibility for death associated with negligent medical treatment of wounds. *Lancet*, **338**, 110

Brahams, D. (1991b) Consent for treatment of minors in wardship. *Lancet*, **338**, 564–565

Clothier, C. (1989) Medical negligence and no-fault liability. *Lancet*, **i**, 603–605

Couch, N.P., Tilney, N.L. and Moore, F.D. (1978) The cost of misadventures in colonic surgery. A model for the analysis of adverse outcomes in standard procedures. *American Journal of Surgery*, **135**, 641–646

Couch, N.P., Tilney, N.L., Rayner, A.A. and Moore, F.D. (1981) The high cost of low frequency events. *New England Journal of Medicine*, **304**, 634–637

Cowley, R. (1989) Courts could back doctors over risky operations. *Hospital Doctor*, October 19, p. 33

Curran, W.J. (1986) Informed consent in malpractice cases. A turn toward reality. *New England Journal of Medicine*, **314**, 429–431

Dingwall, R. (1991) Risk management. *British Medical Journal*, **302**, 255

Dyer, C. (1988) Most sweeping changes in civil law for a century. *British Medical Journal*, **296**, 1730

Dyer, C. (1989) Ruling on consent: protection for patients and doctors. *British Medical Journal*, **298**, 348–349

Dyer, C. (1991) Manslaughter conviction for making mistakes. *British Medical Journal*, **303**, 1218

Gibb, F. (1988) Scarman backs call for reforms in compensation cases. *The Times*, February 20, p. 6

Harvard Medical Practice Study (1990) *Patients, Doctors, and Lawyers: medical injury, malpractice litigation, and patient compensation in New York*. Harvard Medical Practice Study, Boston

Hawkins, C. (1987) The Medical Defence Union. How the United Kingdom copes with mishap and malpractice. *Annals of Surgery*, **205**, 213–217

Hawkins, C. and Paterson, I. (1987) Medicolegal audit in the West Midlands region: analysis of 100 cases. *British Medical Journal*, **295**, 1533–1536

Hodges, C.J.S. (1992) Compensation for injury – a reappraisal: discussion paper. *Journal of the Royal Society of Medicine*, **85**, 93–95

Jennett, B. and Dyer, C. (1991) Persistent vegetative state and the right to die: the United States and Britain. *British Medical Journal*, **302**, 1256–1258

Law Commission (1991) *Mentally Incapacitated Adults and Decision Making: an overview*. HMSO, London

Lee, R.E. (1863) Address to the defeated Confederate army after the battle of Gettysburg

Legal correspondent (1984) Consent to treatment: the medical standard reaffirmed. *British Medical Journal*, **288**, 802–803

Levin, B. (1988) Juries generous to a fault. *The Times*, May 16, p. 16 (col. 2)

Lister, J. (1980) Negligence or error of judgement. *New England Journal of Medicine*, **302**, 733–735

McQuade, J.S. (1991) The medical malpractice crisis – reflections of the alleged causes and proposed cures: discussion paper. *Journal of the Royal Society of Medicine*, **84**, 408–411

Montaigne, M.E. de (1580) *Essays*. Translated by C. Cotton and W.C. Hazlitt

Morlock, L., Lindgren, O.H. and Mills, D.H. (1989) Malpractice, clinical risk management, and quality assessment. In *Providing Quality Care,* edited by N. Goldfield and D.B. Nash. American College of Physicians, Philadelphia, pp. 225–259

Quam, L., Fenn, P. and Dingwall, R. (1987) Medical malpractice in perspective. II. The implications for Britain. *British Medical Journal*, **294**, 1597–1600

Richards, T. (1989) Defence not the best form of attack. *British Medical Journal*, **298**, 1666–1667

Rosenthal, M.M. (1987) *Dealing with Medical Malpractice. The British and Swedish experience*. Tavistock, London

Sloan, F.A., Mergenhagen, P.M., Burfield, B., Bovjberg, J.D. and Hassan, M. (1989) Medical malpractice experience of physicians: predictable or haphazard? *Journal of the American Medical Association*, **262**, 3291–3297

Vincent, C.A. (1989) Research into medical accidents: a case of negligence? *British Medical Journal*, **299**, 1150–1154.

Chapter 18

Measures to encourage professional competence

In this country [England] it is a good thing to kill an admiral from time to time to encourage the others. Voltaire (1759)

This chapter is concerned with what to do when a doctor is failing to give patients effective care. We all make mistakes, but the doctor who refuses to recognise and correct his errors should be disciplined.

A sociologist spent many months as an observer in a teaching hospital in the USA, to try to identify the ways in which surgical mistakes are prevented and sanctions applied against transgressors (Bosk, 1979). He did this by attaching himself to two surgical firms, each of which had two senior staff surgeons and the usual complement of surgeons in training and medical students.

Bosk classified the controls imposed in all professions on unacceptable practices by its members as follows:

1. Informal internal controls: the daily conversations among members. Errors are identified and correction is by example.
2. Formal internal controls: the weekly or monthly conferences. In the medical profession these take two forms – mortality and morbidity meetings, and grand rounds.
3. Informal external controls: examples are the visits of inspectors of schools, of bank auditors or, in medicine, of members of the authority responsible for licensing hospitals for postgraduate training.
4. Formal external controls: examples are Hospital Activity Analyses, Clinical Indicators, and Independent Professional Review assessors in Britain, and Peer Review Organisations in the USA. In extreme cases sanctions can be applied against individual doctors by the General Medical Council or by the law courts.

Errors, wrote Bosk, are either of judgement and the application of techniques, or they offend against the code of conduct of the profession. Surgeons have more chance of making mistakes that cost patients' lives than physicians. They can make errors of judgement in operating on patients who should not have been operated on, and errors of judgement in not operating on patients who die because they have been denied operation. They can, and frequently do, make technical errors during operations.

Offending against professional codes of conduct

It is the surgeon who offends against professional codes of conduct who is likely to invoke disciplinary action. These errors and offences Bosk divides into *normative* and *quasi-normative*. Normative errors are unacceptable deviations from norms laid down, mainly unwritten, for the proper conduct of surgical practice. They include criminal actions, and behaviour – such as getting drunk – that bring the profession into disrespect. They also include – and these errors apply particularly to surgeons in training – lying, concealing errors, undertaking tasks for which they have not been trained, not keeping senior visiting staff informed about complications, not going to see patients when they have been asked to, and squabbling with nursing and other staff.

Quasi-normative errors are made only by surgeons in training. They are breaches of etiquette such as going against instructions given by visiting surgeons or adopting management regimens that are known not to be the visiting surgeon's normal practice.

As a result of his survey Bosk concluded that errors of judgement and errors of technique are unlikely to result in condemnation by a surgeon's peers, provided that they are honestly reported and that they are not repeated. Errors of deviation from normal moral standards, on the other hand, always result in sanctions against the offender. These sanctions may extend only as far as a rebuke from the visiting surgeon, but repeated offences result in the contract of a surgeon in training not being renewed. In the case of senior staff, repeated minor moral offences may result in withdrawal of visiting privileges in hospitals in the USA.

In Britain it is much more difficult to get rid of a consultant surgeon unless he commits a serious criminal act or operates under the influence of alcohol or drugs. Even then it takes a complicated administrative process to displace an incompetent doctor. All criminal convictions are automatically reported to the General Medical Council, which can warn the offender, suspend him for a variable period, or direct that his name be erased from the register.

Among the internal mechanisms for the handling of surgical errors and preventing their repetition are the word of mouth 'horror stories'. These are tales that may or may not be apocryphal. They are probably the same all over the world with regional variations and they are designed to illustrate the worst technical or judgemental errors that can be made.

An important mechanism for internal audit is the weekly or monthly mortality and morbidity ('deaths and complications') conference. If these are honestly presented – if errors and deviations from ideal practice are acknowledged – they are a potent educational tool. They must, however, be kept confidential. Any hint that the proceedings may be disclosed to outsiders is enough to ensure that information is not given with complete honesty.

Practical ways to minimise error

There are several practical ways in which the probability of error in surgical practice is minimised or recognised, resulting in improvement in outcome for individual patients. They are: undergraduate education, postgraduate education, continuing education of established surgeons, peer review, and litigation. We considered litigation in the previous chapter.

Undergraduate education

Medical education is primarily by apprenticeship to recognised teachers, supplemented by practical experience, lectures, tutorials, and the study of the writings of experts.

All countries demand minimum educational standards for entry into medical schools. Most, in addition, require that each aspiring medical student be interviewed so that the school can be assured that his personality is such that he will make a good doctor. The form of these interviews is left to the discretion of the individual members of the selection panel, and the techniques often lag far behind those used by the armed services and by industrialists, who use tests designed specifically to guide personnel management. These tests can be divided into those that assess *achievement*, and those that test *aptitude*. These are not strictly separate, and in the USA they are combined in the Medical College Admission Test (MCAT). The validation of this test is difficult. On the one hand it can probably predict fairly accurately whether a student will succeed in passing medical examinations. But will it predict how good a doctor he or she will be? What criterion will you use – income, research achievements, contributions to community welfare, opinion of colleagues and patients, number of malpractice suits?

In The Netherlands 36 general practitioners were presented with four standardised (simulated) patients and their performance in practice was compared with their competence when the same problems were presented to them in an 'examination' mode (Rethans *et al.*, 1991). There was a wide discrepancy, and it is clear that competence and performance have to be considered separately.

On the whole, interviews that elicit candidates' attainments, intelligence, special abilities and interests, disposition, and circumstances usually allow the interviewing panel to select the most suitable candidates. Data on this are, however, lacking because the fate of the 'control' group – the candidates turned down – is not known.

Medical school education in Britain

One of the main functions of the General Medical Council, established by Act of Parliament in 1858, is to safeguard the educational standards of doctors registered to practise in Britain. Before the passing of the *Medical Act 1978* the law required that at the point of graduation a doctor must possess 'the knowledge and skill requisite for the efficient practice of medicine, surgery, and midwifery' (Kilpatrick, 1989). The Act now requires the General Medical Council to determine 'the extent of knowledge and skill' and 'the standard of proficiency' required of a graduating medical student.

It fulfils this duty in several ways. The Council published *Recommendations on Basic Medical Education* and on *General Clinical Training*, in which the following attributes of a trained doctor are listed:

- Specialist knowledge
- Problem solving skills
- Broad consultation skills
- Scientific approach to practice
- Recognition of the importance of prevention
- Capacity for good team work
- Ability to teach
- Ability to advance knowledge
- Application of personal and mutual audit
- Application of high professional standards.

In 1987, the Education Committee of the General Medical Council published a survey of medical schools in the United Kingdom. Members of that Committee monitored details of the admission of students and of examination results. They scrutinised educational processes, paying particular attention to the extent of student clerkships, the use of non-teaching as well as teaching hospitals, the range of subjects taught, and the methods of assessment used. They encouraged the keeping of log books to ensure that every student saw a wide variety of diseases and other problems.

The Education Committee found certain deficiencies in the organisation of elective periods of study away from the main centre, and in the encouragement of the most able students to undertake original work. They commented that the barrier between the preclinical and clinical years was too rigid and recommended that there should be more integration of basic sciences into the wards.

Foreign medical graduates in Britain

The General Medical Council is empowered to confer full or limited registration on doctors who have qualified abroad. Since April 1985, however, foreign graduates who are accepted on to the limited list can stay only five years in hospital training posts, although about 10% in 1990 were subsequently transferred to full registration. The graduates of many medical schools, including those of Australia, South Africa, Hong Kong, Malaya, Singapore, and the West Indies, are recognised for full registration, as are those of all the medical schools in the European Community.

All other foreign graduates must apply for limited registration having either been sponsored by a recognised organisation such as the British Council (and having been accepted by a trainer) or having passed the examination of the Professional and Linguistic Assessment Board. This board was set up by the General Medical Council and its activities were the subject of a report by a Working Party (1986). The candidate is required to understand and communicate in both spoken and written English, and at the same time to show sufficient knowledge of medicine by answering written and oral questions. In 1990 the examination was taken by 2209 doctors and 551 (25%) passed.

Postgraduate education

It is quite legal for a newly qualified doctor, in most countries after a year's internship, to set up in practice. Most doctors, however, regard the passing of the final medical school examination as a qualification to start their postgraduate training. This is true whether they intend to follow careers as primary care physicians (general practitioners) or as specialists. In either case the most important component of the training is the trainer, and in most countries training posts require recognition by a national medical authority. At first the young doctor assists the established trainer, then he is given more to do under guidance. Finally, after several years, his judgement and technical skill are such that he can take his place as an independent practitioner.

During his years as a resident or registrar the trainee is both a learner and a provider of services. The pace of surgical work has increased considerably in the last 20 years: patients are seldom admitted to hospital for investigations, and they are not kept in hospital for so long; the result is that surgical beds are occupied by sicker people who require more services.

Apprenticeship or exploitation?

In Britain the ratio of trainees to consultants in general surgery is 2.8:1, and in all surgical disciplines 1.9:1, and the length of time spent in training grades is greater than anywhere else. Nowhere in the world is there such a disproportion between the number of surgeons in training and the number of trained (staff) surgeons (Report of the Working Party on the Composition of a Surgical Team, 1988). This might be expected to result in better teaching (or, if you prefer, better training or apprenticeship) of young doctors. It was, however, made clear in the report on the Confidential Enquiry into Perioperative Deaths (Chapter 14), that some preventable deaths have followed operations that were inadequately supervised by senior staff. The conclusion is inevitable – more staff surgeons must be appointed and they must be made more directly accountable for operations on patients under their care.

Many countries limit the number of hours that doctors in training are allowed to work. The Association of American Medical Colleges made several recommendations in 1988. Among these were that teaching hospitals should ensure that residency programs not only have inherent educational value, but also enhance the quality of care provided to patients, that residents be properly supervised, and that they should not work (either in their residency post or moonlighting to pay off loans acquired while they were students) for more than 80 hours a week averaged over four weeks.

In Britain, as a result of longstanding dissatisfaction among interns (house officers) about long hours of being on call, the Department of Health has announced that the weekly hours worked should not exceed 72 by the year 1994. This implies that more patient care will have to be undertaken by senior doctors and by nurses.

Recognition of surgical competence

In the USA the completion of a residency training is marked by passing the appropriate Board examination, whereas in Britain the passing of the examination for Fellowship of one of the four Royal Colleges of Surgeons (England, Edinburgh, Glasgow, and Ireland) has in the past merely been an indication that the doctor is serious in his intention to pursue a career as a surgeon.

Considerable secrecy surrounds the manipulation of pass marks of the examinations for the diplomas of the Royal Colleges, but it is likely that only about one third of candidates do succeed in their first attempt. *The Lancet* (Anonymous, 1990) asked why pass rates are so low, and suggested that there are three possible reasons: the candidates are of poor quality, their training is of poor quality, or the examinations are of poor quality.

The Royal College of Surgeons of Edinburgh instituted a Higher Specialty Examination in Neurosurgery in 1979, and this was followed by Higher Examinations in Orthopaedics and, in 1981, Cardiothoracic Surgery (MacLaren, 1988). With the agreement of the other Royal Colleges of Surgery, the examination of surgeons in training was radically altered in 1991. The Primary and Final examinations for the Fellowship of each college will be replaced by a new combined examination in applied basic sciences and the principles of surgery, taken at the end of a period of basic surgical training, and leading to the conferring of the diploma of Member of the appropriate Royal College. Towards the end of training, a new Higher Specialty Examination, leading to the conferring of the diploma of Fellow, will be taken in the branch of surgery that the surgeon has been trained in. This, it is expected, will have a low failure rate, and consistent failure will be a test as much of the trainer as the trainee. The position in the past was that a surgeon more or less automatically gained a Certificate of Higher Surgical Training from one of the Royal Colleges (on the recommendation of the Joint Committee of Higher Surgical Training) after four years as a senior registrar.

It is during the period of postgraduate training that a doctor's ethos regarding the recognition and correction of errors develops. If his trainers have adopted bad habits such as failing to communicate properly with patients, and failing both to admit mistakes and to remember them so that they are not repeated, then the doctor in training may pick up these habits and regard them as normal. Nearly all postgraduate programmes involve rotations from one trainer to another, and often from one hospital to another, so that the doctor in training is usually able to reject the influence of the morally and technically inferior trainer.

The Joint Committee on Higher Surgical Training is responsible for the recognition of training posts in Britain. It includes in its educational criteria: 'Regular opportunities should be provided for consultants and trainees to meet together...to enable comments and criticisms to be made of patient care and investigation' (Duncan, 1980).

Research is an important component in the training of a surgeon, because it is important that surgeons (and other specialists) shall recognise the limitations of knowledge, and be willing to abandon present ways of dealing with problems in favour of properly tested new ways. With a background of properly taught research experience a surgeon is more likely to be able to judge the validity of claims in the journals that he reads. He is less likely to defend out of date and ineffective methods of diagnosis and treatment on the grounds that 'this is the way I was taught to do it, and I have done it this way ever since'. Healthy scepticism is a prerequisite of continual improvement in patient care.

Continuing education of trained doctors

The salary of a consultant surgeon in Britain is on a par with that of a senior airline pilot. Both have tremendous responsibilities, although admittedly a grave error on the part of a pilot may kill hundreds, whereas an error on the part of a doctor may kill only one. Nevertheless, there is a vast difference between the regulations that govern the fitness and proficiency of pilots and those of doctors. Pilots have to undergo detailed yearly medical examinations, and their proficiency is checked regularly, both in simulators and in real flight. Doctors are subject to neither of these requirements, but simulators are being developed and surgeons who are motivated can attend workshops to improve their skills in such matters as anastomoses, bone fixation, arthroscopy, colonoscopy, and even laparoscopy. Such surgeons are, however, exceptional.

The United States is far ahead of Britain in requiring that surgeons continue their education. It is quite possible for a fully trained doctor to be appointed to the staff of a hospital in Britain and never again open a journal or a textbook, and never again attend a scientific meeting. Provided such people recognise their limitations and send complicated problems to better educated colleagues, no great harm comes to their patients. Their income from private practice will probably vary inversely with their golf handicap, and their local reputation will depend as much on personality as ability.

In the USA, on the other hand, continuing education is taken much more seriously, and much more money is made out of it. Conferences and courses are organised and many of them make profits for the organisers. The American Medical Association has adopted a Continuing Medical Education (CME) Accreditation Program, and defined continuing medical education as:

> 'Any education or training which serves to maintain, develop, or increase the knowledge, interpretive and reasoning proficiencies, applicable technical skills, professional performance standards, or ability for interpersonal relationships that a physician uses to provide the service needed by patients and the public.'

Surgeons are expected to earn not less than 150 'credits' every three years. These credits are awarded in six categories. Sixty of the credits must be in category 1, which includes full time training in an approved residency and attendance at meetings that are sponsored by an organisation accredited for CME and that meet the definition of a planned programme. Category 2 comprises attendance at meetings that do not satisfy both the above requirements and the credits are limited to 45 in three years. Category 3 credits are earned by doctors (other than full time academics) for teaching medical students, and 45 credits can be earned in this way. Forty credits can be earned by publication of up to four papers in medical journals or presentation of papers or exhibits at medical meetings (category 4). Up to 45 credits can be earned in category 5 by 'self instruction' such as reading of journals, or by participation in audit programs, and up to 45 credits can be earned by miscellaneous activities in continuing medical education. The theory is that these conferences and courses will ensure the quality of medical care, but that has not been proved – nor, indeed, is it likely to be possible to prove it.

Periodic recertification is required in all American states. In some this is a mere formality, whereas in others the state medical authorities keep complete records of all their doctors, and may refuse to relicense a doctor who has not earned his credits or against whom there have been serious complaints, until the doctor has undertaken a further period of study.

Peer review

Here again the USA is far ahead of the rest of the world. The American Medical Association (AMA) has been in the forefront of initiatives to educate both the profession and the public in the ingredients of high quality medical care. The Board of Trustees Report (1986) recommended self-policing by not referring patients to incompetent doctors and by denying hospital privileges to such doctors. Their initiative includes:

1. Encouragement of all doctors to report misconduct or incompetence. The AMA will expel any member guilty of serious misconduct or incompetence.
2. The AMA will publish comprehensive guidelines for peer review.
3. The AMA will assist in the defence of any body that incurs litigation as a result of good faith peer review.
4. The Department of Justice will assist doctors in appropriate self regulation.
5. The AMA will expand their physician data bank (Masterfile) to include all disciplinary actions by state medical boards. They hope to make sure that every hospital uses the Masterfile and to expand the file to include hospital disciplinary actions against doctors.
6. The AMA will foster peer review mechanisms that really do review the quality of care.
7. The AMA will continue to review standards of medical education.

The Council on Medical Services (1986) advised fostering a broader public understanding of 'high quality medical care' and of the mechanisms of assessment. The Council proposed the development of guidelines for assessment, and encouraged the systematic use of such assessments. They wrote that 'High quality care ... consistently contributes to improvement or maintenance of the quality and/or duration of life.'

The guidelines issued by the Council for the proper conduct of peer review were as follows:

1. The criteria must be agreed by the doctors being reviewed.

2. They can relate to structure, process, or outcome and preferably be interrelated. Those elements of structure and process that are related to favourable outcome should be defined.
3. Outcome studies should be prospective as well as retrospective.
4. Intermediate outcome is easier to assess than late outcome.
5. Review should be on specific targets or on samples.
6. Both explicit and implicit criteria can be useful.
7. Prior consultation, concurrent peer review, and retrospective peer review can all be valid.
8. The results of quality assessment should be used to improve the quality of care.
9. The quality assessment process itself needs continued evaluation and modification.

'Bad apples' or 'continuous improvement'?

Berwick (1989) wrote that 'In modern American health care there are two approaches to the problem of improving quality ... the Theory of Bad Apples ... and the Theory of Continuous Improvement.' The bad apples theory lies behind the Health Care Financing Administration's annual publication of mortality profiles of Medicare recipients in nearly every hospital in the USA, which causes an inevitable reaction by those hospitals that are criticised. It also lies behind the development of the National Practitioner Data Bank, legislated in 1986 and implemented in 1990, which requires maintenance of a record of all practitioners who have been involved in unfavourable professional review decisions or judgements or settlements of malpractice claims.

The theory of continuous improvement (Total Quality Management – TQM) on the other hand, which is so much admired and pursued in Japan, was formulated by W. Edwards Deming and Joseph M. Juran in the early 1980s (Berwick, 1989). They concluded that problems (and therefore solutions) had been built into the production processes, and that improvements can be made by studying the processes. The theory focuses on learning, not punishing. It is, according to Berwick, essential to assume that workers are doing their best and it is up to the leaders of the profession to improve processes of care. Preferred methods, not standards, must be promulgated, and waste, reworking, complexity, and error must be eliminated. Berwick *et al.* (1992) wrote that 'In a TQM organisation people do not ask "Did I pass inspection?" but rather "How could I do this better?" '

Snags of hospital based peer review in the USA

In a small and relatively isolated community in the United States a surgeon joined a group of doctors who practically monopolised medical care. Disagreements arose, the surgeon left the group, and set up his own practice. Allegations of incompetence were laid against the surgeon, were investigated and found proved by his local peers. He was reprimanded, his practice declined, and he sued for restraint of trade on the grounds that the decision had been made by a group of local competitors. He was awarded damages, the local doctors appealed, and the case was brought to the Supreme Court (Anonymous, 1988). Such antitrust actions have had a chilling effect on Peer Review Committees, but the AMA received a letter from the Justice Department stating that antitrust laws do not stand in the way of physicians' participation in hospital review conducted to identify and restrain incompetence and 'to the contrary, because such peer review enhances both the quality and efficiency of services delivered in our nation's hospitals to the benefit of the consumers, it furthers the antitrust goal of fostering competition in the health care market place'.

Dealing with incompetence or misconduct in Britain

Consultant surgeons, in common with all other consultants, are appointed to National Health Service hospitals in Britain for life, and the mechanisms for getting rid of an incompetent or misbehaving doctor are complex and costly. General practitioners, on the other hand, are subject to many restrictions by Family Health Service Authorities.

Disciplinary functions of the General Medical Council

If a doctor has been convicted on a criminal charge this conviction is automatically communicated to the General Medical Council, which also receives complaints from other doctors and the general public of conduct that might be regarded as unprofessional. Each year the Council receives about 1100 complaints, three quarters of which are from the public. The complaints are considered by the preliminary screener, who may ask for further evidence and, if he (it has only once been she) thinks fit he will report the case to the Preliminary Proceedings Committee. This committee comprises nine doctors and two lay members. It hears evidence and comes to a decision to take no action, to send a letter of advice or admonition, to refer the matter for consideration by the Health Committee, or to refer it to the Professional Conduct Committee.

In 1990 the Preliminary Proceedings Committee considered 147 cases (General Medical Council Annual Report, 1990), 59 resulting from convictions and 88 from information received. Two thirds of these concerned disregard of professional responsibilities to patients, abuse of alcohol, indecency, improper prescribing of drugs, and dishonesty. Just over one third were referred to the Professional Conduct Committee, which determined that nine doctors were not guilty of 'serious professional misconduct', 13 were admonished, 20 were suspended, and 13 names were erased from the register. This automatically ended their contracts with the National Health Service. It is perhaps unfortunate that the Council can bring no charge less than 'serious professional misconduct'. There are many aspects of professional relations between doctors and their patients that do not come under that heading, and yet appear to require some attention by the Council. A doctor who makes a wrong diagnosis or gives the wrong treatment has little to fear from the Council.

The sick doctor

Until 1980 there was nothing that the General Medical Council could do about a doctor who had not committed a criminal offence or been guilty of serious professional misconduct. In that year the Council established a procedure for helping doctors who are 'sick'. This is usually a euphemism for the abuse of alcohol or drugs. If his colleagues conclude that the doctor's impairment is such that it makes him incapable of dealing adequately with patients, they inform the Preliminary Screener, who is apppointed by the Council. He instructs three examiners nominated by various professional bodies to consider the case, hear the doctor's side, and if they conclude that he is a danger to patients advise him to restrict his practice and undergo treatment. Only if this advice is unheeded is the case reported to the Health Committee, which has the power to suspend a doctor's registration. Most doctors readily agree to undergo treatment, and only 75 have needed referral to the Health Committee in 10 years.

The incompetent doctor

The real difficulty arises when a doctor's actions are criticised by patients or relatives, or when he attracts the odium of his peers because of deviations in his practice from those acceptable to the rest of the staff and which in the opinion of his peers are a danger to patients. Such a doctor is likely to continue in practice for a long time because his colleagues follow the General Medical Council (1987) guidelines. In this document is the statement that 'It is improper for a doctor to disparage...the professional skill, knowledge, qualifications, or services of any other doctor.' This discourages reporting of incompetence and there are no sanctions against doctors who fail to take action when they know that one of their colleagues is incompetent, or even dangerous. On the other hand the standing orders of the Council allow it to act when:

(a) the doctor has behaved, or may have behaved, in a manner which cannot be regarded as acceptable professional conduct and that matter is not trivial;
(b) the information received does not raise a question of serious professional misconduct; and
(c) it is desirable in the public interest or in order to maintain the reputation of the medical profession that the council should take some cognisance of the matter.

If the incompetence of a doctor is eventually reported the laborious process of finding the facts may go on for years, and culminate in what is to all intents and purposes a secret trial. There are mechanisms for appeal, the whole affair is likely to cost many thousands of pounds, and often results in the reinstatement of a suspended doctor (McGregor and Bunbury, 1988).

The College of Anaesthetists in Britain has issued guidelines for dealing with anaesthetists who are reported to the College by colleagues because of 'a repeated inability to perform some technical procedure ... an unacceptably high incidence of complications as evidenced by observation or audit, or by failure to comply with generally accepted practice' (Anonymous, 1991). Colleagues will try and improve matters locally, but may then report the anaesthetist in confidence to the College secretary, who will contact one of a group of advisers. The adviser will interview the anaesthetist and possibly offer advice on retraining. Ultimate sanctions include reporting to the College committee, the employer, or even the General Medical Council.

In 1990 a Working Group of the General Medical Council was given the task of 'considering arrangements for the identification and handling of cases of serious deficiency in a doctor's professional performance'. The group is expected to report that if a doctor's performance is found to be below an acceptable standard he should be advised to mend his ways, including attending refresher courses. Only if he fails to comply with these suggestions will he be reported to the Council, which will have the power to suspend his registration.

References

Anonymous (1988) Medical discipline: who shall judge? *Lancet*, **i**, 1329

Anonymous (1990) Examining the Royal Colleges' examiners. *Lancet*, **335**, 443-445

Anonymous (1991) *British Medical Journal*, **302**, 371

Berwick, D.M. (1989) Continuous improvement as an ideal in health care. *New England Journal of Medicine*, **320**, 53-56

Berwick, D.M., Enthoven, A. and Bunker, J.P. (1992) Quality management in the NHS: the doctor's role – I. *British Medical Journal*, **304**, 235-239

Board of Trustees Report (1986) AMA initiative on quality of medical care and professional self-regulation. *Journal of the American Medical Association*, **256**, 1036-1037

Bosk, C.L. (1979) *Forgive and Remember. Managing medical failure.* University of Chicago Press, Chicago

Council on Medical Services (1986) Quality of medical care. *Journal of the American Medical Association*, **256**, 1030-1032

Duncan, A. (1980) Quality assurance: what now and where next? *British Medical Journal*, **1**, 300-302

General Medical Council (1987) *Professional Conduct and Discipline: fitness to practice.* General Medical Council, London, p. 17

General Medical Council Annual Report (1990) General Medical Council, London

Kilpatrick, R. (1989). Profile of the GMC: portrait or caricature? *British Medical Journal*, **299**, 109-112

McGregor, A. and Bunbury, A. (1988) *Disciplining and Dismissing Doctors in the National Health Service.* Mercia Publications, London

MacLaren, I.F. (1988) Quality control in surgical training – do we need higher examinations? *Journal of the Royal College of Surgeons of Edinburgh*, **33**, 98-102

Rethans, J-J., Sturmans, F., Drop, R., van der Vleuten, C. and Hobus, P. (1991) Does competence of general practitioners predict their performance? Comparison betweeen examination setting and actual practice. *British Medical Journal*, **303**, 1377-1380

Report of the Working Party on the Composition of a Surgical Team (1988) Royal College of Surgeons of England, London

Voltaire, F.M.A. (1759) *Candide*, Chapter 23

Working Party on the PLAB Tests (1986) *Report.* General Medical Council, London

Audit of patient satisfaction

Chapter 19

Introduction

Courtesy is the due of man to man.　　　　　　　Thomas Carlyle (1832)

This is the fourth aspect of audit, after those of structure, process, and outcome. It is probably the most important of all; if patients are not satisfied with the service they are getting there is little point in paying much attention to the other three aspects. When a doctor chooses a colleague to look after his wife he asks: Does he care? Does he try? Does he visit his patients? Does he listen to the history? Does he make an appropriate examination? Does he communicate well? Does he give meddlesome treatment? Knowledge is such a small part of proficiency.

There are, of course, many patients who consult their general practitioners with symptoms that have no organic cause. A few of these are referred to hospital consultants who arrange extensive investigations and come up with no diagnosis. Such patients are seldom satisfied. They remain 'ill' in the sense of the opposite of 'healthy', and neither physical nor psychological treatment will help them.

On the other hand, one can have a satisfied patient who has had inappropriate investigations, incorrect diagnosis, incompetent treatment, and an outcome that is worse than might have resulted if that patient had been in the care of a more able doctor. It seldom makes sense to judge a doctor by the opinions of his patients alone.

The Patient's Charter

The Department of Health (1991) sent a copy of a booklet called *The Patient's Charter* to every household in Britain. It emphasised seven existing rights, three new rights, and nine standards of service which the National Health Service will aim to provide. The seven existing rights are:

- To receive health care on the basis of clinical need, regardless of ability to pay
- To be registered with a general practitioner
- To receive emergency medical care at any time
- To be referred to a consultant, or for a second opinion, when the general practitioner thinks it necessary

- To be given a clear explanation of any treatment proposed, including risks and alternatives
- To have access to personal health records and to know that they are kept confidential
- To choose whether to take part in medical research or teaching of medical students.

The three additional rights from April 1992 are:

- To be given information on quality standards and waiting times in local health services
- To be guaranteed admission to hospital in less than two years
- To have complaints about services in the NHS investigated promptly.

The nine standards or guidelines that the health service aims for are:

- Respect for privacy, dignity, and religious and cultural beliefs
- Arrangements to ensure that everyone can use the services
- Availability of information to relatives and friends, subject to the patient's wishes
- Arrival of an emergency ambulance within 14 minutes in urban, and 19 minutes in rural, areas
- Immediate attention and assessment in accident and emergency departments
- Giving times for outpatient appointments and not keeping patients waiting longer than 30 minutes
- Aiming to avoid cancellation of arranged admissions to hospital
- Having a named person responsible for each patient's nursing care
- Arranging continuing care after patients have left hospital.

Among the aims that are not mentioned are: communication in ways that patients can understand (in their own language if necessary); the right of a woman to be examined only by a woman if she wishes; and, even more striking, any mention of standards of care in terms of its effectiveness.

Assessment of patient satisfaction

Research on the estimation of satisfaction of people with commercial services, particularly in the USA, has established that 10 features of a service are important (Ovretveit, 1992). They are:

- Reliability: keeping promises and performing consistently
- Responsiveness: willingness of staff to serve the client
- Competence: staff have appropriate skills
- Access: how easy it is to get to the service
- Courtesy: politeness and friendliness of staff
- Communication: particularly listening
- Credibility: trustworthiness of staff
- Security: safety and confidentiality
- Understanding: staff demonstrate their concern
- Physical tangibles: appearance of fixtures and staff.

Patients are dissatisfied if their treatment does not match up to their expectations. One of the least effective ways of deciding whether patients are dissatisfied is to wait until they send formal complaints (Cartwright, 1983). Most patients who are dissatisfied do not complain to the doctor or the hospital, but spread word of their dissatisfaction among their friends who then tell their friends in turn. In this way the reputation of a doctor or a hospital can be ruined and that doctor and that hospital may never know what caused the tarnishing of their image.

We do, however, stress that patients should be actively encouraged to make complaints and constructive suggestions, and we welcome the existence in some departments of a comments book, in which any member of staff, from cleaner to consultant, can record ways in which the service to patients can be improved. The corollary is that the suggestions in this book must be discussed and, if possible, implemented.

It is all part of communication; patients at a hospital that welcomes constructive complaints are often more satisfied than those at hospitals in which it is made difficult for them to complain. This must not be the only criterion of satisfaction, however, because it could result in diversion of resources from the old, the mentally ill, and the handicapped, who may lack the ability to complain logically.

The 'nursing process' should mean that the patient is made to feel a partner in his or her care, but it is really no substitute for the caring ward nurse who spends a lot of time talking to patients instead of sitting in an office filling in forms. Nurses, porters, and cleaners are in a better position to assess patient satisfaction than people who interview patients but are not directly concerned with their care; such interviews often produce biased data.

The same objection applies to questionnaires completed by patients before they are sent home – relief at gaining freedom may encourage them to gloss over minor deficiencies that they identified during their stay in hospital. Bias may also arise if questionnaires are administered by the doctor who looked after the patients; gratitude for deliverance from their illness may encourage them not to mention causes of dissatisfaction.

Questionnaires should ask specific questions, and should be given to patients to be completed anonymously in the privacy of their own homes. A reliable form of questionnaire is one that makes statements with which patients can signify that they 'strongly agree', 'agree', are 'uncertain' about, 'disagree', or 'strongly disagree' (Fitzpatrick, 1991b). These are the basis of the Likert scale, and are graded from 1 to 5. A numerical total can be derived, which can be subjected to statistical analysis. Questionnaires should always contain a section for comments on matters not dealt with by the specific questions. Fitzpatrick (1991a) concluded that the results of many questionnaires are not disseminated and acted upon. He discussed the merits of self administered and interview questionnaires and stressed the importance of producing structured but flexible documents.

Another way in which less than optimal care can be identified is by an unbiased observer sitting in at outpatient clinics and ward work. This has to be done most tactfully; it is expensive in terms of the observer's time, and often does not produce results that can be used to improve services.

Communication

There are many components of patient satisfaction. The most important is patients' awareness that they are free and equal partners in the process of health care – what has always been recognised as the 'doctor–patient relationship'. This relationship depends on honest, comprehensible, and comprehensive communication by the doctor; above all it depends on the doctor taking time to listen to the patient's story and then to explain things. Armstrong (1991) reported that patients often hold elaborate and often sophisticated theories of their own illness, and that what they need is answers to three questions: 'Why me?' 'Why now?' and 'Why this particular illness?'

Communication, as Brewin (1985) pointed out, 'is of crucial importance in medicine. Partly to inform, explain, and advise. And partly – especially when a patient is frightened, ill, weak, or otherwise vulnerable – to raise morale, give confidence, encourage, and protect'. It is important that a doctor's determination to eschew paternalism should not lead him or her into giving patients information that they do not want. By all means explain the options but you must know when to stop; this is usually when the patient says 'I leave it to you, doctor.'

Patients feel depersonalised when they are admitted to hospital, and nurses and doctors can do a lot to minimise the distress of an illness that requires hospital treatment by being welcoming, by talking to them, by seeing that they are occupied in some way, and above all by taking time (Skipper and Leonard, 1965). Byrne, Napier and Cuschieri (1988) reported that 44 of 100 patients interviewed by an independent medical observer between two and five days after their operations did not know exactly what had been done. This was more common among elderly people and is a reflection either of the inadequacy of the information that patients were given or of the fact that some patients simply do not want to know.

Sutherland *et al.* (1989) asked a sample of 52 patients in a postoperative cancer hospital in Ontario to complete questionnaires about the amount of information that they had been given (relative to how much they wished), and about their desire to participate in decision making. More than half the patients actively sought detailed information, but did not wish to be involved in the decision making, preferring to leave that to their doctors.

Failure to listen and communicate can lead to incorrect or only partly correct diagnoses, to lack of compliance with the proposed treatment, and to dissatisfaction resulting in accusations of malpractice.

The training of surgeons tends to be biased towards technicalities, and a surgeon in training usually gains experience in communicating only by following the example of older surgeons, not by any formal teaching; in many medical schools in the USA, however, there are courses in techniques of interviewing. There is in some quarters a move toward the appointment of 'counsellors'. This shifts the duty of communicating to non-doctors and is usually not as effective as the cultivation of a good doctor–patient relationship.

It is usually the most junior doctors on the team to whom patients are most grateful, simply because they have spent a lot of time with the patients. The senior surgeon may be the one who has made the diagnosis and carried out the operation, and he may (and usually does) communicate information to the patient, but the second aspect of communication – the establishment of a personal relationship – is often neglected. This can leave patients unhappy, bewildered, and antagonistic. The escalation of malpractice suits in recent years is related only in part to the greater expectations of patients; it stems equally from the poverty of communication that sometimes exists.

The essentials of good interviewing are:

- Be punctual
- Greet the patient by name
- Seat the patient comfortably
- Establish rapport
- Listen
- Ask appropriate questions
- Avoid jargon
- Do not judge.

We analysed 56 letters of complaint received by the administrator of a hospital during a recent year. Half the letters concerned medical care, nearly all resulting from failure of communication between doctors and patients and their relatives. All but three were satisfactorily dealt with by explanation and better communication. There were also nine concerning nursing care, six about waiting times, and 13 miscellaneous complaints.

There is in Britain an 'ombudsman', the Health Service Commissioner, to whom complaints (other than those concerning decisions about the care of a patient which, in his opinion, were taken solely in the exercise of clinical judgement) can be made. He sends regular reports to Parliament, and occasional 'epitomes' to health service managers. We have analysed the reasons for patients' dissatisfaction in a recent issue of one of these epitomes, which commented on 26 cases. In all of them the main cause of complaint was lack of communication by medical or nursing staff, or by Health Authorities. The Commissioner is an important link in the chain of quality assurance in Britain.

Dying and bereavement

One of the most difficult tasks facing a doctor is communicating with the dying in a way that is both sympathetic and honest. Buckman (1988) wrote a book subtitled *How to help and support someone who is dying*. He suggested that the most important thing that a doctor (and everyone else) can do is to reassure people who are dying that their lives were valuable and that they would be remembered. He pleaded for openness and honesty. Above all, if the patient wants to talk about his funeral or his family's future, he must be listened to. Listening is often a more important component of communication than talking. We have more to say about the 'good death', which is to be regarded as a pinnacle of achievement and not a failure, in Chapter 21.

There are, according to Brewin (1991), three ways of giving bad news. The first is the throwaway statement from the end of the bed; the second is the kind, unhurried interview, which the patient recognises to be no less than a painful duty for the doctor. The third, and the one that he recommends, is the optimistic one: touch is important, and the good points as well as the bad must be brought out.

Bereavement causes grief, and sudden bereavement is a shattering experience to close relatives (Yates, Ellison and McGuiness, 1990). They must be allowed to grieve, and they must be given a lot of time and a lot of patient listening. Close relatives must not be kept away from the dying, even if their presence inhibits normal medical and nursing processes. They must be told the truth – of course – but in a sympathetic way. If there is a question of the patient being brain dead the concept must be explained and the tests detailed (and witnessed by the relatives if they want to). If the tests prove that the patient is brain dead and a candidate for organ donation the relatives must be allowed to absorb this for several hours before being asked their permission to use the organs. Garrison *et al.* (1991) reported that permission was granted for organs to be donated in 53 of 82 cases when there was a delay between telling the relatives that the potential donor was brain dead and asking permission for the donation; when the request for donation was made at the same time as the information that the patient was brain dead, only 11 of 61 donations resulted.

Other methods of communication

It is usual to give each patient admitted to hospital a booklet describing the routine of the hospital and the functions of various members of the staff. These are, however, no substitute for friendly talk by the nurses and doctors. Few patients retain an accurate memory of their interview with the doctor, and some doctors try to reinforce the message of their conversations by giving patients leaflets describing individual diseases and treatments, including operations. These are usually sketchy and may need to be altered for particular patients.

Many organisations produce valuable leaflets. Among these are self help groups such as the Ileostomy Association; these groups help their members not only by producing leaflets but also by meeting regularly, listening to difficulties, and even putting forward ideas for the improvement of the quality of life of people who have that disease or disability. Most ethical pharmaceutical companies produce leaflets that do not contain unacceptable advertising and can be recommended. On the other hand, most patients would prefer to know that the information they are given was written by the doctor whom they consulted.

There are some rules that should be followed when writing information leaflets for patients. First, the language must be non-technical: it should be easy to write good English without resorting to 'medispeak'. Obviously the sentences must be grammatically correct, but after that the greatest impact is made by observing three rules: use short words; use short sentences; and use common words.

Secondly, instructions must be specific; do not write in a leaflet on intermittent claudication: 'Take more exercise'. Write instead: 'Walk at your own pace at least half a mile every day'. Third, instructions must be explained; when you suggest that a patient should lose weight (and have explained how to do that), explain also why it would benefit the patient's disease. Finally, it is wise to leave a blank space for specific instructions for specific patients.

An example of such a leaflet is entitled *Information for patients having a prostatectomy*. This is reproduced below.

Your prostate operation

As you know, you are coming into hospital to have a prostatectomy. We feel that this leaflet will help you to understand the operation and its effect on your life. Please read it carefully and if you have any questions about your own operation ask the doctor for details.

Your stay in hospital. You will be admitted to .... ward. You are likely to be in hospital for four to seven days from the day of your operation. You will be asked to sign a consent form for the operation and the anaesthetic.

Before your operation. You will be admitted a day before your operation. The house surgeon will ask you about your symptoms and examine you. Please tell him about any other disease or serious symptoms you may have and about any medicines you are taking. If you are to have your operation in the morning you must not eat or drink after midnight. Those having an operation in the afternoon may have a light breakfast. Shortly before the operation nurse will give you an injection that will make you relax but may give you a dry mouth. This injection will not make you sleep.

The anaesthetic. You may be given either a general anaesthetic, where an injection is given into the back of your hand to send you to sleep, or a spinal anaesthetic where a needle is put in your back to numb the lower half of your body. The anaesthetist will decide which is best for you.

The operation. During the operation the inside of the prostate gland is cut away, allowing the urine to pass freely out of the bladder once again. The operation is performed through a fine tube passed down the penis, so there are no scars.

After your operation. During the first day or two you will have an intravenous drip in your arm. You will have a catheter tube leading from the bladder to a bag beside your bed. For the first day or two water is flushed through the bladder into the catheter tube from a bottle at the side of your bed. The doctors will decide when to take down this bottle and when to remove the catheter. This is often on the third or fourth day after your operation. When the catheter is removed try and pass your water regularly every couple of hours during the day. It helps to drink plenty of water after the operation to flush yourself through. Because there is no scar this is a relatively painless operation. If you do have pain you will be given injections or tablets.

Physiotherapy. It speeds up your recovery to take lots of deep breaths after the operation to clear the lungs, and it is important to keep moving your legs to prevent blood clots forming. These may block the veins and occasionally break loose and are carried to the lungs.

Bowel movement. It is natural to be constipated for several days after an operation. Please ask nurse for some bowel medicine on the third day after the operation if you feel that you need it.

Convalescence. You will need four weeks convalescence. Do not be alarmed if there is some blood in the urine for a few weeks after the operation. If the urine burns a lot or if you are passing a lot of blood clots, get in touch with your doctor.

This leaflet mentions expected postoperative events, but not unexpected events and complications. It is becoming increasingly important that patients are not led to believe that every operation invariably has a satisfactory outcome, and in many countries patients are asked to sign lists of the possible complications of their operation, after these have been read and explained to them.

It is usual to ask patients to sign 'consent forms' before any operation or invasive investigation, but these are meaningless unless patients are informed in simple language and with the help of diagrams exactly what is proposed. Leaflets or short pamphlets that have been written by the consulting doctor can be given each patient when a diagnosis is first made and a regimen of treatment accepted. These must be written in simple prose, without jargon, and avoiding words with Latin or Greek stems.

It is not only concerning operations that patients must be fully informed of possible side effects and complications. In Britain it is illegal to supply certain drugs unless they are accompanied by leaflets describing 'contraindications, warnings, and precautions'. These must be approved by the licensing authorities, but are often written in such technical language that patients disregard them. In Germany, and no doubt in other countries, the warnings of undesired effects may be so forbidding that patients refuse to take what may in the opinion of the doctor be essential drugs. The Association of the British Pharmaceutical Industry has recommended that printed leaflets should be provided with medicines (George, 1987). The information should be brief, concise, and comprehensive, and should include a statement that 'the information in this leaflet is limited; further details can be obtained from your doctor or pharmacist'.

In the United States far more detail is given to patients than in Britain. This may partly be a reaction to the high level of litigation. For example, the Alza Corporation markets an intrauterine device called Progestasert. Each device is accompanied by an eight-page booklet describing its correct use and including information about possible adverse effects. Prospective users are asked to go through the booklet with their doctors and sign each section to show they have understood it. The British Department of Health and Social Security refused to license this booklet, and the Alza Corporation has withdrawn the product from the British market.

An alternative that is popular with patients is to give them an audio-tape which they can take home and play back as often as they like. Hogbin and Fallowfield (1989) taped the interviews between doctors and patients with cancer, in which they were told that they had cancer and were offered options and advice. These tapes were given to the patients and nearly all of them found them useful. For more serious and complicated operations some surgeons have gone to the extent of making videotapes which can either be shown in the hospital or lent to the patient. As a means of communicating information moving pictures with text have a greater impact than text alone.

A patient who has been fully informed by doctors and nurses, and who knows that he is a partner in the decision process, is less likely to be under stress than one who has been left in the dark. On the other hand, is it fair to the patient to disclose that there is profound disagreement among doctors about the best treatment for a particular disease (Anonymous, 1989)?

One of the ways in which the patient can be assured that he has been told the truth is to send him a copy of the letter that the consultant sends to the referring general practitioner (Tattersall, 1989).

Communication from doctor to doctor

Communication between hospital doctors and primary care physicians is equally important. The patient's 'own' doctor needs to know the diagnosis, management, immediate outcome, and recommendations for further treatment for any patient who has been in hospital, and he needs to have this information quickly. Sandler and Mitchell (1987) showed in a randomised study that interim discharge letters given patients before they left hospital reached primary care physicians significantly more quickly than those that were mailed. In a later publication Sandler *et al.* (1989) reported that 258 patients were given, when they left hospital, two copies of a card giving details of their admission, diagnosis, and treatment. One was for the patient to study and the other was for the general practitioner. Nearly all the patients and general practitioners were pleased with the innovation.

Confidentiality

It goes without saying that no information given in confidence by a patient shall be disclosed to anyone else, unless with the express permission of the patient or by the order of a judge. As for the confidentiality of casenotes, there used to be a time when hospital casenotes were kept locked away so that patients could not read them. This is surely undesirable and can only make patients think that information is being kept from them. For 30 years we put our casenotes in carriers at the end of patients' beds and have encouraged patients to read them and to ask questions about technical matters and abbreviations recorded in the notes. The *Access to Health Records Act*, introduced in Britain in 1990, gives people the statutory right to see medical records, particularly those relating to employment and insurance. Since 1 November 1991 patients in Britain have had statutory right of access to their manual health records, thus extending the right that was established by the *Data Protection Act 1984*, which applied to computerised records.

Some doctors have advocated entrusting hospital notes to the care of patients, who would bring them along for each consultation or admission. This seems a splendid idea from the administrative point of view – what hospital has enough storage space for all its notes? It suffers, however, from the grave disadvantage that the notes are not available for research and audit purposes, and we wonder how copies of letters to patients' own doctors manage to find their way into casenotes.

Smart cards

Smart cards resemble credit cards; data can be entered and retrieved either by an integral chip or by writing and reading with a laser beam. In either case they act as miniature computers. They are usually used in pairs, one being kept by the patient and the other by the doctor or the hospital. Data must be kept up to date in both cards. In 1989, 9000 smart cards were issued to patients in Exmouth in Devon. Each card could store more than 100 clinical episodes. They were coded by Read codes and the reactions to this pilot study were favourable. The aim is to introduce an internationally accepted standard card, but this is for the future.

Courtesy

When we are among strangers in a hotel or an aeroplane, we expect many things: comfort, warmth, food, and above all courtesy. When a patient is admitted to hospital the same expectations apply. Sick people can be aggressive and discourteous themselves, but they still deserve the utmost courtesy from their attendants. Among the most courteous things you can do are to be punctual, to address everybody by their name, to listen, and to be kind.

It is not common for inpatients to complain of discourtesy, but in the British National Health Service the treatment of outpatients often leaves a lot to be desired. Patients are made to feel like anonymous supplicants rather than valued sick people. Outpatient appointments should be made so that no patient waits more than 15 minutes. During that wait they should be made to feel that their presence is acknowledged and they should be offered a newspaper or up to date magazine to keep them occupied. Letters making appointments for outpatients should include bus timetables and maps of the clinic in relation to the nearest car park. Repeat attendances should be arranged only if there is clinical need; the exception is when long term follow up is needed for research purposes. In that case the patient should be fully informed of the reason for the follow up. In some specialties, notably orthopaedics, patients with non-urgent complaints have to wait several months for an outpatient appointment. We consider the question of waiting lists in Chapter 20.

There are other aspects of courtesy. Such is the pressure on surgical beds in many hospitals that patients who have been sent for to come into hospital on a certain day are instructed to telephone on the morning of the day they are to be admitted to make sure that there is a bed available for them. Often there are none vacant. This system may be necessary for the most efficient use of beds, as nobody can accurately anticipate discharging a convalescent patient or not admitting an emergency. But the discourtesy to the patient whose family and work plans are upset at the last minute by the cancellation is considerable.

The existence of a waiting list instead of planned dates for admission for every patient, and the uncertainty about the length of time before admission, is another discourtesy. But perhaps the greatest discourtesy apart from actual rudeness is unpunctuality on the part of the doctor. Such behaviour suggests that the doctor thinks so little about the patient's time, and so much about his own, that he is willing to let patients wait in his outpatient clinic for hours instead of spacing appointments in a more sensible way.

Concern

When patients are in pain, or suffering some other form of distress, they expect that somebody will be concerned and take the trouble to alleviate the pain or remedy the cause of the distress. They should be encouraged to complain and assured that it is only they themselves who can bring their distress to the notice of doctors and nurses. Dissatisfaction is bound to be generated by callousness on the part of attendants who ignore requests for help, delay giving analgesic drugs, or exhort patients not to make such a fuss. A sympathetic and concerned doctor or nurse will always earn more respect and admiration from patients than one who is merely efficient. One of the ways in which a doctor or nurse can express concern is by touching the patient. Laying on of hands may not cure diseases but it certainly helps to allay distress.

Competence

It goes without saying that patients expect their doctor to be competent, but the assessment of competence is more difficult. Even the assessment of the competence of a surgeon by his peers is likely to be flawed; it can be influenced by the occurrence on the one hand of a single tragedy, and on the other of a single triumph. We have written more fully about the audit of outcome in Chapter 12. There is no doubt that the acquisition of competence is one of the most important parts of a surgeon's training, and that the technically incompetent person should be told early in his career that he would be well advised not to continue in surgery. One of the drawbacks of the system of rotating surgeons in training through many departments is that no single senior surgeon is likely to take the responsibility for counselling a trainee to give up surgery.

Comfort

As long as recovery from an operation is uncomplicated many surgeons minimise the importance of pain and discomfort. To patients, however, they are anything but unimportant and more attention should be paid to effective alleviation of pain. We had a postcard from an elderly doctor after he had read a paper in the *British Medical Journal* (Pollock and Evans, 1987). This is what he wrote: 'I have twice been admitted for acute retention, aged 73 and 75. There are two things that pull one down: l. The condition, in this case the pain. 2. The ambulance journey. Our National Health Service ambulances must be lethal to many ill or injured patients. They are not much better than those we had in North Africa. I understand a new well sprung stretcher is in the offing. See if you can procure one before your emergency!'

Relief of dissatisfaction

Patients should be asked specifically about anything that has caused dissatisfaction. Quite apart from the relief to an individual patient of getting a sympathetic hearing, it should be possible to ensure that future patients will benefit. When a source of dissatisfaction is identified it is essential that appropriate corrections are made. There are of course more formal ways in which patients can air their grievances, culminating in litigation. Much anxiety and ill feeling can be avoided by actively asking patients about any aspect of their care that has not pleased them.

Conclusion

Communication, courtesy, concern, competence, and comfort – patients are more likely to be satisfied with their treatment if doctors and other health workers observe these rules.

References

Anonymous (1989) Informing patients about clinical disagreement. *Lancet*, **ii**, 367–368

Armstrong, D. (1991) What do patients want? Someone who will hear their questions. *British Medical Journal*, **303**, 261–262

Brewin, T.B. (1985) Truth, trust, and paternalism. *Lancet*, **ii**, 490–492

Brewin, T.B. (1991) Three ways of giving bad news. *Lancet*, **337**, 1207–1209

Buckman, R. (1988) *I don't know what to say*. Papermac, London

Byrne, D.J., Napier, A.A. and Cuschieri, A. (1988) How informed is signed consent? *British Medical Journal*, **296**, 839–840

Carlyle, T. (1832) *Corn Law Rhymes*

Cartwright, A. (1983) *Health Surveys in Practice and Potential: a critical view of their scope and methods.* King's Fund, London

Department of Health (1991) *The Patient's Charter.* HMSO, London

Fitzpatrick, R. (1991a) Surveys of patient satisfaction: I – Important general considerations. *British Medical Journal*, **302**, 887–889

Fitzpatrick, R. (1991b) Surveys of patient satisfaction: II – Designing a questionnaire and conducting a survey. *British Medical Journal*, **302**, 1129–1132

Garrison, R.N., Bentley, F.R., Raque, G.H., *et al.* (1991) There is an answer to the shortage of organ donors. *Surgery, Gynecology and Obstetrics*, **173**, 391–396

George, C.F. (1987) Telling patients about their medicines. *British Medical Journal*, **294**, 1566–1567

Hogbin, B. and Fallowfield, L. (1989) Getting it taped: the 'bad news' consultation with cancer patients. *British Journal of Hospital Medicine*, **41**, 330–333

Ovretveit, J. (1992) *Health Service Quality. An introduction to quality methods for health services.* Blackwell, Oxford

Pollock, A.V. and Evans, M. (1987) Major abdominal operations on patients aged 80 and over: an audit. *British Medical Journal,* **295**, 1522

Sandler, D.A. and Mitchell, J.R.A. (1987) Interim discharge summaries: how are they best delivered to general practitioners? *British Medical Journal,* **295**, 1523–1525

Sandler, D.A., Heaton, C., Garner, S.T. and Mitchell, J.R. (1989) Patients' and general practitioners' satisfaction with information given on discharge from hospital: audit of a new information card. *British Medical Journal,* **299**, 1511–1513

Skipper, J.K. and Leonard, R.C. (1965) *Social Interaction and Patient Care.* JB Lippincott Co, Philadelphia

Sutherland, H.J., Llewellyn-Thomas, H.A., Lockwood, G.A., Tritchler, D.L. and Till, J.E. (1989) Cancer patients: their desire for information and participation in treatment decisions. *Journal of the Royal Society of Medicine,* **82**, 261–263

Tattersall, R.B. (1989) Informing patients. *Lancet,* **ii**, 280

Yates, D.W., Ellison, G. and McGuiness, S. (1990) Care of the suddenly bereaved. *British Medical Journal,* **301**, 29–31

Chapter 20

Waiting for hospital treatment

How much of human life is lost in waiting!

Ralph Waldo Emerson (1841)

There are occasions when delay in treatment can adversely influence the outcome of an injury or an illness. This is an aspect of audit that has been extensively investigated and criteria have been established. Emergency insertion of an airway, arrest of haemorrhage, and cardiac massage are examples in which minutes count. In other conditions a delay of as little as an hour can make the difference between death and survival: for example, fibrinolytic treatment of myocardial infarction, intravenous fluid replacement in shock, and relief of strangulated intestinal obstruction.

Delay in the treatment of cancer increases patients' apprehension and should theoretically have an adverse effect on mortality, but this has not been proved, at least not for delays of a few weeks. All these aspects of delay are related more to the clinical outcome than to measurements of patient satisfaction. It is the waiting lists for non-urgent operations that are of greater concern to the general public.

If patients have to wait unduly long times for outpatient consultations and inpatient or outpatient treatment for non-urgent conditions, particularly surgical conditions, they can feel frustrated and dissatisfied. The frustration is increased by the fact that no date is given for the admission and patients feel that they cannot plan their lives around a certain date. The alternative is to establish a booking system (Beecham, 1991). The regional medical advisory committees in Bristol recommended that patients should be booked direct for admission, booked for preadmission clinics, or given an outpatient appointment for further review. A few patients who were willing would be put on a short notice call list. Such a system would remove the uncertainty that is one of the worst aspects of a waiting list. On the other hand, as Frankel *et al.* (1991) pointed out, many surgeons have had to give up the booking system because they found that the pressure of emergency and urgent admissions was forcing the last minute cancellation of booked non-urgent cases.

These problems do not arise when hospitals are privately funded and when payment of surgeons' fees is by item of service: in that case doctors make sure that they arrange consultations and treatments to suit their patients. When, however, medical care is 'free' to the consumer, when doctors are paid salaries, and government funding is restricted, waiting lists can build up. In 1991 there were nearly a million patients awaiting either daycase operations or admission to hospitals in Britain. The Department of Health is committed to reducing to zero the number of those waiting more than two years by mid-1992.

The length of waiting lists varies widely among districts, and it is feasible (and acceptable to patients) to arrange for operations for non-urgent conditions to be done in hospitals with short waiting lists, even if it means that the patients have to travel long distances (Stewart and Donaldson, 1991).

Aetiology of waiting lists

Consideration of the aetiology of long surgical waiting lists must include attention to several variables:

- Restriction of hospital budgets
- The number of consultants in each specialty
- The number of operations a consultant performs
- The criteria for defining the need for operations
- Admission of patients for investigation
- The development of new operations
- The demands of patients
- The referral habits of general practitioners
- The availability of hospital beds
- The availability of operating theatres
- The availability of trained nurses
- The acceptability of daycase surgery
- Excessive follow up by surgeons
- Periodic review of the waiting lists.

Restriction of hospital budgets

Health care resources can never keep up with demand, and one of the ways of ensuring a fair and just distribution of resources is to limit hospital budgets. As we pointed out in Chapter 11, the health care industry differs from all other industries in that the more efficient a hospital – the more patients it treats and the shorter their stay in hospital – the greater are its expenses. The position then arises that to balance the budget many hospitals see no course open to them other than to close wards and treat fewer patients, resulting in growing waiting lists.

The number of consultants in each specialty

One of the biggest problems in deciding the allocation of resources for health care concerns the number of doctors to be trained, and the proportion to be guided into primary care compared with the proportion to be encouraged to become consultants in each of the numerous medical and surgical specialties. As new techniques are invented the need for specialisation increases, and the general surgeon and the general physician find more and more of their work taken over by specialists. What are the mechanisms for deciding, firstly on the total number of doctors a country needs, and then on the numerical needs of each specialty? No country has solved these questions. On the one hand the number of doctors is grossly inadequate in rural areas of developing countries, and on the other there are too many doctors in attractive centres in most countries. Sometimes newly qualified doctors are directed by central agencies to regions that are short of doctors, but in most countries the number and distribution of doctors are decided by economic forces and opportunity. In Britain the number of consultant surgeons per 100 000 population varies from two to six, and there is little dispute that some surgeons have such heavy clinical loads that they are bound to build up waiting lists.

The number of operations a consultant surgeon performs

Some surgeons operate more slowly than others, and no one can say that they are less effective, even if they are less efficient. Central audit by, for example, performance indicators can reveal whether operating theatres are fully used, but they cannot show whether the surgeon or the anaesthetist has wasted time, or indeed occasionally has neglected his National Health Service practice because he has been too busy operating on private patients (Yates, 1987).

Inefficiency seldom increases effectiveness. The National Audit Office (1987) in Britain examined five district health authorities in detail and concluded that operating theatres were being used to half their capacity in spite of huge waiting lists. In these five districts an extra 11 000 operations could be performed each year if the theatres were fully used. They found inadequate forward planning, lack of coordination among hospital departments, and serious imbalances between staffing levels, bed availability, and operating time. Twenty eight per cent of available weekday theatre time was not scheduled for use, while 23% was unused because operations had been cancelled.

The criteria for defining the need for operations

Here again national audit is no help – the definition of need is left to the judgement of individual surgeons who claim that their clinical freedom is endangered by any attempt to persuade them that the way in which they give priorities may not reflect patients' perceptions. Diseases and operations that are interesting to doctors are likely to receive priority. In addition, outpatient non-operative methods are sometimes as effective as inpatient operations. Minor haemorrhoids and varicose veins, for example, are dealt with by most surgeons by injections in the outpatient department, and a useful aspect of audit is the examination of the proportion of a surgeon's work that he does in that department.

Clinical audit can disclose that some surgeons are operating on many more patients with asymptomatic gall stones or minor menorrhagia than others, and that patients are being admitted for investigations that could be done as outpatients. When gynaecologists in Canada agreed on guidelines for hysterectomy the result was a reduction in the rate of hysterectomy in many hospitals (Dyck *et al.*, 1977). Nils and Ulla addressed the World Congress on Surgical Efficiency and Economy in Lund, Sweden, in 1987 and disclosed that the waiting list for total joint replacements in Stockholm was intolerable. They reduced it by investigating every patient's general condition in the outpatient department.

The development of new operations

Since the establishment of the effectiveness and relative safety of joint replacement operations, there has been an enormous increase in the number of these elective operations without a decline in the amount of emergency trauma work for orthopaedic surgeons. The same thing has happened with intra-ocular lens replacement after removal of cataracts. Many elderly people were prepared to put up with their cataracts rather than face a future with distorting spectacles. Coronary artery bypass grafts for intractable angina have allowed many people to resume active lives. With all these and with other techniques the appropriate specialists have been overwhelmed with new work and their waiting lists have grown. It is not, however, only when new operations are feasible that commonplace operations for commonplace conditions are postponed. Jennett (1987) suggested that many complicated operations for elderly people and those with a limited expectation of life are being done while the waiting lists for the repair of hernias in working men escalate.

The demands of patients

As a result of talking to their friends and neighbours, reading newspaper and magazine articles, and watching television presentations, many people who had no idea that their complaints might have remedies are now seeking referral to hospitals.

The referral habits of general practitioners

Britain is fortunate in having a thriving primary care sector, the family practitioner service. This manages 90% of all episodes of ill health for less than 8% of total expenditure by the National Health Service. Information from the National Morbidity Survey showed a largely inexplicable variation in doctors' referral rates to hospitals (Crombie and Fleming, 1988). Ideally, general practitioners would refer all those who were likely to benefit from hospital treatment and no one who would not. It may be that changing the rate of referral would not of itself be beneficial and that what matters is to improve the logic of the decisions that are being taken. Good referral practice is therefore part of quality assurance. Britain has not had to control the over-use of specialists that happens when payment is by item of service, but there are grounds for believing that some patients may not be receiving hospital care though they would benefit from it, whereas others are referred to hospitals without good reason.

The role of the family practitioners as gatekeepers in preventing unwarranted and unlimited access to specialists ensures that the admission rates to hospitals in Britain are among the lowest in the world. The variation among family doctors in the proportion of their patients referred to specialists may arise from variations in the personal commitment of these doctors to their patients, but it may also arise because of patients' demands for specialist opinions.

The availability of hospital beds

This is closely bound up with the restriction of hospital budgets, but sometimes beds are closed quite inappropriately for maintenance and redecoration at busy times of the year. It is not, however, an important cause of long waiting lists, particularly if hospitals are prepared to use convalescent and preconvalescent facilities outside the hospital. The growth of daycase and overnight stay surgery has meant that many more patients can be treated in the same number of beds. It is generally recognised that an average bed occupancy of 80% is desirable, and efficiency is jeopardised, costs rise, and waiting lists increase if the bed occupancy is consistently below this figure.

The availability of operating theatres

Most hospitals were built with too few operating theatres. There should always be a theatre for emergencies, and surgeons can do more operating if they can run twin theatres. This, however, is seldom possible. Operating theatres are expensive to build and to run, but there is hardly a hospital in which an extra theatre would not be welcomed by surgeons.

The availability of trained nurses

In many countries there are shortages of trained nurses. This may be partly due to relatively poor pay, but it is often the result of a lack of job satisfaction. Nurses are traditionally women and the career structure in Britain is such that promotion and better pay depend on giving up practical nursing in favour of administration.

The acceptability of daycase surgery

Waiting lists for some operations can be cleared quite quickly by asking patients to be prepared to convalesce at home or, if postoperative pain is expected, to spend no more than one night in hospital. We considered this subject in greater depth in Chapter 9.

The excessive use of follow-up consultations

Except for the purposes of clinical audit of the late outcome of operations and diseases there is no need for surgical patients to attend outpatient departments month after month. Even for most research and audit programmes it is quite enough to contact patients regularly by mail or telephone. The figures for number of patients seen are inflated if the consultant insists on repeated follow up visits, but the proportion of 'new' and 'old' consultations will be revealed in the figures derived from performance indicators in England and a reduction in the number of follow up visits should allow surgeons to see more new patients. The ratio of total surgical outpatients to new outpatients a few years ago varied from five to one in Leeds to three to one in Bristol (Wilkes, 1980). In 1985 a total of 37 440 million patients were seen in the outpatient departments of all specialties in England (Department of Health and Social Security, 1987). 8 682 million of these were new patients, a ratio of 4.3 to 1.

Periodic review of patients on the waiting list

When a newly appointed surgeon takes over a waiting list inherited from his retired predecessor the first thing he does is to review the patients on that list. Some will have moved, others no longer want an operation, and others no longer need an operation. It is, however, unusual for a surgeon to review periodically the patients whom he has put on the waiting list himself. For this reason the number of patients on the list may not reflect the true number (Davidge *et al.*, 1987). Mangan *et al.* (1992) reduced the number of patients awaiting admission for operations on their feet by 60% by holding a series of special clinics and advising non-operative treatment where that was appropriate.

Conclusions

The perpetuation of a waiting list for admission to hospital is one way of rationing scarce resources. It is doubtful, however, whether patients view hospital waiting lists with anything but abhorrence, and the Department of Health in Britain is committed to reducing the time people have to wait for inpatient treatment. Only part of the responsibility lies with hospital doctors.

References

Beecham, L. (1991) Waiting lists out, booking system in. *British Medical Journal*, **302**, 929

Crombie, D.L. and Fleming, D.M. (1988) General practitioner referrals to hospital: the financial implications of variability. *Health Trends*, **20**, 53–56

Davidge, M., Harley, M., Vickerstaff, L. and Yates, J. (1987) The anatomy of large inpatient waiting lists. *Lancet*, **i**, 794–796

Department of Health and Social Security (1987) *Health and Personal Social Services Statistics for England, 1985*. HMSO, London

Dyck, F.J., Murphy, J.R., Road, D.A. *et al.* (1977) Effect of surveillance on the number of hysterectomies in the province of Saskatchewan. *New England Journal of Medicine*, **196**, 1326–1328

Emerson, R.W. (1841) *Prudence. Essays, first series*

Frankel, S., Coast, J., Baker, T. and Collins, C. (1991) Booked admissions as a replacement for waiting lists in the new NHS. *British Medical Journal*, **303**, 1257–1258

Jennett, B. (1987) Waiting lists: a surgeon's response. *Lancet*, **i**, 796–797

Mangan, J.L., Ashford, R.L., Murphy, J.S.G. and Beverland, D.E. (1992) Waiting list initiatives: application to foot surgery. *Medical Audit News*, **2**, 44–45

National Audit Office (1987) *Use of Operating Theatres in the National Health Service*. HMSO, London

Stewart, M. and Donaldson, L.J. (1991) Travelling for earlier surgical treatment: the patient's view. *British Journal of General Practice*, **41**, 508–509

Wilkes, E. (1980) In *Waiting for Hospital Treatment*. DHSS, London, pp. 14–17

Yates, J. (1987) *Why are we waiting? An analysis of hospital waiting lists*. Oxford University Press, Oxford

Audit of ethics

Chapter 21

The sanctity of life

Thou shalt not kill; but needst not strive officiously to keep alive.
Arthur Hugh Clough (1852)

We have defined audit, and we have written about the three divisions of audit – structure, process, and outcome. We have, however, restricted ourselves to what Kennedy (1981) would call the concept of the doctor as a 'scientist engineer'. It is equally important – some would say far more important – that social and ethical considerations of medical practice and the health of nations shall be audited as stringently as aspects of technique.

The present population of the world is 5.4 billion, and is expected to reach 8.5 billion by the year 2025 (King, 1991). It has increased fivefold in the last 150 years, and threatens to put an unsustainable pressure on resources. The trap is closing in the Indian subcontinent, in Kenya, and in Nigeria. In all these countries the birth rate has remained high while the death rate has fallen. King suggested that the only escapes from closure of the trap – which would cause starvation – are bloody war, disease such as a virulent strain of influenza, emigration (which is impossible on the necessary scale), and one-child families.

In developed countries the picture is quite different, and the populations of Italy and Germany are actually declining. *The Times* (1990) reported that Italian women produce an average of 1.29 children, Germany 1.39, Denmark 1.62, France 1.81, Britain 1.85, and Ireland 2.11.

We must respect above all things the four imperatives that derive from Immanuel Kant's Categorical Imperative: 'Act only on that maxim through which you can at the same time will that it should become a universal law'. These four are respect for autonomy, beneficence, non-maleficence, and justice. Consideration of these four leads us to discuss life, death, and dying.

Gillon published 26 articles in the *British Medical Journal* on Philosophical Medical Ethics. He concluded (Gillon, 1986) that 'Doctors are obliged...to ensure that they practise in ways that do actually benefit patients with minimal harm. Thus continuing postgraduate medical education, including some form of audit, is a moral obligation, as distinct from an optional extra taken on by enthusiasts.' Illich (1976) added to these moral imperatives three related ones: compassion, hospitality, and respect (summed up by Gillon as kindness).

Life

We accept that it is essential for doctors to preserve life and postpone death, but we must first of all attempt to define these words.

When does human life begin? There is one view that is irreconcilable with all others: it is that life begins when an ovum is fertilised and that it is the duty of doctors to preserve that life. 'There is a certain consistency in maintaining that abortion and contraception are both morally wrong, for each has the effect of preventing the development of morally autonomous life' (McLean and Maher, 1983).

This strict view was modified in the thirteenth century by Thomas Aquinas, who accepted the view of Aristotle that a male fetus acquires a soul at 40 days after conception and a female at 90 days (Gillon, 1985b). There are at least four alternative views:

- Life begins with quickening. This is an ancient concept that is still accepted by many people.
- Life begins when the embryo (at about 14 days after fertilisation) reaches a stage when that part that will be the fetus could neither divide into other individuals, nor differentiate into non-human tissue: this is the stage of the primitive streak (Ford, 1988).
- Life begins when a foetus might be capable of survival outside the uterus. This is often arbitrarily defined as the 28th week of pregnancy and in many countries is the legal limit drawn betweeen hysterotomy for termination and caesarean section for delivery. In Britain the *Human Fertilisation and Embryology Act 1990* amended the *Abortion Act 1967* and laid down the four conditions under which a medical termination of pregnancy is not unlawful. These are:

  - The pregnancy has not exceeded the 24th week and continuance of the pregnancy would involve greater risk than if the pregnancy were terminated or injury to the physical or mental health of the pregnant woman or any existing children of her family, or
  - The termination is necessary to prevent grave permanent injury to the physical or mental health of the pregnant woman, or
  - The continuation of the pregnancy would involve risk to the life of the pregnant woman greater than if the pregnancy were terminated, or
  - There is a substantial risk that, if the child were born, it would suffer from physical or mental abnormalities as to be seriously handi-capped.

- Life begins at birth. This is the least controversial and clearly separates late termination of pregnancy from neonatal death.

The registration of births and neonatal deaths

In Britain the *Births and Deaths Registration Act 1953* defined live birth merely as 'a child born alive' with no reference to gestational age. The World Health Organisation recommended that a beating heart or movement of voluntary muscles should proclaim that a fetus, however premature, was alive. Problems arise, however. In the first place, in Britain an infant born dead is regarded as an abortion until the 24th week of gestation and cannot be registered as a stillbirth until after that age. Second, many hospitals are jealous of their statistics of perinatal mortality, which are still used as indices of the quality of obstetric and neonatal paediatric care; they are not anxious to include the deaths of extremely premature ('non-viable') infants.

Dr Marek Gabrielczyk (1987), a senior lecturer in anaesthetics, gave a moving account of the extremely premature delivery of his wife of twin daughters, one of whom never lived and the other who lived for eight hours. He admitted to three emotions: grief at the death of his daughters, gratitude for the consideration and humanity of the obstetric and paediatric staff, and anger that the event had legally to be described as an abortion.

The case of Dr Leonard Arthur

In 1981 a newborn infant, John Pearson, was diagnosed as having Down's syndrome and was rejected by his mother. Dr Arthur, a consultant paediatrician, prescribed nursing care and dihydrocodeine 5 mg in distilled water every four hours to keep the infant comfortable. Death rapidly ensued and Dr Arthur was prosecuted at the instigation of an organisation called Life. Initially the charge was murder but, on the orders of the judge (Mr Justice Farquarson), this was changed to attempted murder and Dr Arthur was acquitted. Gillon (1985a) summarised the case for the prosecution:

1. All innocent human beings have a fundamental right to life and must not be deprived of it by acts or omissions.
2. Doctors in relation to patients and parents in relation to children have greater than normal duties of care.
3. It would be wrong to give a normal child nursing care alone, unless the child were dying.
4. It was wrong to treat the infant's distress by analgesics when it needed food and comfort and possibly antibiotics.
5. It would be wrong to neglect to treat an older child with Down's syndrome.

The moral case for the defence was:

1. A doctor's duty is to preserve life and minimise suffering.
2. Some congenital defects are so severe that the chances of ordinary human flourishing are small.
3. Severely defective children can impose a great burden on parents and on the community.
4. The parents are the proper people to decide whether medical care shall be given, after being given all the facts about the possible outcomes.
5. It would be arrogant for the doctor to reject the parents' decision.
6. There was no reason to suppose the parents were incompetent or malicious.

7. In these circumstances it was right for the doctor to alleviate suffering
   by prescribing analgesics.

Death

Death and bereavement are natural phenomena. The aim of medical and
nursing people must be to make sure that the dying is dignified and that
the bereavement is dealt with sympathetically. Many people would rather
die at home, and their relatives would welcome this. It is the custom in
some cultures, notably among Hindus, that patients who are going to die
are taken home from hospital and die in the comfort and love of their
families. A Natural Death Centre has been established in London (20
Heber Road NW2 6AA), one of the aims of which is to bring compassion
into the process of dying (Richardson, 1991).

Brain death

There was a time when it was easy to diagnose death: it was the cessation
of the functions of the heart and the lungs. During the last 20 years,
however, confusion has arisen because of the ability of doctors to provide
artificial ventilation and so keep the heart beating, even though the
patient's brain is so severely damaged or diseased that no return of
consciousness can be expected. It was the Harvard Ad Hoc Committee in
Boston, Massachusetts that first formulated the concept of brain death, a
concept that has been accepted with few modifications in most countries.
The Harvard Committee was chaired by Henry K. Beecher and all the
appropriate medical specialties were represented, together with members
with particular knowledge of history, ethics, and law. The definition
accepted by this Committee can be summarised as follows (Report, 1968):

1. Unreceptivity and unresponsivity.
2. No movements or breathing after three minutes off ventilator.
3. No central reflexes.
4. Flat electroencephalogram. The chairman of this Committee, Henry K.
   Beecher (1969), subsequently suggested that the electroencephalogram
   is unnecessary.

'All the above tests shall be repeated at least 24 hours later with no
change.' The Committee required that hypothermia and drugs must be
eliminated from the diagnosis, and that at least two doctors together with
the family must make the decision of brain death before the respirator is
turned off.

The British version of the requirements for the diagnosis of brain death
was the outcome of a Conference of Medical Royal Colleges and was
published in the *British Medical Journal* in 1976. The requirements called
for observation by at least two doctors on at least two occasions separated
by intervals of several hours. Three conditions must co-exist before the
diagnosis can be considered, and six confirmatory tests must be applied.
The preconditions are that the patient is deeply comatose and that this is

not due to drugs, hypothermia, or metabolic or endocrine disturbances; that the patient is being maintained on a ventilator; and that there should be no doubt that the patient's condition is due to irremediable structural brain damage. The confirmatory tests to establish that all brain stem reflexes are absent are: the pupils are fixed and do not react to light; there is no corneal reflex; the vestibulo-ocular reflex is absent; no motor response can be elicited; there is no gag reflex or response to an endotracheal catheter; and no respiratory movement occurs when the patient is disconnected from the ventilator for long enough for the PaCo$_2$ to be 6.7 kPa (50 mm Hg), oxygen being supplied by an endotracheal catheter.

In clinical practice the diagnosis of brain death is important in relation to organ transplantation, the ethical principle being that the welfare of another patient requires the removal of living organs (the kidneys often, the liver sometimes, and the heart and lungs occasionally) from the dead person and that this must be done immediately after oxygenated blood has ceased to circulate.

The concept of brain death has, however, also been used to substantiate a charge of murder. The facts of a case in point (Curran, 1978b) were as follows: a youth of 18 hit a 34-year-old man on the head with a baseball bat 'for kicks'. The man was admitted to hospital where he was placed on a respirator. Several days later tests for brain death established that withdrawal of the respirator resulted in no spontaneous breathing or reflex activity, and an electroencephalogram was flat. The tests were repeated two days later, the patient in the interim being artificially ventilated. Again the tests showed brain death and three days later, with the agreement of the man's family, the respirator was turned off. The defence was that death was caused by the turning off of the respirator, and that, if artificial respiration had been continued the patient might have lived for 'a year and a day' – the time limit that Sir Edward Coke introduced in 1595 within which death following an assault was to be regarded as murder. The trial judge instructed the jury to apply a test of brain death, which he defined for legal purposes as occurring when there is a total and irreversible cessation of spontaneous brain functions and further attempts at resuscitation would not be successful in restarting such functions. The jury found that the concept of brain death had been satisfied, and that death had occurred before the respirator was turned off. On appeal the Supreme Judicial Court affirmed the conviction for murder and found that the definition of brain death was essentially medical and must be left to expert medical witnesses. In Britain it has been established in two cases (see Chapter 17) that those responsible for inflicting initial wounds will take responsibility for the victim's death even if it might have been avoided by better medical care.

Dying

'Developments in science and technology tend to acquire a momentum of their own, such that they pass beyond ready control' (Kennedy, 1981). Many doctors conceive it their duty to treat terminally ill patients, not merely to ease their pain and apprehension. Several problems arise: first, it is often difficult to be sure that a patient is dying; second, the treatment may be worse than the disease and impose a new burden on a patient already burdened by an incurable disease; third, 'the position that the dying have a greater right to economic resources runs the double risk of doing an injustice to other patients and using scarce resources without reflection' (Bayer *et al.*, 1983). These authors, from the Hastings Center, New York, believe 'that the relation between the economic and the moral dimensions of care for the terminally ill is a subject that can be addressed openly, without embracing a crude calculus that trades life for dollars'. They proposed better criteria for admitting patients to intensive care units, promoting the autonomy of patients and their families, and promoting alternative institutions like hospices.

Ashby and Stoffell (1991) put forward the concept of three modes of dealing with seriously ill patients. The first is the curative mode: prolongation of life is the aim – a high rate of toxicity associated with the treatment, and even a risk of death attributable to the treatment is acceptable. The second is the palliative mode: this is to be used when either treatment is not expected to prolong life, or alternatively that any gain in life expectancy is at the expense of intolerable toxicity. For these patients investigations and treatment are to be directed solely to the patient's comfort and general wellbeing. The third is the terminal mode, when nothing other than ordinary social care and relief of suffering is to be undertaken. Moral problems arise mainly when the patient is no longer competent to take part in the therapeutic decisions.

The moral dilemmas have occasionally reached courts of law, as in the Saikewicz case (Curran, 1978a). The patient was a 67-year-old man with mental retardation so profound that he could not talk and was cared for in a school. He was terminally ill with acute myeloblastic leukaemia, but was not in pain. The school superintendent, his guardian, was unsure whether to agree to chemotherapy with all its attendant discomforts, so brought a petition in the Probate Court of the state of Massachusetts for the appointment of a guardian *ad litem* with authority to make a decision. After investigation the guardian recommended that it was not in the best interests of the ward to undergo treatment. The Supreme Judicial Court of Massachusetts affirmed the order in July 1976, and published their full opinion the following year. The court held that a competent adult could refuse further treatment, and that a guardian could take this decision. Justice Liacos on behalf of the Supreme Court held that the decision to withhold treatment was one for the courts of law and could not be granted to any other group, and asserted that 'To the extent that this formulation equates the value of life with any measure of the quality of life, we reject it.'

In Britain a similar dilemma faced Dr Desmond Oliver and the staff of the dialysis unit at the Churchill Hospital in Oxford (Brahams, 1985). Early in 1983 a man aged 43 came under the care of the renal unit at the Churchill Hospital. He had severe mental impairment and lived in a hostel for the homeless. Gradually his renal function deteriorated and haemodialysis was started in March 1984. Thereafter his mental function got worse and his mental age was put at three years. He was at times violent, generally uncooperative, dirty, incontinent of urine and faeces, unable to take medication reliably, could not adhere to diet, exposed himself, and masturbated while being examined. He had to be sedated during dialysis to prevent him removing blood lines from his arm. The dialysis sessions were proving a torment to both patient and medical staff, and the unit's capacity to deal with other patients was being affected. By December 1984 nurses told Dr Oliver who was in charge of the unit that they did not think continuation of dialysis was in the patient's best interests. He was dialysed again on 2 January 1985 and then discharged back to the hostel. His case was taken up by the British Kidney Patients Association and he was referred for private treatment to a unit in London.

Persistent vegetative state

Correct medical or surgical treatment of a patient in coma (resulting from a severe head injury, or a hypoxic or hypoglycaemic episode, or as a result of a disease of the brain) may result in complete recovery, recovery with neurological deficit, or a persistent vegetative state. Patients in this state breathe spontaneously but cannot eat or drink: they need feeding by nasogastric or gastrostomy tube. The question that the Institute of Medical Ethics in the UK asked a working party to decide was whether, and when, tube feeding could be discontinued. In the USA the decision often hinges on the expressed wishes of the patient while he or she was competent and, if there is a conflict between the wishes of the guardians and the carers, usually requires a court order. Nancy Cruzan had been in a vegetative state for five and a half years when a court in Missouri refused such an order, which had been requested by her parents. Two years later the US Supreme Court upheld this decision, but the parents presented new evidence of Nancy's previously expressed wishes and the court in Missouri granted the order (Rouse, 1991).

Marcia Angell (1990) showed up the dilemma facing doctors who have the technology to keep such a person apparently living and noted that 'the very high suicide rate among older Americans is probably due partly to their opinion that they may be unable to stop treatment if they are hospitalized...some people now fear living more than dying because they dread becoming prisoners of technology'.

The Institute of Medical Ethics Working Party on the Ethics of Prolonging Life and Assisting Death (1991) concluded that withdrawal of hydration and nutrition was morally justified if the decision was unanimous among guardians, carers, and at least two experienced doctors.

In the earlier case of Karen Ann Quinlan the court in New Jersey entrusted the decision to discontinue life support to the patient's family, the attending doctors and the hospital ethics committee. Whether the requirement that only a court of law can make the decision to withhold treatment for a person who is not competent to make the decision himself remains unclear.

Courts may occasionally have to make a decision to withdraw treatment even in the presence of resistance from the family (Charatan, 1991). Mrs Helga Wanglie, aged 87 years, had been in a persistent vegetative state for nearly a year when the Hennepin County Medical Center in

Minneapolis requested permission from her husband to discontinue ventilation. This he refused, on the grounds that his wife had told her husband that 'Only He who gives life has the right to take life'. The medical director of the hospital asked for the appointment of a guardian *ad litem* to decide the issue.

The introduction of the techniques of external cardiac massage, external cardiac defibrillation, and endotracheal intubation and artificial ventilation have allowed the resuscitation of a patient whose heart has stopped and who would previously have been certified dead. The difficulty is that most people who suffer cardiac arrest are indeed dead, and the ethical dilemma arises over the instruction (whether given in writing or not) not to attempt resuscitation of patients with terminal illnesses. This has nothing to do with euthanasia, which most people believe always to be wrong. If, on the other hand, a patient dies marginally before his time because a doctor has prescribed analgesics and sedatives, that must be accepted as a price to pay for proper medical care. In *R v Adams (1957), LR 365:375*, Mr Justice Devlin ruled that 'a doctor...is entitled to do all that is proper and necessary to relieve pain and suffering, even if the measures he takes may incidentally shorten life'.

The living will

In 1969 the Euthanasia Educational Council published what it called a 'living will', the essence of which was contained in these two paragraphs:

> 'If the time comes when I can no longer take part in decisions for my own future, let this statement stand as an expression of my wishes, while I am still of sound mind.
>
> If the situation should arise in which there is no reasonable expectation of my recovery from physical or mental disability, I request that I be allowed to die and not be kept alive by artificial means or heroic measures. I do not fear pain. I, therefore, ask that medication be mercifully administered to me to alleviate suffering even though this may hasten the moment of death.'

Sissela Bok (1976) published a document embodying these requests and called *Directions for my Care*, which, however, has not yet been ratified by the courts, although most American states already have natural death acts that recognise living wills and allow a person to let a family member or friend make medical decisions for him or her; from November 1991 federal legislation will require hospitals to inform all patients on admission of their right to make an advanced treatment declaration or to appoint a decision making proxy (Jennett and Dyer, 1991).

The Clinical Care Committee of the Massachusetts General Hospital (1976) issued a report that recommended classification of patients into four classes: class A patients were to be given maximal therapeutic effort without reservation; class B patients were to be given maximal therapeutic effort but were to be evaluated daily for possible transfer to a lower class; class C patients were to be given appropriate treatment short of cardiopulmonary resuscitation, and class D patients were to receive only 'measures which are indicated to insure maximum comfort'.

A policy statement was developed after consultation with legal and ethical experts on the applicability of Orders Not to Resuscitate (Rabkin, Gillerman and Rice, 1976). The authors stressed that 'Even if a medical judgment is reached that a patient is faced with such an illness and imminence of death that resuscitation is medically inappropriate, the decision to withhold resuscitation ... will become effective only upon the informed choice of a competent patient or, with an incompetent patient, by strict adherence to ... guidelines ... and then only to the extent that all appropriate family members are in agreement with the views of the involved staff.'

A recent legal model in the United States, the *Uniform Rights of the Terminally Ill Act*, suggested the form: 'If I should have an incurable or irreversible condition that will cause my death within a relatively short time, and am no longer able to make decisions regarding my medical treatment, I direct my attending physician...to withhold or withdraw treatment that only prolongs the process of dying and is not necessary to my comfort or to alleviate the pain.' The difficulty is that a dying person may be mentally incompetent to understand such a directive, and no one other than the patient has the legal right either to consent to or to refuse treatment.

In Canada the issue of the living will has caused a lot of public discussion. The Manitoba Law Reform Commission (1990) published a discussion paper which considered 'the situation of the individual who through age, illness, or accident loses the ability to communicate his or her wishes respecting medical treatment'. The difficulty with a living will, or 'advance directive' is that it puts a great burden on the doctors and the person holding power of attorney.

The legalities have still not been sorted out, but the federal *Patient Self-Determination Act* in the USA, which came into effect in December 1991 and applies to patients receiving treatment under Medicaid and Medicare, is likely to influence other systems to adopt the measures that are required by that Act. They are that hospitals and other health care facilities are now obliged to tell patients when they are admitted that they can prepare a living will specifying their preferences for terminal care, including proxy arrangements for making decisions.

Euthanasia

A working party of the British Medical Association chaired by Sir Henry Yellowlees considered the problems of euthanasia for 16 months and produced a report (Higgs, 1988). Essentially their conclusion was that the taking of life must always and under all circumstances be illegal and that doctors must refuse to accede to a patient's wish to have his or her life ended, even though they recognise that in all other matters the patient must be a partner in any medical decision. The aim of medical care for the dying must be 'dying well'; doctors must respect patients' autonomy, but they must also keep beneficence constantly in mind.

The *Journal of the American Medical Association* published an unsigned account by a resident in gynaecology (Anonymous, 1988). This doctor was called to a young woman dying of ovarian cancer. He gave her a large dose of morphine and she died. The publication of this act of active euthanasia caused a storm of mainly condemnatory correspondence. In an editorial, Lundberg (1988) concluded that doctors must continue to support the tradition that has persisted for thousands of years – that their duty is to preserve the best possible life for the longest possible time. 'When one backs away in any sense from the utter sanctity of maintaining human life, the slope becomes very slippery indeed.'

Lundberg identified six types of euthanasia, defined as 'a quiet and easy death', and gave examples:

1. Passive: not attempting resuscitation of a patient with carcinomatosis who has had a cardiac arrest. This is perhaps the most common, and the instruction 'do not resuscitate' should be made openly and with the knowledge of the patient's family.
2. Semipassive: withholding food and fluids from a patient in irreversible coma.
3. Semiactive: disconnection of a ventilator from a patient in a stable vegetative state after massive brain destruction.
4. Accidental: relieving pain by an injection of a narcotic, which incidentally hastens death.
5. Suicidal: allowing a patient access to drugs that can cause death.
6. Active: injection of a lethal dose of a drug.

Active euthanasia has been repudiated by doctors since the time of Hippocrates, part of whose oath reads: 'I will give no deadly drug to any, though it be asked of me, nor will I counsel such.' Even active euthanasia is now accepted with reservations in The Netherlands, where it is illegal but doctors acting in good faith after determined requests from patients are unlikely to be prosecuted. It is clear that the debate is by no means over. Nor has it been helped by the television antics of Dr Jack Kevorkian, who invented and has used a 'suicide machine'.

Conclusion

Audit of ethical matters is just as important as of technical matters, and nowhere is this more apparent than in the consideration of life, death, and dying. A doctor's conscience and integrity can usually be relied on to do the right thing, but guidance from ethical philosophers is essential. Ethical aspects of consent, telling the truth, and respecting of confidentiality will be considered in the next chapter.

References

Angell, M. (1990) Prisoners of technology: the case of Nancy Cruzan. *New England Journal of Medicine*, **322**, 1226–1228

Anonymous (1988) It's over, Debbie. *Journal of the American Medical Association*, **259**, 272

Ashby, M. and Stoffell, B. (1991) Therapeutic ratio and defined phases: proposal of ethical framework for palliative care. *British Medical Journal*, **302**, 1322–1324

Bayer, R., Callahan, D., Fletcher, J. *et al.* (1983) The care of the terminally ill: morality and economics. *New England Journal of Medicine*, **309**, 1490–1494

Beecher, H.K. (1969) After the 'definition of irreversible coma'. *New England Journal of Medicine*, **281**, 1070

Bok, S. (1976) Personal directions for care at the end of life. *New England Journal of Medicine*, **295**, 367–369

Brahams, D. (1985) When is discontinuation of dialysis justified? *Lancet*, **i**, 176–177

British Medical Journal (1976) Diagnosis of brain death. Statement issued by the honorary secretary of the Conference of Medical Royal Colleges and their Faculties in the United Kingdom on 11 October 1976. **2**, 1187–1188

Charatan, F.B. (1991) Hospital sues to remove life support. *British Medical Journal*, **302**, 552

Clinical Care Committee of the Massachusetts General Hospital (1976) Optimum care for hopelessly ill patients. *New England Journal of Medicine*, **295**, 362–364

Clough, A.H. (1852) *The Latest Decalogue*

Curran, W.J. (1978a) The Saikewicz decision. *New England Journal of Medicine*, **298**, 499–500

Curran, W.J. (1978b) The brain death concept: judicial acceptance in Massachusetts. *New England Journal of Medicine*, **298**, 1008–1009

Ford, N.F. (1988) *When Did I Begin?* Cambridge University Press, Cambridge

Gabrielczyk, M. (1987) Personal view. *British Medical Journal*, **295**, 209

Gillon, R. (1985a) The Arthur case. *British Medical Journal*, **290**, 1117–1119

Gillon, R. (1985b) To what do we have moral obligations and why? *British Medical Journal*, **290**, 1646–1647

Gillon, R. (1986) Doctors and patients. *British Medical Journal*, **292**, 466–469

Higgs, R. (1988) Not the last word on euthanasia. *British Medical Journal*, **291**, 1348

Illich, I. (1976) *Limits to Medicine. Medical nemesis: the expropriation of health*. Marion Boyars, London

Jennett, B. and Dyer, C. (1991) Persistent vegetative state and the right to die: the United States and Britain. *British Medical Journal*, **302**, 1256–1258

Kennedy, I. (1981) *The Unmasking of Medicine*. George Allen and Unwin, London

King, M. (1991) Human entrapment in India. *National Medical Journal of India*, **4**, 196–201

Lundberg, J. (1988) 'It's over, Debbie' and the euthanasia debate. *Journal of the American Medical Association*, **259**, 2142–2143

McLean, S. and Maher, G. (1983). *Medicine, Morals and the Law*. Gower, Aldershot

Manitoba Law Reform Commission (1990) Discussion paper on advance directives and durable powers of attorney for health care

Rabkin, M.T., Gillerman, G. and Rice, N.R. (1976) Orders not to resuscitate. *New England Journal of Medicine*, **295**, 364–366

Report of the Ad Hoc Committee of the Harvard Medical School to Examine the Definition of Brain Death (1968) A definition of irreversible coma. *Journal of the American Medical Association*, **205**, 337–340

Richardson, R. (1991) Death in context. *British Medical Journal*, **302**, 1232

Rouse, F. (1991) The Cruzan case. *Lancet*, **337**, 105–106

The Times (1990). December 31, page 1, 2–5

Working Party of the Institute of Medical Ethics (1991) Withdrawal of life-support from patients in a persistent vegetative state. *Lancet*, **337**, 96–98

Chapter 22

Ethics of clinical surgery

*I know but one code of morality for men whether acting singly or
collectively.*   Thomas Jefferson (1801)

Ever since the first man or woman was recognised in the community as a
healer, there has been an implied ethical imperative, that the healer will
act only in the patient's interests. This was embodied in the Hippocratic
oath in the fourth century BC, which has been translated as: 'Into
whatever houses I enter, I will go into them for the benefit of the sick,
and will abstain from every voluntary act of mischief and corruption; and
further, from the seduction of women or men, of freemen and slaves.' A
good deal of the rest of the Hippocratic oath is concerned less with the
good of patients than with the preservation of the privileges of healers.

Over the centuries it has been accepted that medical people will not act
to do harm, even if they cannot do good. In most countries legal sanctions
are imposed on transgressing doctors. This is further considered in the
chapter on medical negligence. The philosophical basis of this ethical
imperative was propounded by Emanuel Kant in 1785 (Gillon, 1985a).
Kant's Categorical Imperative was 'Act only on that maxim through which
you can at the same time will that it should become a universal law.' His
supreme moral law was that no person should be treated as a means, but
as an end, and that people should always act as if they were kings creat-
ing universal laws for their kingdoms.

Jeremy Bentham, the prophet of utilitarianism, on the other hand,
regarded 'the greatest happiness of the greatest number' as the foundation of moral philosophy (Gillon, 1985b), and John Stuart Mill regarded
respect for the autonomy of others, consistent with autonomy for all, as a
fundamental component of utilitarianism.

Beauchamp and Childress (1983) put forward four principles of medical
ethics: respect for autonomy, beneficence, non-maleficence, and justice.
Illich (1976) added three related ones: compassion, hospitality, and
respect, and Johnson (1990) distilled the imperatives into aim, value,
autonomy, and truth.

Gillon (1985c) wrote: 'The doctor may advise, but the patient is then
given the opportunity to decide whether to accept that advice .... Doctors
are obliged ... to ensure that they practise in ways that do actually benefit

patients with minimal harm. Thus continuing postgraduate medical education, including some form of audit, is a moral obligation, as distinct from an optional extra taken on by enthusiasts.'

The *Declarations of the World Medical Association* include the *Declaration of Geneva* (1948, revised 1983), which is an updated version of the Hippocratic oath. The *Declaration of Helsinki* (1964, revised 1983) concerned the ethics of research, the *Declaration of Lisbon* (1981) addressed the rights of patients, the *Declaration of Sydney* (1968, revised 1983) considered the diagnosis of brain death in relation to organ transplantation, the *Declaration of Tokyo* (1975, revised 1983) placed a prohibition on doctors taking part in torture, the *Declaration of Hawaii* (1977, revised 1983) concerned the ethics of treatments for psychiatric diseases, and the *Declaration of Venice* (1983) accepted Pope Pius XII's statement of 1958 that 'The good of saving life is morally obligatory only if its pursuit is not excessively burdensome or disproportionate in relation to the expected benefits.'

Respect for autonomy

Illich (1976) wrote a scathing attack on medical practice in the United States and claimed that 'the layman and not the physician has the potential perspective and effective power to stop the current iatrogenic epidemic'. The subtitle of his book is *Medical Nemesis*. (Nemesis was the goddess of chastisement and vengeance on the perpetrators of wanton boastfulness.) Illich considered that costly and high risk medical and surgical treatments, as opposed to certain prophylactic and public health measures, do as much harm as good. 'The study of the evolution of disease patterns provides evidence that during the last century doctors have affected epidemics no more profoundly than did priests during earlier times.'

McKeown (1976) examined the possible causes of the decline in mortality (and the consequent rise in population) in Britain during the nineteenth century and concluded that improvements in medical care had little to do with it, and that the main reason for the improvement was better nutrition. Other authors (Farrow, 1987) have emphasised the role of improvements in personal hygiene and in public health.

Illich was particularly scathing about hospitals and pleaded for more respect for autonomy, more compassion, more hospitality, and more respect. 'The hospital only reflects the labor economy of a high-technology society: transnational specialization at the top, bureaucracies in the middle, and at the bottom a new subproletariat made up of migrants and the professionalized client.'

Illich's view that 'the medical establishment has become a major threat to health' was echoed in Britain by Ian Kennedy in the Reith lectures in 1980 (Kennedy, 1981). He claimed that doctors, having abrogated to themselves the right to decide who is ill and who is not, wield the power. He considered that there was a long list of issues that were deeply troubling but which the medical profession kept under wraps. He was particularly critical of the training of doctors as engineers with the emphasis on high technology: 'Developments in science and technology tend to acquire a momentum of their own, such that they pass beyond ready control.'

Kennedy's criticisms included the following:

- Students are trained to be scientists and to ignore sociology
- Doctors regard themselves as dispensers of cures
- Doctors seek problems and then try and solve them instead of trying to prevent them
- Patients are thought of in terms of diseases
- Doctors try and give treatment for all 'illnesses'
- Medicine is increasingly hospital based: 'Hospitals are the epitome of the problem-solving disease-orientated scientific engineer approach'. In Colombia a programme of hospital care for premature infants resulted in survival rates equivalent to those in the United States but 70% died within three months of discharge
- The concept of 'illness' has been broadened to include old age and particular forms of behaviour, and these people can be locked away out of sight and neglected. Modern medicine concentrates on disease, not on health.

Kennedy proposed that many medical decisions should be taken out of the hands of doctors and should be made by the community, possibly through the law courts. He cited the decisions about whether to operate on a baby with severe spina bifida, whether to give chemotherapy for leukaemia to a severely mentally retarded man of 67 years (the Saikewicz case), and whether to continue ventilation of a girl in prolonged deep coma (the Karen Quinlan case).

There can be moral dilemmas inherent in the absolute requirement of respect for autonomy. Take the case of an unwanted pregnancy: respect for the mother's autonomy demands that she be assisted to expel the 'invader'. But what about the extinction of a potentially autonomous life? McLean and Maher (1983) wrote that 'There is a certain consistency in maintaining that abortion and contraception are both morally wrong, for each has the effect of preventing the development of morally autonomous life'.

Withholding or stopping treatment

If we acknowledge that respect for autonomy is an important ethical obligation, and that murder is wrong because it transgresses this obligation, what attitude are we to take to the withholding of food from a newborn baby with Down's syndrome who has been rejected by its mother? Or the instruction not to attempt resuscitation of a patient with advanced cancer? It is usually held that acts resulting in death are morally worse than omissions to act that result in death, but the distinction is dishonest. On the other hand, 'A doctor ... is entitled to do all that is proper and necessary to relieve pain and suffering, even if measures he takes may incidentally shorten life.' (Mr Justice Devlin, *R v Adams 1957, LR 365, p 375*). Respect for autonomy demands that the patient – and sometimes the whole community – must share in the making of decisions.

Consent

Respect for patients' autonomy demands that they consent to every step of the pathway of diagnosis and treatment. As Bernarde and Mayerson (1978) wrote: 'It is essential that the patient be made to believe that he is an independent, worthy person entitled to the most clearly stated information possible.' The consent to history taking and physical examination is implied by the patient's attendance at a clinic. On the other hand, consent to special examinations – both imaging and laboratory – must be specifically sought. This also applies to physical examination by medical students and doctors in training.

There are exceptions, of course; the autonomy of a child with meningitis who refuses an injection of an antibiotic cannot be respected. Normally the parent or guardian of a child is the one who gives consent for investigation or treatment, but the child should always be consulted and advised.

An enormous difficulty arises when the patient is not a child, but has the mental development of a child, or has a mental illness that precludes him or her from coming to a reasoned judgement. No one has the right to consent on behalf of such a patient. This dilemma reached the House of Lords in the case of *Re F* (Whitfield, 1989). The question was who, if anyone, had the right to give consent for the proposed sterilisation of a woman with a mental age of 4 or 5 who was at risk of pregnancy which, in the opinion of her psychiatrists, would be disastrous. The law was exhaustively examined and the following propositions emerged:

- In the case of a minor, such an operation should be carried out only with the leave of a High Court judge after the child had been made a ward of court
- In the case of an adult incapable of giving consent there is no Court that has jurisdiction to give or withhold substitute consent; nor can any relative, however close, or any medical attendant give consent on the patient's behalf
- Nevertheless, just as it is perfectly lawful to treat an unconscious patient in his or her best interests without consent, so it is lawful to sterilise a woman even though she is incapable of consenting, provided the procedure is in her best interests
- The test of whether the doctor is acting in her best interests is whether he acts in accordance with the opinion of a responsible body of medical practitioners in the relevant specialty
- There are, however, features that distinguish sterilisation from many other operations. It has moral, social, and emotional connotations, and is indeed an operation that might indirectly benefit the carer or relations to whom the pregnancy might be an embarrassment. Thus a carer or relation who advocated it overstrongly might be suspected of having mixed motives
- The final opinion of the Law Lords was that *'Although involvement of the Court is not strictly necessary as a matter of law, it is highly desirable as a matter of good practice.'*

There are, of course, occasions on which it is not necessary to ask consent to investigation. This includes the examination of a person suspected of a serious crime. One of the ways that carriers smuggle heroin into Britain is by swallowing polyethylene sachets containing the drug. If the Customs and Excise officials at London Heathrow Airport are suspicious, the suspect is taken to a nearby hospital and an X-ray taken of the abdomen – no consent is requested (Lancashire *et al.*, 1988).

Nevertheless, in normal everyday practice, surgeons have a moral duty to give their patients truthfully all the relevant options and to share decisions about investigations and treatment with their patients. This is usually done by word of mouth, but the amount of such information that the patient retains is small.

One of the ways this can be counteracted is by encouraging patients to read their own records. Another is to expand the content of pamphlets that some hospitals give patients who are to be admitted; these are sometimes so cursory and authoritarian as to be insulting to an intelligent person. Some pharmaceutical companies produce pamphlets dealing with specific diseases and treatments. These are usually well written and contain little advertising. It is possible to write pamphlets without jargon that do allow patients to participate in decision making. An important component of such a pamphlet is the assurance that no steps will be taken without the patient's freely given consent. Furthermore, when the treatment of a disease is controversial the options should be spelled out, the opinion of the surgeon logically stated, and the patient encouraged to give his or her own decision. Some patients will read such a pamphlet and conclude 'I leave it to you, doctor', but they should at least have an opportunity to make up their own minds.

Audiotapes that can be given or lent to patients are popular and allow the patient to hear the information many times (Baskerville *et al.*, 1985). When the disease, its treatment, or its long term effects are more serious it is preferable to impart the information in the form of a videotape.

Brewin (1982) concluded that 'the best policy ... is for a responsible caring doctor to be flexible, considerate, and discreet, never imposing unnecessary "informed consent" yet always ready to discuss anything with patients who wish it. Far from being patronising or arrogant, such a policy enhances the dignity of the patient as a unique individual, with changing moods and a changing ability to cope with fear, doubt, and uncertainty.'

There was a move at a recent British Medical Association Annual General Meeting to allow doctors to test blood preoperatively for antibodies to the human immunodeficiency virus without asking patients' consent. This was defeated, but permission for such tests is not required in some European countries including Austria, Hungary, Belgium, and Switzerland. Blood donors are always screened for the possibility of infection by this virus and other agents, but this is with their consent.

Over 50 years ago Richard Clarke Cabot, the distinguished physician at the Massachusetts General Hospital and originator of the weekly clinico-pathological exercises that are still published in the *New England Journal of Medicine*, wrote a book called *Honesty* (Cabot, 1938). He was primarily concerned with the widespread tendency of doctors to deceive their patients. He argued that doctors are prone to self deceit and self justification, and that lying to a patient is usually not to spare the patient's anguish but the doctor's conceit. The habit of lying may become entrenched and affect other aspects of a doctor's work, even including research publications.

One of the corollaries of the ethical obligation to seek consent to every investigation is that it would cut down the number of tests that are ordered merely to satisfy the doctor's curiosity (Reichen, 1984).

The improving results of renal, cardiac, and hepatic transplantation, partly resulting from the use of cyclosporin, have highlighted the shortage of suitable cadaveric organs, and different countries have responded in different ways. In some European countries the law lays down that organs may be removed from victims of brainstem death unless a specific objection had been raised by the next of kin. In some states in the United States doctors are required to request permission from the next of kin to remove organs. There is little doubt that in most cases this permission is granted. The problem in Britain is that many clinicians looking after these potential donors do not discuss matters with the local transplant team, and a greater awareness of need would help to provide many more organs. We shall have more to say about consent, particularly consent to randomisation, when we discuss the ethics of clinical research.

Beneficence

This is the second of the four ethical imperatives. How can we define it? It takes us into the realms of audit of process and outcome, and into a consideration of justice. The concept of beneficence means placing the interests of patients before those of the doctor. It also includes the old fashioned virtues of kindness, consideration, friendliness, and politeness. When we audit ethics we must identify the intention to do good, and distinguish from the intention to do harm. 'It would be morally naive to look at some medical action in retrospect, see that its results were in fact disastrous, such as the patient dying, and conclude that therefore the action must have been wrong' (Gillon, 1986).

Non-maleficence

Barnes (1977) examined the *Transactions of the American Surgical Association* from 1880 to 1942 and found testimonials to the value of numerous operations which have long since disappeared.

More recently Moossa (1987) quoted Lord Cohen: 'The feasibility of an operation is not an indication for its performance.' He examined surgical options for the treatment of chronic pancreatitis. These include duct drainage by sphincterotomy, by distal pancreaticojejunostomy, or by longitudinal pancreaticojejunostomy, by resections of varying magnitude, and by autotransplantation of the resected gland. Moossa concluded that 'The undeniable reality is that chronic pancreatitis is not primarily a surgical disease and only becomes so when a surgically correctable complication develops ... the results of surgical treatment must be properly analysed and reported.'

The surgeons who practised these operations were misguided, but most of them were not acting from motives of maleficence, and it is the motive that should be judged in an audit of ethics. Sometimes, however, the motive itself can be questioned. Attempts have been made in the USA (mainly for economic reasons) to reduce the number of unnecessary operations. Rutkow (1982) suggested that operations should be appropriate for the disease, they should be appropriate for the patient, and they should be performed by appropriately trained surgeons. Jennett (1988) wrote that inappropriate operations can be classified as unnecessary, unsuccessful, unkind, unsafe, or unwise.

Vayda, Mindell, and Rutkow (1982) reported that the number of operations per 100 000 population in 1976 in England and Wales was about 4000, in Canada about 6100, and in the USA about 8800. There are far more caesarean sections, carotid endarterectomies, and coronary artery bypass operations done in the USA than in any other country. A subcommittee of the Committee on Interstate and Foreign Commerce in the USA reported that 'there were an estimated 2.4 million unnecessary surgeries [sic] performed in 1974 at a cost to the American public of almost \$4 billion. These unnecessary surgeries led to 11 900 unnecessary deaths' (Report, 1976).

Tissue committees to audit unnecessary operations have been in existence in most American hospitals for 40 years or more. The function of a tissue committee is to report on the removal of normal tissues, but Rutkow (1982) criticised this method of audit on the grounds that 'the present misconception concerning the relationship of normal tissue rates to the justification of surgery stems from the now disproved theories of pioneers in hospital standardization who stated that the incidence of removal of normal tissues was an indication of unnecessary surgery and should not exceed 10 per cent ... a normal tissue rate is not the sole criterion of the justification for surgery. This can be determined only by the physician's evaluation of the clinical indications for surgery in each case.'

The debate about unnecessary operations became 'little more than a political slogan. The real issues of quality control, including certification, monitoring, and discipline of negligent surgeons, cost control, and patient access to information, should be addressed directly' (Annas, 1979). Nevertheless, many states introduced 'second opinion programs'. Grafe *et al.* (1978) presented the results of such a programme at Cornell Medical Center. From February 1972 to January 1978, 7053 patients were evaluated for proposed elective surgery, and in 27.6% the operations were not approved. Analysis of these operations showed that 42% of 707 orthopaedic operations, 34% of 894 gynaecological operations, 29% of 324 urological operations, and 18% of 1375 general surgical operations were not approved. In the discussion on this paper Moore wrote that second opinion was a new word for consultation; what was needed was expert first and second opinions; he wondered how many patients who should have had an operation did not see a first expert.

Justice

It is easier to identify injustice than to define justice. According to the utilitarian school of moral philosophers it means the greatest good for the greatest number, and according to Karl Marx it means 'from each according to his ability, to each according to his needs'.

Injustices in relation to medical care arise mainly for political and economic reasons. The greatest inequalities in expectation of life at birth are between developed and developing countries, but even within developed countries there are still unjust inequalities. These persist despite the decline in the importance of the infectious diseases as causes of death. In Britain in 1985 the perinatal mortality in social class I was 7.7 per 1000, compared with 12.4 in social class V (Office of Population Censuses and Surveys, 1987). At all ages manual workers are more likely to die than professional people, and those who are unemployed fare even worse. The divergence of mortality among the social classes is widening (Delamothe, 1991), and this continues despite the fact that the percentage of total spending in the National Health Service is greater for semiskilled and unskilled men and women (Appleby, 1991).

In the USA there are considerable differences in mortality between whites and blacks (US DHHS, 1990). The leading cause of death among young black men is homicide or 'legal intervention' – usually gunning down by the police. In the age group 25–34 homicide accounts for 98.9/100 000 deaths, compared with 13.2 among whites. In nearly every other category, however, mortality for both men and women is higher among blacks.

From the point of view of audit of the ethics of individual surgeons, however, the problem of the dispensation of justice rests on the distribution of scarce resources: if there is an imbalance between resources and need, who should be given priority? Some might say the illest, but they might be the least likely to benefit. Some would say the patient most likely to benefit from an operation that was most likely to succeed. Some would attempt to quantify benefit by calculating the quality adjusted life years likely to result from the intervention. McLean and Maher (1983) offered five criteria for the allocation of scarce resources:

1. The likelihood of success: why are some people denied dialysis or transplantation?
2. Potential future contribution: is a lawyer worth more than a doctor?
3. Past services rendered: preference to be given to the elderly
4. Ability to pay
5. Random selection.

None of these except the first should be purely medical decisions. Whatever formula is adopted, justice demands that decisions about whom to treat shall be shared between doctors and the community.

References

Annas, G.J. (1979) The extravagant, wasteful and superfluous debate about unnecessary surgery. *Hastings Center Report*, **9**, 13–16

Appleby, J. (1991) Equal treatment for equal need. *British Medical Journal*, **302**, 1559

Barnes, B.A. (1977) Discarded operations: surgical innovation by trial and error. In *Costs, Risks and Benefits of Surgery*, edited by J.P. Bunker, B.A. Barnes and F. Mosteller, Oxford University Press, New York, pp. 109–123

Baskerville, P.A., Heddle, R.M. and Jarrett, P.E.M. (1985) Preparation for surgery: information tapes for the patient. *Practitioner*, **229**, 909–919

Beauchamp, T.L. and Childress, J.F. (1983) *Principles of Biomedical Ethics*. 2nd edn. Oxford University Press, Oxford, pp.148–158

Bernarde, M. and Mayerson, E.W. (1978) Patient and physician negotiation. *Journal of the American Medical Association*, **239**, 1413–1415

Brewin, T. (1982) Consent to randomised treatment. *Lancet*, **ii**, 919–921

Cabot, R.C. (1938) *Honesty*. Macmillan, New York

Delamothe, T. (1991) Social inequalities in health. *British Medical Journal*, **303**, 1046–1050

Farrow, S.C. (1987) McKeown reassessed. *British Medical Journal*, **294**, 1631–1632

Gillon, R. (1985a) Deontological foundations for medical ethics? *British Medical Journal*, **290**, 1331–1333

Gillon, R. (1985b) Utilitarianism. *British Medical Journal*, **290**, 1411–1413

Gillon, R. (1985c) Doctors and patients. *British Medical Journal*, **291**, 466–469

Grafe, W.R., McSherry, C.K., Finkel, M.L. and McCarthy, E.G. (1978) The elective surgery second opinion program. *Annals of Surgery*, **188**, 323–330

Illich, I. (1976) *Limits to Medicine. Medical nemesis: the expropriation of health*. Marion Boyars, London

Johnson, A.G. (1990) *Pathways in Medical Ethics*. Edward Arnold, London

Jefferson, T. (1801) Engraved on the wall of the Jefferson Memorial, Washington DC

Jennett, B. (1988) Balancing benefits and burdens in surgery. *British Medical Bulletin*, **44**, 499–513

Kennedy, I. (1981) *The Unmasking of Medicine*. George Allen and Unwin, London

Lancashire, M.J.R., Legg, P.K., Lowe, M., Davidson, S.M. and Ellis, B.W. (1988) Surgical aspects of international drug smuggling. *British Medical Journal*, **291**, 1035–1037

McKeown, T. (1976) *The Modern Rise of Population*. Edward Arnold, London

McLean, S. and Maher, G. (1983) *Medicine, Morals, and the Law*. Gower, Aldershot

Moossa, A.R. (1987) Sugical treatment of chronic pancreatitis: an overview. *British Journal of Surgery*, **74**, 661–667

Office of Population Censuses and Surveys (1987) *Infant and Perinatal Mortality 1985*. OPCS Monitor, London

Reichen, D.B. (1984) Learning diagnostic restraint. *New England Journal of Medicine*, **310**, 591–593

Report by the Subcommittee on Oversight and Investigations of the Committee on Interstate and Foreign Commerce (1976) *Cost and Quality of Health Care: unnecessary surgery*. Government Printing Office, Washington DC

Rutkow, I.M. (1982) Unnecessary surgery: what is it? Surgical Clinics of North America, **62**, 613–625

US Department of Health and Human Services (1990) *Health, United States, 1989, and Prevention Profile*. Government Printing Office, Washington DC

Vayda, E., Mindell, W.R. and Rutkow, I.M. (1982) A decade of surgery in Canada, England and Wales, and the United States. *Archives of Surgery*, **117**, 846–853

Whitfield, A. (1989) The sterilisation of mentally-impaired patients. *Medical Protection Society Annual Report*, p. 15

Chapter 23

Human experimentation

The ethical obligation always and entirely outweighs the experimental.
A. Bradford Hill (1963)

Consumers have the right to safety, the right to be informed, the right to choose, and the right to be heard. J.F. Kennedy (1962)

The four moral principles – respect for autonomy, beneficence, non-maleficence, and justice – must be applied with as much rigour in clinical research as in everyday practice. Clinical scientists point out that clinical research does not differ profoundly from everyday routine practice. Medical decisions in everyday practice are often experimental: 'If I follow this pathway of treatment I anticipate that my patient will get better, so let's try it.'

The disclosure of some despicably unethical human experimentation in Nazi Germany resulted in the introduction of international, national, and local regulations for the conduct of research in human beings. The *Declaration of Helsinki* of the World Medical Association (revised in Tokyo in 1975) embodies all the moral principles that should govern the behaviour of clinical scientists, including the injunction that 'concern for the interests of the subject must always prevail over the interests of science and society'. Subjects of research must be fully informed of the aims, methods, anticipated benefits, and potential hazards of the study and of any discomfort that it may entail. The protocol for any research on people must be scrutinised, altered if necessary, and passed by an appropriate independent Ethics (sometimes incorrectly called Ethical) Committee in Britain or Institutional Review Board in the USA. It is possible to conduct clinical research without submitting a protocol to an Ethics Committee in Britain, although this is rare. In the USA most types of clinical research must by federal law be subjected to scrutiny by an independent Institutional Review Board, which has the power and duty to continue to monitor the progress of research projects, and to suspend any investigation that appears to be harming patients. There is a move in Britain to set up a national Ethics Committee that would have the power to veto any unethical clinical research (Warnock, 1988).

The functions of ethics committees

Clinical research, like most biological research, is concerned with disproving, not proving, hypotheses. A null hypothesis is put forward and then an experiment is designed to try to disprove it. Because the hypothesis generally reflects the current norm in clinical practice, it is obvious that a lot of original research is concerned with upsetting this norm. The ethics committee may take it on itself to stand by the norm and refuse to sanction an original research project. This is undesirable.

The first and foremost consideration of an ethics committee is the relative safety and low risk:benefit ratio of the planned research. It must also be assured of the feasibility that the study can be brought to a valid conclusion: this depends not only on the number of patients with the disease that the investigator proposes to study, but also on the event rate in those patients and the time scale of those events. The committee must be convinced that the investigator has the proper training and facilities to undertake the research. It should enquire into the ways in which data are to be validated, recorded, retrieved, and analysed. It should take steps to ensure that bias (or even occasionally fraud) cannot occur. Finally, one of its most important functions is to make sure that the patients being studied are treated with the utmost care and respect. Patients in a research study should be made to regard themselves as privileged, not put upon. If this is the frame of mind of the subjects of research, neither scandal nor legal action will ensue.

Herxheimer (1988) proposed six rights for subjects or patients taking part in clinical research. They are:

1. Patients have the right to know what their rights are.
2. Patients must be fully informed of the nature of the experiment, the ways in which it could affect them personally, and the availability of alternative options.
3. Patients have the right to refuse to be given more information than they want.
4. Patients have the right to withdraw from an experiment at any time and continue to have the best treatment.
5. The confidentiality of information about individual patients must be respected.
6. Patients or their next of kin should be given a copy of the final report on the experiment.

We must keep in mind that not all controversies in surgery can be answered by random control clinical trials. If the treatment options are not a matter of indifference to patients, they must be allowed to choose their option, thereby invalidating randomisation. This applies particularly to trials of partial versus total mastectomy for cancer (Taylor, Margolese and Soskolne, 1984) and of extracranial-intracranial bypass versus medical treatment for inoperable extracranial arterial lesions (Dudley, 1987).

Explanatory research

It is usual to distinguish between explanatory and pragmatic clinical research. Some years ago we investigated the relation between preoperative anergy – shown by absence of delayed type hypersensitivity reactions to four common recall antigens injected intradermally – and postoperative infective complications (Ausobsky *et al.*, 1982). This was explanatory research and the preoperative testing could not be held to be beneficial to individual patients. We had, therefore, to be absolutely sure that patients understood what we were doing and why. In the event, thanks to the tactful way in which information was given to patients, nobody refused to take part and many patients asked later about our conclusions – that preoperative anergy is a relatively poor predictor of postoperative infective complications.

The four moral principles are sometimes ignored in explanatory research. Hamblin (1987) brought to public attention an obscure publication from the Committee on Energy and Commerce of the United States House of Representatives entitled *American nuclear guinea pigs: three decades of radiation experiments on US citizens.* This report detailed many experiments in which people were exposed to potentially toxic doses of radiation simply to satisfy scientific curiosity. There was no question of the experiment offering benefit to the subjects under experiment, and little evidence that they were properly informed of the possible harmful effects of radiation, or that they gave fully informed consent.

Hamblin reported some examples of these deplorable experiments. Between 1961 and 1965, 20 elderly volunteers were injected with radium or thorium to study the metabolism of these substances by scientists at the Massachusetts Institute of Technology. In 1946 and 1947 six homeless chronic alcoholics with good renal function were injected with increasing doses of uranium-234 and uranium-235 to determine the dose necessary to produce renal injury. From 1963 to 1971 over 100 inmates of Washington and Oregon state prisons were subjected to testicular irradiation to determine the dose that would sterilise them. No account was taken of the possible oncogenic effect on the testes.

In 1966 a study of the natural history of cervical carcinoma in situ was approved by the medical staff at the National Women's Hospital in Auckland, New Zealand (Paul, 1988). Dr Herbert Green was convinced that carcinoma in situ does not progress to invasive carcinoma and was given permission to try to prove this by observing, not treating, women with abnormal cervical smears. The women were not told that they were subjects of an experiment, and the development of invasive carcinoma in the study group was not noted or acted on. The trial was finally reported in a local magazine, an inquiry was set up, and recommendations were made that should make sure that such a thing does not happen again.

Such reports could emanate only from countries committed to the disclosure of truth. One wonders how much unethical research goes on in other countries that are more committed to secrecy.

Much research in psychology is carried out without the consent of the subjects being investigated, the reason being that people who know that they are being investigated behave differently from those who do not. The use of one-way mirrors and periscopes to observe without being seen are commonplace in some branches of psychological research, but this contravenes a most important moral principle – respect for autonomy (Levine, 1986).

Explanatory research on children or the mentally ill can never be justified because these people cannot give properly informed consent, and the consent of a parent or guardian is not valid unless the procedure advised is in the interests of the patient. The ethical and legal problems of using medical students, members of the staff of the hospital, or prisoners as subjects for explanatory research are complicated. It is common in the USA for volunteers for non-therapeutic research to be paid, and the practice is increasing in Britain. This in itself does not alter the obligations and duties of the investigator, but the use of people who are in a position of dependence on the investigator does raise important ethical issues, and should probably be discouraged. The subjects of research must never be allowed to feel that they are under an obligation to continue to cooperate; they must feel free to abandon a research project at any time.

Pragmatic research

Pragmatic clinical research, generally in the form of random control clinical trials, must be governed by several inalienable moral rules, all derived from the simple one, that a doctor's first duty is to help individual patients who consult him. First, the investigator must be ignorant of the respective merits of the two or more treatments being tested (and must remain ignorant throughout the course of the trial – he or she must not be party to any interim analyses). The corollary is that a trial must if possible be 'double blind': a doctor does not need a 95% ($p = 0.05$) certainty that one regimen is better than another. If he is constantly made aware that half his patients are receiving what appears to be a less effective treatment, his ethical obligations to his patients must override his scientific obligations (Schafer, 1982).

Second, the investigator must be assured that none of the treatment options are expected to do more harm than good. There are risks associated with every effective treatment, but the anticipated benefit should always outweigh the possible risks. There is no place for placebo intramuscular injections, for example.

Third, the treatment of the control group must be the best standard treatment: if there is a recognised treatment for the disease being investigated, that – and not a placebo – must be the treatment offered to the control group. A lot of the money for clinical research comes from pharmaceutical companies, which are not enthusiastic about comparing their new drug with the best previously available. This is a fairly recent addition to the requirements, and no one would now repeat the trial of Cobb *et al.* (1959) (in which patients with angina pectoris were randomised to have internal mammary artery ligation or a sham operation: the internal mammary artery was exposed and left intact).

Finally, research projects demand much more careful documentation, often involving invasive tests, than is usual in everyday practice: the existence and stage of the disease under investigation must be absolutely established; the events being studied must be fully proved, not merely suspected; and frequent follow up visits are often necessary. For all these reasons patients must be told that their investigations and treatment are related to a clinical trial, even if they are in the control group. On the one hand most patients will perceive that, because of the existence of the study, they will be getting the very best attention, but on the other hand some will prefer not to be subjected to extra investigations. Patients should be partners in all dealings with doctors and their wishes must always be respected.

Doctors must always keep in mind their moral obligation to beneficence, but they must never forget the rule of non-maleficence. There will be occasions when a patient does not want too many details, and the doctor may be acting correctly by not going more deeply into matters than the patient wishes (Baum, Zilkha and Houghton, 1989).

The special problems of testing drugs in children were addressed by the American Academy of Pediatrics Committee on Drugs (1977). The guidelines drawn up by this committee were as follows:

'The conditions under which the use of placebos is ethical in drug research in children include (1) when there is no commonly accepted therapy for the condition and the agent under study is the first one that may modify the course of the disease process; (2) when the commonly used therapy for the condition is of questionable or low efficacy; (3) when the commonly used therapy for the condition carries with it a high frequency of unacceptable side effects; (4) when the incidence and severity of undesirable side effects produced by adding a new treatment to an established regimen are uncertain; (5) when the disease process is characterized by frequent spontaneous exacerbations and remissions.'

The fallacies of informed consent in the context of random control clinical trials were emphasised by Appelbaum, Roth, and Lidz (1983). 'Despite disclosures of randomization, placebos, double-blind procedures, and invariant treatment schedules, subjects often continue to believe that research procedures are intended primarily for their benefit ... a frame of mind we have called "the therapeutic misconception" ... we are convinced that the usual perfunctory explanations and quick readings of the consent form are not ethically adequate.'

Many doctors claim that clinical freedom is restricted by random control clinical trials, but as Hampton (1983) wrote: 'Clinical freedom died accidentally, crushed between the rising costs of new forms of investigation and treatment and the financial limits inevitable in an economy that cannot expand indefinitely. Clinical freedom should, however, have been strangled long ago, for at best it was a cloak for ignorance and at worst an excuse for quackery.'

Not all pragmatic clinical research is in the form of random controlled trials. In phase 1 trials of new drugs that have been thoroughly evaluated in chemical and animal laboratories, there is an extra burden on investigators to make sure that the first human beings to receive the drug understand what they are doing.

The same moral imperative applies to new operations. Monkeys with experimental Parkinsonism have been cured by injection of nigral cells from fetal monkeys (which secrete dopamine) into the substantia nigra. Extension of this work to humans requires assurances on several ethical issues (Gillon, 1988): first, that the patient recipient shall be fully informed of the experimental nature of the operation; second, that a pregnancy is not entered into in order to be terminated for the purpose of providing fetal brain cells; third, that it was necessary to perform the abortion by a method other than vacuum extraction (obviously the fetus has to be delivered intact in order to extract brain cells); and lastly, that the woman who has accepted an abortion for her own good shall be informed that living cells of the fetus will be used to help another person. The fetal nigral cells need to be obtained from fetuses 8–12 weeks old, when many gynaecologists would advise vacuum extraction. The woman would have to agree to have a 'medical abortion' by taking mifepristone by mouth, followed by a pessary containing gemeprost the following day.

It is important to ensure that all human and animal experiments are ethical. Progress achieved by unethical means is not progress but regress.

References

American Academy of Pediatrics Committee on Drugs (1977) Guidelines for the ethical conduct of studies to evaluate drugs in pediatric populations. *Pediatrics* **60**, 91–101

Appelbaum, P.S., Roth, L.H. and Lidz, C.W. (1983) Letter. *New England Journal of Medicine*, **308**, 344

Ausobsky, J.R., Bean, P., Proctor, J. and Pollock, A.V. (1982) Delayed hypersensitivity testing for the prediction of postoperative complications. *British Journal of Surgery* **69**, 346–348

Baum, M., Zilkha, K. and Houghton, J. (1989) Ethics of clinical research: lessons for the future. *British Medical Journal*, **299**, 251–253

Cobb, L.A., Thomas, G.I., Dillard, D.H., Merendino, K.A. and Bruce, R.A. (1959) An evaluation of internal mammary artery ligation by a double blind technic. *New England Journal of Medicine*, **260**, 1115–18

Dudley, H.A.F. (1987) Extracranial-intracranial bypass one; clinical trials, nil. *British Medical Journal*, **294**, 1501–1502

Gillon, R. (1988) Ethics of fetal brain cell transplants. *British Medical Journal*, **291**, 1212–1213

Hamblin, T.J. (1987) A shocking American report with lessons for all. *British Medical Journal*, **295**, 73

Hampton, J.R. (1983) The end of clinical freedom. *British Medical Journal*, **287**, 1237–1238

Herxheimer, A. (1988) The rights of the patient in clinical research. *Lancet*, **ii**, 1128–1130

Hill, A.B. (1963) Medical ethics and controlled trials. *British Medical Journal*, **2**, 1043–1049

Kennedy, J..F (1962) *The Consumer's Bill of Rights*. Government Printing Office, Washington DC

Levine, R.J. (1986) *Ethics and Regulation of Clinical Research*. Urban and Schwarzenberg, Baltimore

Paul, C. (1988) The New Zealand cervical cancer study: could it happen again? *British Medical Journal*, **297**, 533–539

Schafer, A. (1982) The ethics of the randomized clinical trial. *New England Journal of Medicine*, **310**, 1363–1367

Taylor, K.M., Margolese, R.G. and Soskolne, C.L. (1984) Physicians' reasons for not entering eligible patients in a randomized clinical trial of surgery for breast cancer. *New England Journal of Medicine*, **310**, 1363–1367

Warnock, M. (1988) A national ethics committee. *British Medical Journal*, **297**, 1626–1627

Section VII

Audit of publications

Chapter 24

Peer review of papers submitted to scientific journals

An editor is a man who knows exactly what he wants but isn't quite sure.
attributed to Walter Davenport

Magna est veritas et praevalet (The Vulgate). This is the ingenuous motto of the Forensic Science Society of Great Britain and it is the duty of editors and peer reviewers of scientific papers to try to recognise truth and to do their best to ensure that it does prevail. The same applies to peer review of projects that have been submitted to bodies that control the distribution of grants for research (Smith, 1988).

History of peer review

In 1628 William Harvey published *Exercitatio anatomica de motu cordis et sanguinis* in Frankfurt in Latin, no suitable vehicle for publication being available to him in England (Booth, 1982). The Royal Society started publishing the *Philosophical Transactions* (many of the papers still being in Latin) in 1665, soon after it received its royal charter from Charles II. It was, however, not until 1752 that the Earl of Macclesfield, a mathematician and astronomer, persuaded his colleagues to set up a 'Committee on Papers', which could call on 'any other members of the Society who are knowing and well skilled in that particular branch of Science that shall happen to be the matter of any paper which shall then come under their deliberations' (Kronick, 1990). This was the start of the process of peer review, which became generally accepted only in the twentieth century.

In 1796 Edward Jenner sent a paper to the President of the Royal Society, Sir Joseph Banks, describing the first successful inoculation of a boy who had failed to develop smallpox when he was inoculated with material from a patient with the disease; Jenner concluded that this was because the boy had previously had an attack of cowpox. Instead of submitting it to the Committee on Papers, Banks sent it to John Hunter's brother-in-law (Everard Home), who wrote that 'I want faith', pointing out that a single case report did not prove the case and suggesting that he would be more convinced if 20 or 30 children were inoculated with cowpox material and then failed to develop smallpox. Jenner successfully vaccinated 23 children; he did not submit a revised paper to the Royal Society but published the findings in a 64-page monograph (Jenner, 1798). This provoked a great deal of controversy, which did not subside until well after Jenner's death. As late as 1820 it was estimated that as many children were being inoculated (with smallpox material) as were being vaccinated.

Peer review today

Far more research papers are submitted to reputable journals than they can publish. Sometimes a paper is so bad or so inappropriate to the interests of the journal that the editor has no difficulty in rejecting it; occasionally it is so good that the editor has no hesitation in accepting it. Most papers, however, fall between these two extremes, and editors then see the need for independent assessment. Crawford Jamieson (personal communication) confessed when he was editor of the *British Journal of Surgery* that two kinds of paper gave him particular difficulty: one that was so badly written that it concealed what might be an important message, and the other that was so well written that it concealed a total absence of useful ideas: an American expression about such a work is that it is all tip and no iceberg.

Other questions that must be faced by an editor are: Was the work described in the paper carried out in accordance with acceptable ethical standards? Was the paper under consideration by another journal – in which case multiple publication might result? Was there evidence of bias in the paper, or possibly even fraud? On the other hand, in the words of an editorial in *Nature* (Anonymous, 1981): 'It would be catastrophic if journals habitually declined to give house room to data that could not be accommodated within the existing body of received wisdom.'

For all these reasons most journals retain a panel of experts (mostly unpaid), to at least one of whom manuscripts are sent for independent opinions. The appointment of referees, and the selection of the appropriate ones for a particular paper, are entirely up to the editor, often guided by an editorial committee. The qualities that a good referee must have are, first, expertise; second, dedication in that he must study the manuscript, consult other original work, and come to reasonable and well argued conclusions; and third, that he must send in a report on each paper within a reasonable time – say three weeks.

Usually the name or names of the author(s) and the institution from which the work comes are revealed to the referees, but the identity of the referees is not revealed to the author(s). This is an obvious safeguard against acrimonious recriminations by authors against referees. The knowledge of the identity of the authors and their place of work can, however, influence referees in their judgement.

The obligations of peer reviewers

Many editors of journals send out with manuscripts submitted to referees some modification of the recommendations of the Council of Biology

Editors (Lock, 1985). These include injunctions that the manuscript is a confidential document and that no part of it should be communicated to another person, nor should the referee make use of the information contained in it in any way; that the referee should avoid prejudice and partiality in assessing the paper, maintain anonymity, avoid abrasive criticism, and try not to abrogate the editorial decision about publication. Referees should pay particular attention to the originality and potential importance of the work, to the appropriateness of the experimental design, to the soundness of the analysis of data and the conclusions derived from them, and to the relevance of the discussion. Because so many papers are submitted by authors whose first language is not English (and even if it is, they have never been taught to express themselves clearly), referees should include comments on style and grammar – but these are not usually for transmission to the authors.

Guidelines for referees

The *British Journal of Surgery*, in common with many others, sends selected papers to a statistical referee as well as a clinical one, and Murray (1988) found many deficiencies in papers that had been published in the *British Journal of Surgery*. These arose mainly from confusion of statistical significance with clinical relevance, post hoc analyses of events that had not been specified in the hypothesis, failure to report confidence intervals, and stopping a trial before enough patients had been recruited.

We reproduce below the 'guidelines for referees' of the *British Journal of Surgery* (by permission of the editors).

'The quality of the articles published in the *British Journal of Surgery* depends on the care the reviewers take in establishing that an article is of scientific repute. Two referees are asked to comment on each original article, and occasionally a third referee is asked for a further opinion. As referees' comments are confidential and equally, as the paper to be refereed is confidential, it should not be discussed with colleagues or with the authors.

The editors ask the referee to:

1. Write detailed comments on the paper which will be transmitted to the author anonymously. The objective of these comments is to enable the author to resubmit an improved manuscript. Specific advice is more helpful than generalities.

2. Write an opinion on the article for the editors; this will not be transmitted to the author. The editors wish to know if you think the paper should be published, whether modification would enable the article to reach the required standard, the importance and thus priority of the article, and its originality. On the basis of both referees' reports, the editors will decide whether the paper is suitable for publication. You will be sent the other referee's report with their final decision.

The following check list is intended to help you compile your report:

(a) Scientific reliability – of paramount importance.

(b) Originality – highly desirable although we accept that an important function of the journal is to keep our readership up to date with broad advances and that review articles are extremely helpful. We go to great pains to avoid multiple publication of the same material in different journals.

(c) Importance – to surgery and the advance of science.

(d) Suitability – we have a worldwide readership. While many of our readers are general surgeons, we are anxious to encourage specialists to continue to contribute to the Journal.

(e) Presentation – the *Introduction* should be succinct, the *Patients and Methods* section should be a detailed description of the study, the *Results* section should be concise with appropriate statistical analysis, the *Discussion* should be relevant and come to reasonable conclusions on the basis of data presented, and the *Abstract* should be concise and contain hard data. Many of our papers come from overseas and the quality of the English language leaves something to be desired. This is not necessarily a major obstacle if the paper contains an important message. Please comment on whether the references are up to date and relevant.

(f) Illustrations – we ask our referees to comment critically on the quality and need for illustrations and tables.

(g) Statistics – please comment critically on the need for, or inappropriate use of, statistical methods in data analysis.

(h) Ethical considerations – the Journal continues to distance itself from papers based on inappropriate animal experiments or clinical studies which are deemed unethical.'

Audit of ethics

There was a time when a clinical research paper could be published without any reference to ethical considerations, apart from an assurance that a treatment was carried out in good faith and that its object was to do good for patients. In the first properly organised random control clinical trial (of streptomycin treatment of pulmonary tuberculosis) there was no question of asking patients to agree to participate (Medical Research Council, 1948). The report included this statement:

> 'Patients were not told before admission that they were to get special treatment. Control patients did not know throughout their stay in hospital that they were control patients in a special study .... It was important for the success of the trial that the details of the control scheme should remain completely confidential ... this information was not made public throughout the 15 months of the trial.'

This is no longer acceptable, nor is it enough to state baldly in papers reporting clinical research that the project was 'approved by the Hospital Ethics Committee' or the Institutional Review Board. Patients are entitled to as much information as they want, and full disclosure of the details of a clinical research project, including the method of randomisation in random control trials in which the choice of options is important to patients, should be mentioned in publications.

In reports on animal experiments, authors must have regard to Lane-Petter's (1972) five questions: Is the problem under study worth solving? Is the animal chosen the best experimental system for the problem? Must the animal be conscious at any time during the experiment? Can the pain and discomfort caused by the experiment be lessened or eliminated? Could the number of animals used be reduced? It is essential that animal experiments are humane and that the standards of preoperative and postoperative care match the best of veterinary practice.

Multiple publication

An announcement (1987) in the *British Journal of Surgery* regretted the following incident, which contravened the instruction to authors that 'acceptance of original material is on the understanding that contributions are to this journal only':

> 'In the July edition the Journal carried an article by Ono and colleagues ... describing a new approach in the management of oesophageal varices. This article based on 16 patients was accepted in good faith by the Editors on 4 March 1987. We were greatly distressed to see an article by the same three authors in the newly arrived May issue of *Surgery* ... describing exactly the same technique and its use in what are unquestionably the same 16 patients. This article was accepted by *Surgery* in October 1986. The only difference between the articles lies in the more profuse illustration and the inclusion of a group not undergoing added splenopneumopexy in the *Surgery* version. However, the main purpose of the articles, namely description of the new technique, is achieved by almost identical means in the two publications. It appears to us that this is another flagrant example in the long and sorry list of attempts at multiple publication of a given piece of work in different scientific journals.'

There is no doubt that multiple publication is dishonest and does nothing but clutter up the literature with repetition. It is up to authors to abide by the rule of almost all reputable journals that papers submitted for publication shall not be submitted to another journal at the same time.

Fraud in scientific publications

One of the tasks of a referee is to point out to the editor the possibility that the data in a paper that has been submitted may be fraudulent.

Sir William Haley (who was editor of *The Times* for many years) had an unswerving sense of rectitude. In 1967, in his last speech as editor, he expressed his outlook with the utmost simplicity (Obituary, 1987):

> 'I believe it so deeply that I will go on saying it till I die. The truth is that there is a difference between right and wrong, and there are things that we should not be ready to compromise. There is no halfway house between honesty and dishonesty. There are things which are bad and false and ugly and no amount of argument or specious casuistry will make them good or true or beautiful. It is time that these things were said, and time for the Press to say them.'

Investigative journalism is probably more searching in the USA than in Britain. Whatever the explanation, the examples of fraud in scientific publications were nearly all discovered in America (Broad and Wade, 1982). They can be divided into two classes: plagiarism and falsification.

Plagiarism

Elias Alsabti worked as a microbiologist at Jefferson Medical College in Philadelphia. He was dismissed after an internal audit revealed evidence of falsification of data, but after his dismissal it was found that he had copied almost word for word at least seven papers and had them published in obscure journals.

Vijay Soman worked at Yale under Dr Philip Felig. Dr Felig was sent a paper to referee by the *New England Journal of Medicine* on insulin receptors in anorexia nervosa, passed it on to Soman for his opinion, and he, without Felig's knowledge, made a copy, altered it slightly, and sent his manuscript to the *American Journal of Medicine*. The plagiarism came to light when this manuscript was sent to be refereed to the author of the paper that had been submitted to the *New England Journal of Medicine*, and resulted in a retraction of Soman's paper.

Raymond Shamberger resigned from the Cleveland Clinic Foundation (Anonymous, 1987). Plenum Press published his book *Nutrition and Cancer* in 1984, large parts of which were identical with the 1982 report of the National Academy of Sciences on *Diet, Nutrition, and Cancer* (which he did not acknowledge in his book).

Falsification

Falsification is worse than plagiarism, because it is so much more difficult to detect. Occasional examples have been suspected for many years. Ronald Fisher concluded that Mendel's published figures on the genetics of peas were so close to the expected ratio of 3:1 that it would have taken 'an absolute miracle of chance' to produce them. Lysenko's work on the inheritance of acquired characteristics was clearly corrupted by communist ideology, and Cyril Burt's publications on identical twins and the inheritance of intelligence have not withstood searching enquiry. In 1960 a student working in Melvin Simpson's department reported the cell-free synthesis of cytochrome C, but this could not be substantiated and Simpson published a retraction a year later. In 1974 Summerlin's partly black mice were found to owe their colour to a felt-tipped pen (Broad and Wade, 1982).

One of the most spectacular fakes of all times was the discovery that the skull that had been found at Piltdown, and that was claimed to show the 'missing link' between apes and man, had been planted there (probably by Teilhard de Chardin). Another example of planting was that of fossils that came to light after 25 years (Talent, 1989). During these years Professor Viswa Jit Gupta of the University of Chandigarh in Punjab published numerous papers and books relating to finds of species of conodonts and ammonoids in the Himalayas. He had probably bought these fossils, because they have been found elsewhere only in New York (conodonts) and Morocco (ammonoids). His placing of them in geological time made no sense and it is only now that the fake has emerged.

Another crop of frauds prompted the *New York Times* to comment in an editorial in 1982 that '... none of the frauds was originally brought to light through the standard mechanisms by which scientists check each others' work'.

A Congressional investigation headed by Representative John Dingell of Michigan was charged with examining the authenticity of a paper from the Massachusetts Institute of Technology on alterations in the immune system by genetic manipulation of mice (Sibbison, 1989). In evidence, Dr John T. Edsall, professor emeritus of biological medicine at Harvard University, told Mr Dingell: 'If a young scientist believes that he or she has witnessed a case of fraud, and comes to ask me about reporting it to the authorities, I would have to warn him or her emphatically about the dangers of doing so. If the potential whistle-blower decided nevertheless to proceed, I would admire and greatly respect the person in the decision, but I would have serious anxiety about the future of that individual as the system operates today.'

Among recent frauds were those of John Long who forged data about a cell line for the study of Hodgkin's disease that proved useless; of John Darsee, in 16 of 18 of whose papers errors and internal discrepancies were found (Stewart and Feder, 1987); of Joseph Cort who confessed that a synthetic analogue of vasopressin that he reported did not exist (Wingerson, 1983); of Robert Slutsky who published 13 fraudulent and 55 questionable papers, often with coauthors who had not been asked to verify the data (Marshall, 1986); and of Stephen Breuning who published some 50 articles based on fraudulent data on the use of psychoactive drugs in mentally retarded patients (Lock, 1988). When this was discovered the University of Pittsburg returned $163 000 to the National Institute of Mental Health.

Accusations were made by two junior colleagues of Dr William McBride that some of the data that he had published in the *Australian Journal of Biological Sciences* in 1982 were fabricated. McBride believed that Debendox (which has been used for the control of nausea and vomiting in early pregnancy and contains dicyclomine hydrochloride, doxylamine succinate, and pyridoxine hydrochloride) was teratogenic. He reported that oral administration of hyoscine – another anticholinergic drug – to pregnant rabbits caused birth defects. An inquiry headed by Sir Harry Gibbs, the former Chief Justice, found that 'Dr McBride published statements which he either knew were untrue, or which he did not genuinely believe to be true' (Morris, 1988). In 1991 Dr McBride acknowledged to the New South Wales Medical Tribunal that he had fabricated some results for the 'long term interests of humanity' (Swan, 1991).

Stewart and Feder (1987) delivered a swingeing attack on coauthors, referees, and editors for allowing papers containing internal discrepancies to be published. The editor of the *New England Journal of Medicine*, however, concluded that 'unless a maladroit cheat fabricates results that are manifestly impossible or inherently contradictory, even the most rigorous peer review is not likely to uncover fraud' (Relman, 1983).

A committee of the National Institutes of Health presented the following guidelines (US Department of Health, Education and Welfare (1978):

- Faculties must present work frequently at seminars inside and outside the hospital
- All coauthors must be prepared to back the published work
- Heads of departments must take responsibility for work presented from their departments; a committee should be set up to prevent misconduct in research.

Rennie (1989) invited editors of original research journals to participate in an experimental audit of research, in order to define the prevalence of misconduct. Studies to be audited would be chosen at random from among those accepted for publication, and auditors (senior doctors) would visit institutions and require the production of original data such as casenotes and laboratory notebooks.

Conclusions

Referees play an important part in guiding editors in the selection of scientific papers for publication. They must eschew their own biases and prejudices while at the same time being on their guard against the possibility of error, bias, or fraud, in the papers they review. There are occasions when editors and referees must demand from authors the whole of their raw data, including original pro formas and laboratory notebooks.

References

Announcement (1987) Multiple publication. *British Journal of Surgery*, **74**, 980

Anonymous (1981) Editorial. *Nature*, **290**, 433–434

Anonymous (1987) Researcher accused of plagiarism resigns. *Science*, **237**, 1098

Booth, C.C. (1982) Development of medical journals in Britain. *British Medical Journal*, **2**, 105–108

Broad, W. and Wade, N. (1982) *Betrayers of the Truth*. Simon and Schuster, New York

Jenner, E. (1798) *An Enquiry into the Causes and Effects of the Variolae Vaccinae*. S Low, London

Kronick, D.A. (1990) Peer review in 18th-century scientific journalism. *Journal of the American Medical Association*, **263**, 1321–1322

Lane-Petter, W. (1972) The place and importance of the experimental animal in research. *Proceedings of the Royal Society of Medicine*, **65**, 343–344

Lock, S. (1985) *A Difficult Balance. Editorial peer review in medicine*. Nuffield Provincial Hospitals Trust, London

Lock, S. (1988) Fraud in medicine. *British Medical Journal,*, **296**, 376–377

Marshall, E. (1986) San Diego's tough stand on research fraud. *Science*, **234**, 534–535

Medical Research Council (1948) Streptomycin treatment of pulmonary tuberculosis. *British Medical Journal*, **2**, 769–782

Morris, C. (1988) 'Smear' claim by drug researcher. *The Times*, 4 November, p. 5

Murray, G.D. (1988) The task of a statistical referee. *British Journal of Surgery*, **75**, 664–667

Obituary (1987) Sir William Haley. *The Times*, 8 September

Relman, A.S. (1983) Lessons from the Darsee affair. *New England Journal of Medicine*, **308**, 1415–1417

Rennie, D. (1989) Editors and auditors. *Journal of the American Medical Association*, **261**, 2543–2545

Sibbison, J.B. (1989) The Baltimore dispute. *Lancet*, **i**, 1148–1149

Smith, R. (1988) Problems with peer review and alternatives. *British Medical Journal*, **296**, 774–777

Stewart, W.W. and Feder, N. (1987) The integrity of the scientific literature. *Nature*, **325**, 207–214

Swan, N. (1991) Australian doctor admits fraud. *British Medical Journal*, **302**, 1421–1422

Talent, J.A. (1989) The case of the peripatetic fossils. *Nature*, **338**, 613–615

United States Department of Health, Education, and Welfare (1978) *Ethical Principles and Guidelines for the Protection of Human Subjects of Research*. United States Department of Health, Education, and Welfare, Washington DC

Wingerson, L. (1983) Biotechnologist faked results in race for patent. *New Scientist*, 6 January, pp. 3–4.

Chapter 25

Audit of surgical publications

Learning is but an adjunct to ourself,
And where we are our learning likewise is.

(Shakespeare 1594)

In 1872 von Langenbeck complained that 'One suffocates through exposure to the massive body of rapidly growing information'. How much more suffocating it is today. In order to 'keep up with the literature' a surgeon is confronted with at least 30 of the thousands of weekly or monthly journals. What does he do about it? Some do nothing, relying on their own experience to know what is best for each patient; some rely on talking to colleagues informally. Some read the abstracts either in a few original journals or in one of the abstracting publications. Some look at the tables of contents and single out papers that interest them. A few consult *Index Medicus* to retrieve articles that concern their particular interests. Some read both abstracts and conclusions. If these conclusions coincide with their own beliefs they absorb the information into their practices.

The structure of a scientific paper

In reporting original work in medicine and biology there is no substitute for the time honoured formula IMRAD – Introduction, Methods, Results and Discussion. As Sir Austin Bradford Hill (1965) put it: 'Why did you start, what did you do, what answer did you get, and what does it mean anyway?' Recognising, however, that most doctors will read only the abstract, Dr R B Haynes of McMaster University Medical Center, Hamilton, Ontario circulated a document to colleagues all over the world, in which proposals for more informative abstracts in clinical papers were put forward. The final version was published in the *Annals of Internal Medicine* (Ad Hoc Working Group, 1987). The abstract should contain the following information:

'1. Objective: the exact question(s) addressed by the article.
2. Design: the basic design of the study.

3. Setting: the location and level of clinical care.
4. Patients or participants: the manner of selection and numbers of patients or participants who entered and completed the study.
5. Interventions: the exact treatment or intervention, if any.
6. Measurements and results: the methods of assessing patients and key results.
7. Conclusions: key conclusions including direct clinical applications.'

Altman and Gardner (1987) suggested the addition of an eighth requirement – a statement of the primary and secondary outcome measures or end points.

The recording and retrieval of original papers

There are two methods: the first is to write on a card a summary of each paper that you may want to refer to again. A suitable sized card is 8 by 5 inches (200 by 130 mm) and these are filed by subject. Papers torn out of journals, or photocopies, or reprints, are filed alphabetically by name of first author. The second method, which requires considerably more time for recording but allows easier retrieval, is to type an abstract of each paper into a personal computer, again filing the papers alphabetically. There are many suitable computer programs. Whether you use the computer system or not depends on when you do your reading. Hand written cards are more flexible if you do most of your reading of journals at home. If the computer is kept at the hospital it would mean writing an abstract and then having it entered into the computer: this is not cost effective.

The assessment of published results

Attempts have been made to give objective scores to aspects of published research papers. We devised a score system for the assessment of published random control clinical trials of antibiotic prophylaxis of abdominal surgical wound infection (Evans and Pollock, 1985). We based the score system on eight principles, which apply to the assessment of all random control trials. They are:

1. The investigator shall have no preconceived opinion about the superiority of one or other arm, either at the start of the trial or during its conduct.
2. The investigator shall remain in ignorance of any trend in results.
3. The investigator shall be unable to influence the allocation of patients to one or other arm of a trial.
4. The investigator shall have no knowledge concerning the arm of the trial to which the patients has been allocated when judging the occurrence or non-occurrence of an event.
5. No treatment may be given to any patient without his or her properly informed consent.
6. The control group shall receive the best standard treatment whereas the test group shall have the best treatment varied only by inclusion of the regimen being studied.

7. Data shall be treated with due deference and shall not be rearranged to support an opinion.
8. The principal requirements in presentation are accuracy, clarity, and brevity.

In that paper we asked 15 questions about design and conduct, 10 about analysis and 8 about presentation. Out of a maximum score of 100 we found that only 16 of 100 papers studied scored over 70, the highest being 89 and the lowest 34. In a subsequent study of published random control trials of antibacterial prophylaxis in colorectal surgery (Evans and Pollock, 1987) we found that only 13 of 56 papers examined (23%) scored more than 70 out of 100.

The score was made up by giving weights to the answers to the following questions:

Design and conduct
- Is the sample defined?
- Are exclusions specified?
- Are known risk factors recorded?
- Are therapeutic regimens defined?
- Is the experimental regimen appropriate?
- Is the control regimen appropriate?
- Were appropriate investigations carried out?
- Are end points defined?
- Are end points appropriate?
- Have numbers required been calculated?
- Was patient consent sought?
- Was the randomisation blind?
- Was the assessment blind?
- Were additional treatments recorded?
- Were side effects recorded?

Analysis
- Withdrawals: Are they listed?
    Is their fate recorded?
    Are there fewer than 10%?
- Is there a comparability table?
- Are risk factors stratified?
- Is the statistical analysis of proportions correct?
- Is the statistical analysis of numbers correct?
- Are confidence intervals reported?
- Are values of both test statistic and probability given?
- In negative trials is the type II error considered?

Presentation
- Is the title accurate?
- Is the abstract accurate and helpful?
- Are methods reproducible?
- Are the sections clear-cut?
- Can the raw data be discerned?

- Are the results credible?
- Do the results justify the conclusions?
- Are the references correct?

Fowkes and Fulton (1991) laid down guidelines for the evaluation of all research papers, not confining themselves to controlled trials, but dealing also with cross sectional, case control, and cohort studies. They emphasised the value of structured abstracts (Ad Hoc Working Group, 1987) and put forward the following guidelines:

- The study design should be appropriate to the objectives
- The study sample should be representative
- The control group should be acceptable
- The quality of measurements and outcomes should be high
- The data should not be too incomplete
- There should not be too many distorting influences.

The detection and rejection of bias

'Error is unavoidable; it can be rational, and when responsibly made and honestly reported, is not even culpable' (Laor, 1985). Bias, however, is another matter because it can lead to conclusions that are misleading. The bias may, of course, be unintentional or even unavoidable, but it may arise from the wish to prove, as opposed to disprove, a hypothesis. 'The wrong view of science betrays itself in the craving to be right' wrote Sir Karl Popper (1980); his view is that the advancement of knowledge is by formulating a hypothesis and then seeking to falsify it.

Feinstein and Horwitz (1982) claimed that 'readers may be too awed or confused by the statistics to look closely at the scientific quality of the underlying evidence.' They classified the biases as those of susceptibility, detection, and migration, and particularly condemned the use of death certificates in epidemiological research, pointing out that these are notoriously inaccurate.

Gøtzsche (1987) studied the reference lists at the end of each of 111 papers on non-steroidal anti-inflammatory drugs and discovered that 66 of them omitted some references that reported findings that were contrary to the conclusions presented by the authors.

Bias afflicts epidemiological research as much as it does prospective clinical research. Sackett (1979) described 56 different biases in six categories, all of which can discredit case control (and any other) studies:

- Background reading bias
- Sampling bias
- Withdrawals bias
- Measurement bias
- Analysis bias
- Interpretation bias.

Background reading bias
Investigators can be influenced by rhetoric, 'hot stuff', their own preconceived ideas, and positive results. Editors nearly always prefer to publish

papers that report significant differences between study group and control group, rather than those that report no significant differences.

Sampling bias
There are 22 ways in which bias can enter the specification and selection of the study sample. The most important of these are the wrong sample size bias ('samples which are too small can prove nothing; samples which are too large can prove anything'), the Berkson fallacy (patients in hospital are not necessarily representative of all those who have a particular disease), and the use of non-contemporaneous controls. To these should be added refusal of patients to participate in a study, and neglect of investigators to ensure that all eligible patients are enrolled.

The results of a random control clinical trial of the treatment of a disease are not necessarily applicable to all patients with that disease. The National Surgical Adjuvant Breast and Bowel Project recruited 2163 patients with breast cancer from 94 centres between April 1976 and January 1984 (Fisher *et al.*, 1985). Recruitment was by prerandomisation: after a surgeon had established the eligibility of a woman with breast cancer he telephoned the centre and was told to which of the three arms (total mastectomy, segmental mastectomy, or segmental mastectomy with postoperative radiotherapy) his patient was allocated. He then explained the protocol to the patient, discussed all three options, and obtained written consent to the procedure to which she had been assigned. Only 41 patients refused to participate, 74 refused total mastectomy, 41 segmental mastectomy, and 55 segmental mastectomy with radiotherapy. During the nearly seven years that the trial ran 2163 patients were recruited – an average of just over three patients from each centre each year. What happened to all the other women with breast cancer who were treated at these centres? Taylor, Margolese and Soskolne (1984) mailed questionnaires to all participating doctors, asking them their reasons for not entering eligible patients. The six most frequent reasons were:

- Concern about the doctor–patient relationship (73%)
- Difficulties with informed consent (38%)
- Dislike of admission of ignorance (22%)
- Conflict between roles of scientist and clinician (18%)
- Difficulties with prolonged follow up (9%)
- Fear that one arm might prove inferior (8%).

The extracranial/intracranial bypass trial in the USA recruited 1377 patients in 71 centres and the report (EC/IC Bypass Study Group, 1985) concluded that the operation offered no advantage over conservative treatment in patients with symptomatic inoperable extracranial arterial disease (Dudley, 1987). When Sundt (1987) contacted 57 of the 71 centres he discovered that a large number of eligible patients (the exact number is in dispute) had been excluded and not followed up. This means that the negative results of the trial did not preclude the possibility that the operation might help other patients with the disease.

In the last 10 years there have been great changes in the attitudes of the profession and of the public to ethical questions, particularly related to consent in surgical practice and research. These changes are likely to spell the demise of random control clinical trials for the answering of important questions. The alternative in surgical research will be complete, accurate, and honest audit (Pollock, 1989).

Bias in the conduct of the study

Among the five causes of bias in executing the experimental manoeuvre that Sackett identified, perhaps the most important is withdrawal bias: if more than 10% of randomised patients are withdrawn and their fate is not mentioned, the study becomes meaningless. An even greater source of bias is the withdrawal of patients in the experimental group who die before the outcome of their treatment can be determined. The bias potentially introduced when the investigator (or the patient) is not blind to the regimen to which the patient has been allocated is obvious.

The technique of randomisation was designed to avoid bias, but some methods allow it. In the New York trial of anticoagulants for acute myocardial infarction, patients were assigned by alternate days to receive dicoumarol or no anticoagulant (Spodick, 1982); good risk patients could be saved up for the anticoagulant days and the result was that patients who did not receive anticoagulants had a 50% greater mortality. Bias is more likely to occur if a random control trial is not double blind, and if the investigators do repeated analyses of the data.

Bias in measuring outcomes

Bias can arise in 13 ways, particularly when the outcome is not a 'hard' fact like death (Tonkin, Tritchler and Tannock, 1985). In oncology the use of 'recurrence free survival time' to measure the efficacy of prophylactic or therapeutic regimens can lead to false conclusions; subsequent publication of time to death can reverse those conclusions. Tobias and Tattersall (1985) commented on the widespread use of disease-free survival times in cancer trials, when what really matters is total survival time with a worthwhile quality of life. Frequently there is premature disclosure (especially in trials on the treatment of breast cancer) of gains in disease-free survival time with a particular regimen when subsequent reports show no difference in total survival time.

In the Manchester regional breast study, 714 patients without clinically detectable axillary node metastases were randomised to be treated by simple mastectomy or simple mastectomy followed by radiotherapy. There were more local recurrences in the group not given radiotherapy, but the 5- and 10-year survival did not differ between the groups (Lythgoe and Palmer, 1982). Early results of the Milan trial of adjuvant cyclophosphamide, methotrexate, and 5-fluorouracil showed an advantage in the experimental group for all patients, but the results at four years indicated that only premenopausal women had improved survival (Henderson and Canellos, 1980).

The doubts raised by these earlier publications were laid to rest by the meta-analysis of all randomised trials of adjuvant treatment of early breast cancer that began before 1985 (Early Breast Cancer Trialists' Collaborative Group, 1992). This analysis, comprising a total of about 75 000 women, concluded that both recurrence-free and overall survival at 5 and 10 years were highly significantly increased by tamoxifen (in young and old, and whether oestrogen receptor positive or negative), by polychemotherapy, and by ovarian ablation in premenopausal women.

Bias in analysing data

In analysing the data, bias can arise in five ways. Sackett listed post hoc significance bias (when the levels of alpha and beta are decided after the trial has ended), data dredging bias (data that are 'tortured until they confess' – Amery, 1984), scale degradation bias (the collapsing of measurement scales can obscure differences in outcome between regimens), tidying up bias (withdrawal of patients with anomalous outcomes), and repeated peeks bias (interim analyses of trials while they are in progress are bad both ethically and statistically).

Bias in interpretation of data

There are six ways in which the interpretation of an analysis can be faulty, the most outstanding being the equating of clinical importance with statistical significance. It has been said that one of the commonest defects of the orthodox scientific mind is the inability to realise that absence of proof is not proof of absence. Closely related is correlation bias, the equating of correlation with causation. The confusion between clinical and statistical significance can lead to error in either of two directions that are related to wrong sample size bias. A small and clinically indeterminate difference may be statistically significant and, much more commonly, a large and clinically important difference may not achieve statistical significance because too few patients were entered into the study. This is the type II or beta error that is so common in trials reporting (statistically) negative results.

Condon (1986) introduced the concept of the type III error, and this also is quite common: '...the conclusions drawn are not supported by the data presented'.

Stratification to minimise bias

It is sometimes necessary to stratify patients in a trial to avoid or recognise bias. In a random control trial in patients with prostatic cancer that compared treatment with stilboestrol (with or without orchidectomy or prostatectomy) against no stilboestrol, the Veterans Administration Cooperative Urological Research Group (1972) found a significantly higher mortality from cardiovascular causes in patients without metastases who were treated with stilboestrol. The report concluded that stilboestrol caused more deaths from cardiovascular disease than it saved, and that the drug should be reserved for patients with metastases. It is now accepted that prolonged use of stilboestrol results in excess mortality from all causes.

Reader bias

Owen (1982) contributed a light hearted riposte to Sackett's review, listing 25 ways in which readers of scientific journals may be biased. These range from prominent author bias (common) to benevolence bias (overrating a study out of kindness: this is rare).

Conclusions

Surgeons, and of course physicians, must keep abreast of advances in knowledge, and one of the principal ways to achieve this is to read appropriate journals. Doctors must, however, be aware of the possibility of bias on the part both of the authors of original papers and of themselves. Scientific fraud is rare, but bias can arise in so many ways that the reader must be constantly on guard. Audit of medical advances is no less important than audit of a surgeon's own practice. Constructive scepticism sums up the attitude required – an attitude not very different from that required for honest personal audit.

References

Ad Hoc Working Group for Critical Appraisal of the Medical Literature (1987) A proposal for more informative abstracts of clinical articles. *Annals of Internal Medicine*, **106**, 598–604

Altman, D.G. and Gardner, M.J. (1987) More informative abstracts. *Annals of Internal Medicine*, **107**, 790–791

Amery, K.V. (1984) Smoking and ulcerative colitis. *British Medical Journal*, **288**, 1307

Condon, R.E. (1986) Type III error. *Archives of Surgery*, **121**, 877–878

Dudley, H.A.F. (1987) Extracranial-intracranial bypass one; clinical trials, nil. *British Medical Journal*, **294**, 1501–1502

Early Breast Cancer Trialists' Collaborative Group (1992) Systemic treatment of early breast cancer by hormonal, cytotoxic, or immune therapy. *Lancet*, **339**, 1–15 and 71–85

EC/IC Bypass Study Group (1985) Failure of extracranial-intracranial bypass to reduce the risk of ischemic stroke: results of an international randomized study. *New England Journal of Medicine*, **313**, 1191–1200

Evans, M. and Pollock, A.V. (1985) A score system for evaluating random control clinical trials of prophylaxis of abdominal surgical wound infection. *British Journal of Surgery*, **72**, 256–260

Evans, M. and Pollock, A.V. (1987) The inadequacy of published random control trials of antibacterial prophylaxis in colorectal surgery. *Diseases of the Colon and Rectum*, **30**, 743–746

Feinstein, A.R. and Horwitz, R.I. (1982) Double standards, scientific methods, and epidemiological research. *New England Journal of Medicine*, **307**, 1611–1617

Fisher, B., Bauer, M., Margolese, R. *et al.* (1985). Five-year results of a randomized clinical trial comparing total mastectomy and segmental mastectomy with and without radiation in the treatment of breast cancer. *New England Journal of Medicine*, **312**, 665–673

Fowkes, F.G.R. and Fulton, P.M. (1991) Critical appraisal of published research: introductory guidelines. *British Medical Journal*, **302**, 1136–1140

Gøtsche, P.C. (1987) Reference bias in reports of drug trials. *British Medical Journal*, **295**, 654–659

Henderson, I.C. and Canellos, G.P. (1980) Cancer of the breast. The past decade (second of two parts). *New England Journal of Medicine*, **302**, 78–90

Hill, A.B. (1965) The reasons for writing. *British Medical Journal*, **2**, 870

Laor, N. (1985) Prometheus the impostor. *British Medical Journal*, **290**, 681–684

Lythgoe, J.P. and Palmer, M.K. (1982) Manchester regional breast study – 5 and 10 year results. *British Journal of Surgery*, **69**, 693–696

Owen, R. (1982) Reader bias. *Journal of the American Medical Association*, **247**, 2533–2534

Pollock, A.V. (1989) The rise and fall of the random controlled trial in surgery. *Theoretical Surgery*, **4**, 163–170

Popper, K. (1980) *The Logic of Scientific Discovery*. 10th edn, Hutchinson, London, p. 281

Sackett, D. (1979) Bias in analytic research. *Journal of Chronic Diseases*, **32**, 51–63

Shakespeare, W. (1594) *Loves Labours Lost* IV, 3, 314–315

Spodick, D.H. (1982) The randomized controlled clinical trial. Scientific and ethical bases. *American Journal of Medicine*, **73**, 420–425

Sundt, T. (1987) Was the international randomized trial of extracranial-intracranial bypass representative of the population at risk? *New England Journal of Medicine*, **316**, 814–816

Taylor, K.M., Margolese, R.G. and Soskolne, C.L. (1984) Physicians' reasons for not entering eligible patients in a randomized clinical trial for breast cancer. *New England Journal of Medicine*, **310**, 1363–1367

Tobias, J.S. and Tattersall, M.H.N. (1985) Doing the best for the cancer patient. *Lancet*, **i**, 35–37

Tonkin, K., Tritchler, D. and Tannock, I. (1985) Criteria of tumour response used in clinical trials of chemotherapy. *Journal of Clinical Oncology*, **3**, 870–875

Veterans Administration Cooperative Urological Research Group (1972) Treatment and survival of patients with cancer of the prostate. *Surgery, Gynecology and Obstetrics*, **124**, 1011–1017

Index